CLIMBED THE HILL

Christian Title

FⓄRTIS

A NONFICTION IMPRINT FROM ADDUCENT

WWW.ADDUCENT.CO

TITLES DISTRIBUTED IN

NORTH AMERICA

UNITED KINGDOM

WESTERN EUROPE

SOUTH AMERICA

AUSTRALIA

CHINA

INDIA

ITALY

CLIMBED THE HILL

Christian Title

Climbed the Hill
Christian Title

ISBN 9781937592592 (paperback)

Published by Fortis (a nonfiction imprint from Adducent)

Jacksonville, Florida

www.Adducent.co

Published in the United States of America

About the Front Cover:

The painting, by the author, is of his wife examining the Degas sculptures in the Paris Museum. It is titled: "Joyce 1975"

TABLE OF CONTENTS

Dedication & Acknowledgments
Introduction

I
The Early Years

II
Art, Music & Love

III
Sailing

IV
Coming Home / Hollywood and the Studio

V
The Middle Years

VI
Back to Sea Again

VI
The Last Words...

DEDICATION

I dedicate this book to my wife, who has fulfilled my dreams and made me whole. Her love and friendship have never wavered, and she has always been there in every moment of need. She is the Sun and the Stars, the Trees, and the Sea, and she shines brightly to everyone who knows her. I wish there were a forever so I could share it with her.

ACKNOWLEDGMENTS

So many people in this journey have made it unique. I thank all of those who have touched my life and encouraged my ambitions. They are too numerous to name but I want to give special thanks to:

Jim and Barbi Allen
Jay and Molly Precourt
John Moller
Barry and Ue Coe
Alan and Diane Gordon,
Alan and Joanne Kane,
Ric and Suzanne Kayne,
David Tebet,
Marty and Helen Rackin,
Bullets Durgom,
Bill Holden,
Errol Flynn,
John Williams & Barbara Ruick

Tim and Melissa Pennington,
Harry and Birgetta Cooper,
Howard and Jane Smith,
Linda and Bill Feldhorn,
Vince and Dana Zurzolo,
John and Wendy Powell,
Christian and Nahrin Powell,
Roz & Gary Valentine
Jesse Powell,
Ron Ely,
Henry Silva
Wendell Niles.
Paul & Lisa Warnstedt

I had the lee cloths up tight around me to hold me in place, I lay there looking up at the teak beams and the white finish to the underside of the deck. The crushing sounds were unnerving. We could do no more topside. Now it was just a matter of waiting it out with a slim chance of survival. Trent was on the bunk next to me, his eyes open, but he was comatose and paralyzed with fear.

The sight of eighty-foot waves breaking and rolling over the entire boat was scary beyond any understanding if you were not there. The lifeboat and much of the deck gear had broken loose and was gone. Fortunately, the booms and gaffs had been sufficiently secured. Everything would depend on the warps we trailed from the stern which kept us downwind. If they failed, the boat would roll and the four of us would die. My parents would not know about my death; they just knew I was sailing with friends to the Mediterranean.

What possessed me to take this chance? I should have learned my lesson on *Black Tarquin* when I saw how vicious the seas could be. I had worked so hard to secure my future. I knew I had a great talent and that success would be mine, now it was lost in this crazy adventure. I thought about my life, my friends, and family and growing up, and so much about Carolyn, who was in my heart.

INTRODUCTION

The vignette on the preceding page is a part of an adventure that I share in this book, I hope the reader will enjoy the adventures and excitement that have given me a life of beauty and challenge.

The writing of the episodes of my life fulfills a selfish purpose in my eighty-third year. I find that names do not come quickly, memories are clouded and often take more time than I wish to admit. I have a fear that some of the wonderful experiences of my life will fade and the process of recollection will diminish. I felt that it was time to get the most memorable phases down on paper so they could be reviewed in the future. The paintings which set the milestones of my career are in print or photographs which document my years clearly for future recall. I can review the many sights of my travels and the moments of my times with loved ones through photographs, but the excitement and mental reviews of my passions must be recorded in words.

I have an order in my life of what I consider important. It may not coincide with what others have written or said. That is perhaps because they have not had the same physical drives or passions as I, or maybe not the imagination to pursue all fronts, or maybe they are not honest enough or bold enough to put it in the same perspective. Health issues are of course a primary concern in life, but I have had uncommonly good health and energy, and I have not given it much thought or concern until I was into my 70s. I was always a good athlete and kept myself trim and strong. Not because of anything but the fact that I loved sports; the competitive arena was exciting and fulfilling. Meeting the true love of my life, my third wife, Joyce, changed many aspects of my lifestyle, and I started to plan more for the long term. She was the partner that could share everything and keep me happy forever.

I think it is important for the friends and audience of my art career to understand my philosophies and beliefs. First, let me state that I am not religious. I was brought up with a spattering of various contradicting philosophies, which only confused me and caused me early on to develop my own set of rules and beliefs. My mother was a hard-working Mormon woman with good values and a strict regimen of truth and duty. She provided me with lifelong ideals, but she never pushed me to any dogmatic regime. I also accept the faiths of all peoples and I believe that if there is no God then the word alone has served as one. But, as history has drawn on this great landscape, religion has fostered the seekers of power and influence to delineate the rules. They have preached brotherhood but have in fact segregated humanity. I believe there is a force; one that governs ordinary matter, dark matter and dark energy. It is universal. I have no need to try to label or explain it, as to do so would be conjecture, and would serve no purpose. Part of the force is a combination of things that I believe, such as honesty, love, and goodness. I believe from the force I was given the imagination and energy to create, to know no bounds. I personally feel no restrictions; only the obligation to enjoy the beauty and excitement of the world and its peoples. The personality and sexuality of women are something that has always fascinated me; in my younger years I was addicted to the adventure and the challenge of relationships. I was in love with falling in love. When the excitement and challenge were gone, I moved on. Art and music have guided my years and sailing has been a passion of the soul.

Christian Title
December 2015

I

THE EARLY YEARS

1

SAN FERNANDO VALLEY

I was only 4 years old when we moved to Fulton Avenue in North Hollywood, California. The area was a remote and mostly undeveloped countryside. Many people had ranches and farms, but housing developments were beginning to flourish.

My parents bought an eighteen hundred square-foot Mexican-style home. It was on a quarter acre lot with apricot and fruit trees. My dad built a chicken coop with a wire fence around it, and my mother raised chickens. He built a grape arbor and patio in the back that looked out over melon fields to the west, with only a few homes in view. It was a comfortable home with three bedrooms, but just one bathroom. I remember thinking when I went to friends' homes that having more than one bathroom was pure luxury.

The Chase Dairy farms were less than three blocks away up on the hill; the only knoll in the area and where the guys would often hang out after the last class. The big barn was full of hay, and a long rope hung from the second story loft. It was good for an hour or so of play. The Chase's never complained about us being in the barn. Mr. Chase would just come around and say, "Ain't smoking round this hay, are ya?" We would help Mr. Chase feed the cows by pitching hay into the bins. He had two dogs that loved our dog. We would have them do a sit and stay and then hide in the barn, in one of the outbuildings, or in the haystack. The dogs would go crazy looking for us, and this was a great source of fun. When I started kindergarten at

Riverside Drive Grammar School, a half-mile away, my brother Win, our dog Brownie and I would walk past the dairy. The Chase's dogs would accompany us to school. The school had only about thirty students but had a large play yard and baseball diamond. There were four bungalows, one for the office, and three where they held the classes. Many walnut orchards and melon fields surrounded it. We never crossed the fields because the farmers got angry. Life was perfect and growing up in the country was a gift.

My dad was a pharmacist, and he left early for work, usually around seven in the morning. He had his pharmacy, called the *Twentieth Century Drug*, across the street from the *20th Century Fox* movie studios in Hollywood. Sometimes on a Saturday, we would accompany him into town and spend the day in the store. We would have the time of our lives at the soda fountain fixing sundaes, milkshakes, and stuffing ourselves with goodies. He would coach us on the way home about what to say so my mom wouldn't know how much junk we ate. If she found out, that would be the end of our visits.

Both my parents were outstanding athletes and met at the Olympic tryouts. My mother was a state champion swimmer, and my dad represented the Los Angeles Athletic Club in swimming and diving. He was an AAU tumbling champion, which made his diving feats quite spectacular. It was also a feature of his vaudeville act. When he tap-danced, he would do a back flip into the splits. He could also jump into a one arm handstand on either arm. He appeared with his sister on the Orpheum circuit to make money while attending the University of Southern California. Once he appeared in the international newsreels for walking on his hands around the brass railing on the roof of the Los Angeles Athletic Club, fourteen stories above the street.

Christian Title

[Much later in life, one evening, Joyce and I went to a party given by Dick Sherman for his father. He showed a Pathé newsreel of the landing of Lindbergh after his famous flight. They played the song "Lucky Lindy" on his arrival, which was a song his father wrote that became a national favorite. Dick and his brother Bob were songwriters. They wrote many famous tunes and scores including *Mary Poppins*, for which they received an Academy Award. My friends were amazed as on that same newsreel was my father's daring stunt.]

When we went to the beach as kids, my dad would do amazing flips and tumbling acts in the sand, always attracting a big audience. We would swim as a family at the beach. Both my brother and I could swim by the time we could walk. When I was five years old, we would swim the two miles from the pier in Santa Monica to the Ocean Park Pier out beyond the breakers. Then we would walk back up the promenade to the Santa Monica Beach. We would stop at Muscle Beach; famous for all the high bar activities, rings, and weight lifting. Dad would get on the high bar and rings and show off, no one there was ever as good! We were always so proud of him; he was a character and a half.

He was also a great talent with instruments, and could tap-dance well. He would do his song and dance routines for us in the kitchen, which was the only floor where my mom would let him put on his tap shoes. He taught me to sing and tap-dance, *Way down upon the Suwanee River*, and some Al Jolson numbers. I used to practice on the back porch, which had a well-painted wood surface. I liked to sing and play my trumpet, but I didn't like to practice, and my mother said she wouldn't give me lessons unless I practiced. That went by the wayside, and a couple of years later I took up the guitar, which has been a joy for the rest of my life.

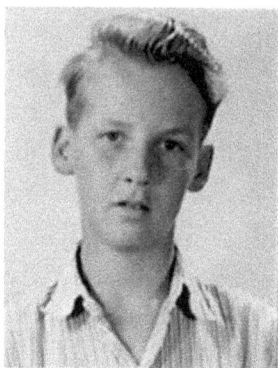

When I was about 8 years old, I decided to put on a show with my repertoire of songs and dance. I told everyone at school and got the neighbors to come. It was a Saturday morning, and about seven or eight showed up. I charged them a penny each, in today's money that would be ten or fifteen cents. My brother said it was a gyp, (an old expression for a rip off) and after the show, some of the kids said it wasn't worth it. They wanted their money back. I said I would give it back but then they couldn't come to any more of my shows. Sad faced; they backed down for fear of being left out.

Around that same time, a parcel for my brother came in the mail while we were in school. The package was a drawing gizmo that traced any image into a larger image with the same proportions. It had cost fifty cents and a box top. It was the single most significant occurrence for me that shaped my life. When we left school that day in 1940, we walked the usual route through the walnut orchards. We climbed a tree or two and made a wide swing past the dairy. When we arrived home, there was the package on the kitchen table addressed to Win, my older brother. I watched eagerly while he opened it. Inside was a rigid orange cardboard square with a large pad of cheap paper. At the top was a chrome bell fastened in the middle, it had a supported arm with an angular bar that had a pointer on it. There was a space above the pad to pin a picture. My brother put a drawing he cut out from the *Prince Valiant* series in the Sunday Los Angeles Examiner newspaper. He placed the pencil in the holder at the end of the arm and proceeded to make the pointer copy the lines of the picture. The exact reproduction began to take form on the pad; it was much larger, but the proportions were the same. After he had all the outlines, he filled in all the details with colored pencils. That evening he showed the drawing to my mother and father. They were amazed and praised his work all evening. For the next three months, the gizmo was the center of my brother's life. All the family was excited and gave him their support. I wanted to use it and do my drawing, but big brother wasn't going to share the glory and let me. My mother said it was his and if he didn't want to share it that was his choice.

I think my brother thought of me as if I was an irritating fly. Always buzzing about, and listening to popular music and the big bands that he hated, the only music he liked was classical. I thought it was stuffy and that he was a real creep.

I started drawing on my own, without the gizmo's assistance, but I wasn't very good. I persisted and filled dozens of drawing pads. At one point, my mother said she wouldn't buy me more if I didn't use the full page. I don't remember how long it was after the arrival of the magic gizmo that my aunt came to visit. She was an animator at the Disney studios and brought me a series of cartoon cells from there. She looked at my drawings. As a talented animator, she carried some weight as an artist. Sensing my frustration that day, she told me I didn't need the gizmo. All I needed was a pencil and paper, no eraser; if I made a mistake, she said I should do the drawing again so I could see the change and the improvement. I used a lot of paper, and did some awful pictures and ran to my parents with everything. They always said, "That's nice," but never did I get the praise my brother received that indelible night.

Sometime in the next couple of years, my brother lost interest in the gizmo, or it got broken. I don't remember what happened to it. But after hundreds of drawings, my work started to show some real promise and people began to take notice.

About that time, my parents began to argue a lot. Jealous and suspicious, my mother always confronted my father for being late. The fights went on and the stressful atmosphere started to affect my brother and me. It seemed to get worse, we didn't know what was going on, and life took a wrong turn. My dad, who at bedtime had always told us terrific imaginative stories, wasn't in the mood anymore, and our connection with him became strained. When I was 9 my mother and father separated, and the battles ended.

After my parents had divorced, I lost my insecurities in my passion for drawing. With it, I could create the world where I was at ease. From then on, I became addicted to art and knew it would be my future. Something as insignificant as that cereal box top purchase guided my entire life. During this period, I buried myself in my drawings, but I didn't like them. I knew they weren't very good. My aunt gave me a book on the painters of the world. For the first time, I could see the work of Leonardo DaVinci, Michelangelo, and the masters, as well as the newer French Impressionists, Cubists, and Abstract Expressionists. That book became my bible; I had my head in it continuously. I even took it to school and doodled all over the edges of the textbook pages. At that time, I was curious about the more modern art but wanted to draw like the masters. Slowly, after hundreds of drawings, people started to show appreciation for what I was doing.

My dad had moved into town, and my mother started working much longer hours at her beauty shop. My grandmother had one in Provo, Utah, and my mom had learned to be a beautician when she was growing up. I think she saw the writing on the wall with my father and started the business a year or two before they separated.

Christian Title

The Monterey Beauty Salon made her an excellent living for thirty-five years.

When my parents divorced, my world fell apart. My father found a new life, and he cared for little beyond himself. My mother worked long hours in her beauty shop. When she came home, she drank hard and had little time to be concerned about our cares and dreams. She was a good provider and a strict mother, but she didn't have the sensitivity to understand what was developing beneath the surface. She was sleeping with Charlie, her drinking partner, who had rented the extra bedroom within a year after my dad left. We knew what was going on. Kids are always a lot more hip than the parents think they are. My father saw us once every month or two, and when he did it was just the obligatory visit.

My brother and I spent a month each summer in Provo and Salt Lake City, Utah with my grandmother and family and went with them often to Mormon services at their local ward. When I was 11 years old, I went with my cousin Jimmy to his choir practice one afternoon because I loved to sing. Back home, I went to the director of the choir at our local ward and asked if I could be a part of their program. I had taken some singing lessons, but the teacher had moved away, and I didn't find another convenient replacement. I also had taken lessons in radio acting for two years and loved the class and the other students. That taught me about phrasing and voice control. When the director asked me to sing for him, he was quite impressed, and within weeks I was singing lead soprano parts. Everyone complimented me on my voice and that built my confidence. It altered my understanding of my future and myself.

But the oppressive nature of the Mormon doctrine disturbed and was wearing on me. I didn't like people calling me Brother and touching me. They were strangers as far as I was concerned. I didn't like many of the people and their phony, overbearing, friendliness. By the time, I was 13 I had had enough, and my mother said I didn't have to go back. The music director called her several times, but she told him I wouldn't return. The director of the choir had made many promises of recordings and musical reviews he was interested in presenting, but it was just more pie in the sky. I quit, and to this day, I've never set foot in a Mormon church.

The emotional stress of not seeing my father very often was perplexing. He was my idol and my teacher. I missed him, but he didn't seem to want to include us in his life. He married again to a woman from Missouri. She was quite lovely, but that's all she had to offer. She tried to alienate us from the very beginning. Her daughter was a show business social climber and her son was gay. They were a different breed from the people we knew and so the relationship with our father never reconnected.

Around that time, when I was 10 and 11 years old, I attended a private Protestant school. There, Mrs. Hawks, a wonderful teacher, saw my plight. She encouraged me, praised my drawings, and helped me to resolve my academic shortcomings. The school had an art exhibit to raise money and since I was by far the best artist in the school I provided twenty drawings for the show. About twenty-five drawings and watercolors by students and teachers sold, including all of mine. It gave me confidence that I was good enough to think about making art my life's work. All of this was beginning to build my self-esteem. At first it was a façade, but as the years went on, I became what I projected.

My mother married Charlie, our renter, who was a chef. He and his ex-wife, Thora, had been friends during my parent's marriage

8

and had divorced around the same time. Charlie was a good guy, and he treated Win and I well. He wasn't much in the smarts department, but he was patient and loving. He taught us both how to drive. And he never made a promise he didn't keep.

My father continued to ignore both my brother and myself. Art and music had replaced my need for him. Win took the brunt of the desertion, and I think it affected him more than me. Occasionally we would take the streetcar to the city, and my father would pick us up at a stop near his home. He would do the obligatory entertaining on Saturday night and then drive us back on Sunday afternoon. There was no real communication, and he and his new family could care less about our desires and dreams. I brought him a recording of one of my solos with the choir. He said he would play it when he had the chance, but it was never mentioned again.

It was his way to promise and grandstand and then do nothing. I never liked Christmas my whole life because of one of his promises. I had spent a considerable amount of time at friends' homes listening to their phonograph players and wanted desperately to have a record player of my own so I could play the popular records and learn the songs. He said he would get me one for Christmas. The holiday came, and there was no record player. I asked him if he had forgotten. It was during the Second World War, and he said he couldn't find a good one. But he would keep looking. When my birthday came in June, he again said he was going to get me a good record player as both a Christmas and birthday present. He didn't. Again, the next Christmas he said he had one lined up and it would be under the Christmas tree. It wasn't. I think that was the most singularly disappointing event of my young life. A phonograph at that time would have been crucial to my future singing, and I knew it. After that, I never wanted to ask him for anything again.

Gary Smith was my best friend from the time I was 5 years old, and I was at his house often. He had a big yard, and we played baseball and football there. I told his father about my disappointment with my dad and Mr. Smith said I must understand my dad also had problems. And that I must learn from the experience and make it a motivation in my life and not a negative. I had learned a critical lesson. If you want something, you cannot depend on others; you must go out and get it for yourself. You must be independent, strong and smart, or you will be at the mercy of others. In its way, disappointment is a character-building element in your life.

While my brother buried himself in his studies, I was quite the opposite. He was a bright and exceptional student, which presented a problem in school. In every class where I followed him, they'd always tell me they hoped I would be as good a student. After a while, I just began to tell them I wasn't and not to expect too much. That seemed to help me feel better about my studies. I always did just enough in school to get by and no more.

I loved girls and spent a lot of my time pursuing them. Next door was a girl, Barbara, who was a year or two older than I was. I think she was about 10 or 11 when we started our mutual investigations. Our double garage had a big flat roof where I had a pup tent set up, which I considered my hideout. I would take Barbara up there, and we would do a little show and tell. The first time she showed me her pussy, I wanted to touch it, but she wouldn't let me. But a few days later, she had thought it over and decided to let me look more closely. I separated her folds to reveal her entrance, and she fondled me. This was as far as it went, and we did this several times. We talked about it, and she told me about sex. About two years after that, we had another episode. She came over to my house; no one was home, and she wanted to know if I would like to play with her pussy. I was quite amazed at how it had changed. It had some hair around it, and she asked me to rub her. She played with me, and I got an erection. We did this little exercise like two inquisitive kids. But when I could see her reacting to my rubbing, she suddenly stopped, became embarrassed and made a hasty exit. Barbara lived next door for several more years, and we saw each other often. We said hello but I could never get her to be alone with me again.

That was about the time I started to masturbate. It felt good, and I would always visualize Barbara's pussy. My friends and I looked at porn photographs Bob Smith's older brother had bought in Tijuana, and it would make us all very horny. We talked about fucking and what it would be like and we couldn't wait until an opportunity presented itself. Some of the older guys would go to Tijuana to get their first experience, but I thought this was stupid. I didn't think that would be a rewarding experience, and the chance of getting some disease was likely.

2

CAROLYN

My life went on its merry way. I enjoyed each day, and my interest in art took on real dimensions as I spent every minute pursuing my drawing and studying every article or book on art, I could get my hands on. My mother also had us take lessons in dancing and music. The guitar, singing lessons and art became my world until Carolyn came into my life.

I was 14 years old, becoming aware of my sexuality, showing a more serious interest in girls and pursuing the subject of sex with friends. My brother was quite different; he was very studious and seemed not to care about women and sex. I was much more outgoing. I was comfortable with people and I had a talent for manipulating those around me. I liked girls, my mother said I was girl crazy from the time I was a tot.

I was making money by doing yard work for people in the neighborhood and had one customer for each day after school. I would mow their lawn, trim the edges and bushes, and clean up. When people went on vacation, I would water and check everything. I earned a dollar twenty-five an hour. I worked hard and did a good job; my customers were pleased, so I was making more than other kids offering the same service.

One day after one of my clients, Mr. Bennett died his wife told me she'd sold their house and wouldn't need me anymore. I promptly went out to a few houses where I had noticed neglected lawns and gardens. A woman I had been aware of for a long time owned one of them. Not that I knew her by name, but I had seen her many times in the neighborhood. I don't think she had noticed me, but she lived only a block and a half from my house. I had heard her husband had been killed in the war; some of the kids said he was a fighter pilot and a hero. I knocked on her door and she answered. When I talked to her, she understood her place needed more upkeep and hired me. Her name was Carolyn Baker and from our first talk, she was warm and friendly. We discussed my pay and how many hours each week I could work. I had Wednesdays free and could put in about three hours. I suggested I also work three or four hours on Saturday until the place was in shape. She agreed, and I started the next Saturday.

It was May, and the valley was starting to get hot in the afternoons. I started early and brought lunch with me. I ate quickly, and Carolyn brought me a glass of juice. She put a pitcher of ice water on the porch and asked me to slow down a little.

"Take a break here and there; open the umbrella on the patio and sit under it to get out of the heat."

She was sweet and concerned. None of the others I worked for had ever paid much attention to me, except for Mr. Bennett before he died. I think he knew his time was ending, and he related in some way to me; perhaps thinking back to when he was my age. He was feeble and would ask me to help him to the back yard so he could sit in the shade of a big tree. He would make noises under his breath and sometimes I thought he was talking to me. I would stop and look over at him, but he would just smile and look up into the tree and watch for birds.

When school let out for summer vacation, I rearranged my schedule with the people I worked for so I could have more days free. I had been working for Carolyn for almost two months, and the place was looking much better except for the garage door with peeled paint that constantly dirtied the driveway. I told her I was a good painter, and I could refinish it for her. She picked up the material for the job, and I took two full days to make it look like new. Impressed and pleased at the results of the work I had done she invited me inside the house for a root beer (Carolyn had asked me what I liked to drink when she went for the paint and supplies).

"Do you have any other ideas for improvement?" she asked.

I told her the trim around the garage, the front door, and many of the windows would require a lot more work if they were neglected much longer. She asked what color I would suggest, and I quickly told her what I had in mind. The house was white, and I felt a very soft blue-white, would give the place a lift. She laughed and decided the existing beige color would be best.

Most of the days, she had been home when I came to work after school, but she often left around three o'clock or a little later. Now that I was there many full days, I realized she worked different hours during the week. From ten at night to six in the morning some of the time, and from four in the afternoon until midnight on some days. I realized she must be a nurse since I had seen her many times going to work in a white dress, stockings and shoes.

One day I asked her about her job. We sat there that day and talked for many hours. She seemed lonely and eager to tell me about her life. Her husband, Robert, had been killed in action on one of the islands in the Pacific. He received the Purple Heart, but other than that, he wasn't a hero; just a Marine doing a job. But in her eyes, he was a great man. They had met when they were both my age, and love and friendship had blossomed over many years. They were steady through high school, and both went to the University of Southern California. At Van Nuys High School, he was a fine athlete and received a scholarship. Carolyn studied nursing, and when the Japanese attacked Pearl Harbor, he decided to join the Marines before being drafted into the Army. During the nearly two years of his service, Carolyn finished her education. Before he shipped overseas, they were married. She told me of the regrets she had of not marrying sooner, and of not enjoying each other physically. She became embarrassed suddenly when she realized she was discussing their sex and passion with a boy just 14 years old.

I put my hand on hers and told her I understood, and that she was very special to me. I was happy she should feel comfortable enough to tell me these things. I had thought a lot about her. She was the first person in my life I felt I had a complete, real, and honest relationship with and I had a vague plan to get even closer to her. I knew she was lonely and had no male friends or even many girlfriends. She was still carrying a torch for the only man she had ever known. She admitted it was taking her a long time before she'd be prepared to have a new man in her life. She told me about her mother, who had never liked Robert. She wanted Carolyn to date and know other men and to not get involved so young; especially when the war started. She knew Robert would be part of it. Carolyn's father had died very young, and her mother had recently married a man in construction, a drinker, and a no good bum and moved to Reno, Nevada. Carolyn said her mother was a hypocrite to criticize Robert and then end up with someone who wasn't worth shining his shoes. When the subject came up about the drinking, I told her about how much it disturbed me that my mother drank so much.

"Don't be tough on her, she works hard and has made you a good person; you have the right values! I respect her because you're her son."

We talked about how much I knew about girls, about kissing and the experiments with Barbara, my neighbor. She asked me if we French kissed. I knew about that, but Barbara didn't like it when we tried.

She said, "I wish Robert and I had started then, but we were just different from the others. We knew many of our friends were getting it on. We wanted to be careful. I had a best girlfriend who admitted her mother took her in to be fitted with a diaphragm when she was 15. I think she had an abortion, and her mother didn't want it to happen again. Several of my friends got married early, and most are divorced now. Do you know much about sex?" she asked me directly.

"Only what I've seen in photos and the books some of my friends pass around. My friend George Harwood gave me a book that tells in intimate detail about a man who had an affair." I was going to say the affair was with an older woman, but that would be too transparent. She prodded me about the book, and I skirted the issues, trying to clean up some of its crudeness in what I told her about it.

She was on to me. "I think you can say anything to me you could say to your friends, you don't have to be embarrassed or avoid the words you would use," she said.

"I don't like those conversations with them; they just look at everything in an ugly way," I told her. "I prefer to read romantic

16

stories that are also sexual." I knew this was what she wanted to hear. And it was partially correct, even though young, I was aware girls didn't like men who discussed their exploits with others. Somehow, talking to her, I became totally relaxed and truthful about my fantasies and dreams of the future.

She was impressed that I already knew my life would be as an artist and that my interests involved so much music and art and so little in anything academic. Our conversations were complete and honest. I had never had anyone to relate to and even with best friends, I couldn't reveal my insecurities and fears as I could to Carolyn. I'm sure it was mutual as she confided in me about her life and fears of the future.

We parted around six that evening after three hours of conversation. I thought about it all night, trying to analyze why she had been so open. It was as if I was one of her girlfriends at times. Then, on other occasions, I realized she was filling in the gaps with where I was at in this phase of my life. It was reasonable that she never had this conversation with her husband when they were teenagers, and she was only curious.

I read George's book again that night and got horny thinking of what it would be like to have sex with Carolyn. The book described every move the man made in his lovemaking. Although I had read it many times, it took on new meanings when contemplating the possibility of an affair with Carolyn. I went to sleep fondling myself. I would have masturbated, but I shared my room with Win.

The next day I went early to Carolyn's house. She would be up around eleven in the morning if she had the earlier shift, but she'd often get up at two in the afternoon if she worked all night. I started scraping the windows in the front so I wouldn't wake her. I would finish one at a time so the screens could be done at the same time. I always saved my lunch and ate it with her, regardless of the time. She liked to have me come in and sit with her while she had her coffee and said it was very sweet of me. I think she had spent so much time alone, that having company was a treat.

Our mutual attraction was growing; I found I could express my innermost feelings, without any criticism or judgment. I told her about my embarrassment at being so thin. She laughed and said she had experienced that herself. She had developed very late and had a terrible complex about being so flat chested.

"I used to rub my breasts and nipples to get them excited; I was told this would help them to grow larger. But, as you can see, it didn't do any good. I tried everything to gain weight, ate like a horse but stayed skinny."

Carolyn at 24 still had the body of a 14-year-old. She was about five-feet-four-inches and weighed not much over a hundred pounds. She had a beautiful face, with a straight nose and bright, blue-green eyes. Her naturally curly hair was a dark brown color with a silky shine and was always slightly mussed. Her skin was smooth and white, and she had a mouth full of beautiful teeth.

To me, she was just gorgeous. I told her how attractive I thought she was. She smiled and said I was very kind. But I think she was a little uncomfortable when I poured out my feelings about her. I couldn't understand why there weren't dozens of guys clamoring about such a special lady. The only reason I could think of was she was very aloof. It was only my youth and that she didn't feel threatened that gave her such freedom with me. She knew I was just a young boy. And I was brutally honest with her. I had never admitted to anyone, not even close friends, that I enjoyed masturbating. She told me this was natural, and she had done it since she was young. I asked bluntly if she still did it and she reluctantly said yes before changing the subject.

A week or so later I needed to take the front door off to paint it properly. I had scraped and sanded it well, but still needed to do the edges. I put it on top of a couple of boxes in the garage. Everything was set up as I had been working on the window screens there. Carolyn hadn't been able to use the garage for a couple of weeks. I put a canvas drop cloth over the front door entrance, nailing around its edges from the outside so that the flies wouldn't come in. I had waited for Carolyn to get up and help me lift the door off the hinges, as I couldn't do it alone. Afterward, we sat and talked too long, and I got a late start painting the door. When I left to go home for dinner, the door was still very tacky. Since Carolyn didn't leave for work until about nine, we decided I would come back at eight that evening and put the door back on.

At dinner, I told my mother I had to go back out to finish some work and left about a quarter of eight for Carolyn's house. The door was still wet, and we would leave fingerprints if we tried to put it back on, but she didn't want to leave the house with just the canvas over the door. I called my mother and told her the situation and that I would sleep on Carolyn's couch in case anyone tried to get in. That wasn't very likely; we had never heard of a robbery or problem in the valley in those days. I promised my mother I would have a window at the back ready to jump out and run home if anything happened in the night. I would then call the police from home. I assured her everything was all right. She was muddled, and I knew she was pretty far gone with booze. She would have to leave by eight or so in the morning to open up the shop; Saturday was always her busiest day. She had two other beauty operators working for her, and she had to get everything ready for nine o'clock appointments. Charlie worked the early shift at the veteran's hospital in West Los Angeles and went to work at four in the morning. My brother, Win could care less if I was around. But mom sent him over with some pajamas, a toothbrush, and my guitar (a kind of midget guitar which I could easily take anywhere).

That evening I listened to the radio and my favorite shows and sang along with all my favorite tunes. I remember KMPC; a local broadcasting station was a favorite. At home, I could listen to it on my crystal set with earphones, and because it was so close to us, it would be clear without static noises. I often fell asleep at night with the earphones on, mom would come in and take them off, but I wouldn't remember. For the first time in my life, I had complete privacy and I just enjoyed being alone and playing the music I liked. It was warm, as all nights in the valley were in the summer. It stayed light until well after nine and never seemed as late as it was. I hated going to bed early, but mom had her nine o'clock curfew, and that was the law. It must be great to live alone, do, and eat anything you wanted. I thought someday I would sit down and eat a pound of crisp bacon, and no one would care or judge me. About one in the morning, I fell soundly asleep on the sofa.

Carolyn came home around six-thirty in the morning. I heard her come in, as she slammed the back door. She had forgotten I was there. When she saw me, she apologized.

"You should be going home anyway." She seemed nervous.

"No one's at my home; is it okay if I sleep a bit more on your sofa?" I could tell she was very disturbed about something. "Are you alright? I asked. Her manner was abrupt, and she was trembling. "Have I done something wrong?"

"No," she said. "I've had an awful night!"

I stood there not knowing what to say. Without another word, she took me by the hand and led me to the bedroom. She took her dress off, her shoes and then unsnapped her stockings from her garter belt. She sat on the bed next to me, slid the stockings from her legs and fell back on the bed with her slip still on. She patted the bed next to her. I lay down beside her, and she arranged me on my left side, brought her body up next to mine, and put an arm around me with her hand on my chest. She fell asleep quickly, still holding me tightly. I could feel the quiver of her body subside as she drifted off.

I didn't go back to sleep right away, even though I was still drained. I reveled in the warmth of her body next to me, and my imagination soared to new heights with sexual fantasies. When I awoke, she was softly caressing my stomach, and I felt her undo the string on my pajama bottom. I thought, it's actually happening, all my fantasies for her. What did George's book say to do, what did the super stud do? I was so filled with excitement I could hardly control myself. Carolyn knew I didn't have any experience, as we had talked about it. I felt her hand rubbing my organ. I had been hard for a good part of the morning, and I think she was aware of it. As she touched me, it was beyond anything, I had ever known. Why was it so much better with her hand rather than mine?

"Turn and put your hand on me," she said.

I rolled over, and she was nude. She had been up before I

awoke and taken her slip off, and maybe got herself ready for lovemaking. It was too good to be true. I still didn't believe it. I put my hand on her breast as she turned on her back, still clasping my member in her hand. Her breasts were tiny and flat with large nipples, which hardened with my caressing. I put my mouth to hers, and she opened it and pushed her tongue through my tight lips. I opened them wider.

"Suck on my tongue," she said softly.

I did and found an incredible excitement to it; I never thought, in all of my fantasies; it would be so magical. I put my tongue in her mouth, she sucked back, in and out our tongues went; our lips passionately widening. Her soft, full, lips were beyond description in my memory. She broke away, and for a second I thought she had changed her mind; she felt she shouldn't be doing this and was going to stop. I was wrong. She looked at me lovingly and helped me take off my pajamas. She pulled the sheet up over us. I put my body against hers, and we resumed kissing.

"Come on top of me," she said in a low stern voice.

I knew the position and got above her as she spread her legs.

"Don't lie flat, raise up on your knees," she instructed.

I felt her reach down, and I lifted my head so I could look at her. She seemed very pleased as she guided me inside. It was so warm, soft, and wet. Was it supposed just to fit in there so perfect? I asked myself. The feeling was so intense I came instantly. It was unlike any I had ever had before. Usually, it was jerky and tedious. But, it wasn't like that; it was fulfilling and ever more exciting. I continued to move in the rhythm I knew she was enjoying. I never softened. I think I was getting bigger and more sensitive.

"Slowly, slowly," she said.

I took gentle and smooth strokes. Her eyes opened wide with a glazed look; she didn't see, just felt. Every nuance of our movement was so perfect. How could it be so good? I guess because I loved her. This is what love is; I thought. A total merging of two people where I couldn't tell where my sensations left off, and hers began. It was good and perfect beyond all things I had ever known.

She started a slow murmur and then a soft gasping sound. They increased, and her body tightened, her head raised, and I could see the strain in her neck. Then it was as if demons that possessed her were expelled from her body. She shook and quivered like a spring-born leaf meeting its first breeze.

Was a woman supposed to reach a climax this way? I stopped for a little while when she tightened up; her legs were rigid against mine. She stayed that way for what seemed a long time. As she relaxed, I began to move again. I was close again, and I wanted to feel it this time. The first time was so sudden I wasn't ready for the full sensation. As I continued to move, she was motionless; spent, at least for the moment. I couldn't imagine she could have another dramatic climax like that again. I knew women were supposed to have multiple orgasms, but surely they couldn't keep having them at that level. I started to slow down, feeling every move.

"Don't stop, I just need a minute to come down a little."

A few minutes later she started to make the sounds again. It didn't throw me off this time. Instead, I found it ever more exciting knowing I could make her feel so good. When she came, again, it wasn't as intense but her moaning lasted for a long time. I thought it was leading up to the climax, but that was it; a different, soft loving, giving up of tension. I could feel myself come again with her first moan and continued to move until I was sure she wanted me to stop. I hugged her close for a long time. We were both silent. When she spoke, she asked me if I had come two or three times. I told her only twice. She thought that was amusing. I asked about her climaxes. She was trying to describe them but kept laughing each time she made the attempt.

"It was wonderful for me and something I guess I needed. I haven't been with anyone for a long time. And I've never reached a climax like the first one."

"Was there anyone after Robert?" I asked.

"Yes, and it was an awful experience with a man who didn't have any sensitivity. He was just a bull; rough and clumsy. But this was your first time, and you were wonderful because you were concerned with my pleasure and my feelings. It's amazing you can stay hard for so long. I think you'll end up being a fantastic lover; you're pretty good right now."

We talked for several hours and had lunch, as it was close to two in the afternoon. I asked every imaginable question about what we had experienced and what I could have done better. "I want to be a perfect lover and I want you to teach me everything."

"This can't be a constant thing; we must choose our time and place carefully. If anyone knew, they wouldn't understand what we've shared. No matter how much we explained. So it's absolutely necessary no mention ever be made of this."

"Carolyn, I never want you to think I would tell anyone. I know they'd think unfairly of you. It's my treasured secret. I won't ever expect or try to be your man, just your student, and your friend. I hope you'll accept all the love I feel for you."

The next day I went to the Milsley's house. They were on vacation and in the hot weather, it was important to see everything was watered properly, and the yard maintenance done. It took about three hours, and when I went to Carolyn's house, I was already sweaty and tired. She was still in bed; I didn't hear her moving about, so I went ahead and mowed the lawn and did the trim work. I had been out in the sun too long, so I took one of the chaise lounge cushions, put it on the garage floor, and stretched out for a while. I don't know how long I was there; my mind was jumping about all over the gamut of memories of what had taken place the day before. I was in Never Never Land when Carolyn came in. She startled me, and I jumped up quickly. I was embarrassed as I didn't want her to think she was paying me for laying down on the job. I made a special effort to explain exactly what time I had come from my other job, and what I had accomplished.

"You've probably had enough for a hot day like this. Come in and we can have something to eat." She said smiling. I think my self-consciousness entertained her.

She had some cereal, and I ate my packed lunch as usual. She asked how I felt about yesterday. I told her honestly how I could think of nothing else, and relived every second in my mind. I told her how special it made me feel when she said I was a good lover and had good instincts.

"It was good and reminded me of being with my husband."

She hesitated. "I know you won't say anything, but we have to be careful and objective about what we did... what we're doing." She looked at me, and I met her look. "You're young and impressionable and I'm... I'm..."

She stopped, but I knew what she wanted to say because though young I could tell. She was fragile, I could easily hurt her through poor judgment, and that would end things. I swore to myself I wouldn't make any mistakes. But I decided not to say anything more on that until I had time to think things over and evaluate it. I wanted more than anything to understand her, have her love me, teach me, and stay with me.

She brightened. "Come and take a shower with me, I think you need to cool off. You look like half the lawn is in your socks."

I looked down and couldn't help but laugh. "Wow, I'm pretty grubby I guess."

I took my shoes off on the outside steps, shook my socks out and put them on the back porch. When I came back in Carolyn wasn't there. I didn't know if I should go into her bedroom to the shower or wait for another invitation. I took a deep breath. I can't be shy, I told myself and headed to her room. In the bathroom, she was adjusting the shower and fully nude. She had such a cute little body. I took my clothes off and got into the shower with her. She pushed me under the water and started to soap my body. As we rubbed each other all over, I looked at her breasts while I caressed them. They were not small as I had thought. They were flat but quite large and firm in circumference. Her nipples were like small corks, perfectly round and almost squared off at the ends.

I loved the feeling of the two of us in the water; it made me look forward to showering. I was hard and sticking straight up from the moment her hand touched me. I wished I could command it to come up when it was more appropriate. It stayed like that after we got out of the shower and into the bed. She slid next to me, and we started to kiss as we had done before. I enjoyed it even more because this time I was relaxed. Carolyn rolled me on my back and positioned herself on top. She put her knees up under my arms, and I could feel her hair and mound against me. We continued to kiss, and she pressed her hips into my body. She then rose and looked at me with a soft smile. Oh, what a feeling it was to be with her. Our eyes drank each other in with a passion for what was beginning. She kissed me all over, and I didn't know what to do with my hands. Should I hold her head? She sensed my uncertainty, reached out and placed my arms at my site.

"Close your eyes and just feel," she said. Her voice seemed lower in tone, a husky whisper.

She did things that brought me to an incredible level. I knew this was part of the sexual array of activities, but it was so intense that even now I remember it like it was yesterday. I could tell she was enjoying it and in rhythm rubbed herself against my leg. When I would get close, she'd somehow sense it and ease off. Finally, she wasn't able to stop in time; it was too late. She loved watching it twitch and kick and laughed as if she had just won some amusing game. She bounced up quickly, grabbed a towel, and wiped me. She saw I was still ready.

"I think he needs more." She sat on top of me and slowly lowered herself. It was very different from being on top of her. This way she was in control. She gyrated, and I was able to see the full view of her at the pinnacle of passion. Afterward, we stayed quiet for a long time. She moved a little now and then but mostly just hugged me tightly. When she lifted, she let out a little whimper. She rolled onto her side and straightened her legs. They had been in that position so long she was cramping slightly. Rising from the bed and stepping into the bathroom she cleaned up with a hot washcloth and spread a towel on the wet bed. When she noticed I was still hard, she giggled and said, "I have nurse friends that tell me their husbands and boyfriends can't stay hard for more than five minutes." She could see she had embarrassed me, and quickly commented. "I love it; keep it like that just for me."

She came alongside, reached down and played with me for a while, and then asked me to come on top again. The words were what I was waiting for; I was still so horny and wanted to feel it inside again. I slid into her, and the excitement was so intense; the pulsations lasted for a long time. I felt her climax again even though we were still, not moving. It was as if an inner heartbeat pulsating with me inside her sent its vibrations through every part of our being. Everything in the world was perfect. I closed my eyes and without realizing I was going to, I soon I fell asleep.

When I awoke, she wasn't beside me. I could hear her in the kitchen humming a tune I recognized at the time but can't recall now. I had never heard her so happy. Like a bird, chirping away at the sun and enjoying a new found world. I put my grubby clothes back on and walked in on her while she was ironing her uniform. She stopped, pulled the blind down on the kitchen window and put her arms around me.

"That was the best sexual experience of my life. I don't even know how it happened." She smiled. "But, I felt such love and complete giving up... of letting go of all my thoughts and worries. It was wonderful."

I was a little stunned she'd imply it was better than with her husband. I just held her and told her how special it was for me, too. I loved her, but I knew that was something I couldn't say that aloud.

* * *

That day when I went home, I sat on the back patio and Charlie came and sat next to me. He asked if everything was okay, as he hadn't seen much of me the last few weeks. He seemed to be pumping me for a little information, or maybe I was just paranoid. I told him I was doing a lot of work for the Milsley's and Mr. Johnson. I told him all about Mr. Johnson's flower garden in such detail I hoped he would soon get bored and go away. It worked, and he left me to my thoughts.

After Carolyn's expressions of delight in me as a lover, I had very mixed feeling and investigated every possibility in my mind. I didn't spend the time reviewing the excitement nearly as much as trying to understand better what I had apparently achieved. Did she say what she said just to make me confident so I would become a better lover? I didn't know. I glanced through George's book again; it seemed shallow and not nearly as appreciative of the woman and her desires. It sounded like the man she had described being with after the loss of her husband; rude, crude and unrefined.

What about that statement from the other nurses that had men who would make love to them for five minutes? Did they not enjoy it? I usually masturbated in nothing less than a half hour, and then it was usually because that was all the private time I had available. Sometimes when I knew I would be alone for many hours, I would take mineral oil, Vaseline or anything available and have a fantasy that would last for at least an hour and a half. If I had time, it would be a marathon and a tired arm before I would complete the imaginary affair. I shook my head. Here I was, beyond all my imaginings, having an affair with an erotic and passionate mature woman. I was sure she enjoyed our lovemaking and during it, I don't think she even thought about that I was so much younger. But maybe she didn't have control when she was with older men. The man she told me about had been rough and hurt her; she didn't feel any pleasure with him. She was slight, and a man could hurt her a lot. Yes, I think that was the answer. She needed someone she could teach and control so that she wouldn't be hurt physically. I remembered the fragile look on her face at times when she looked at me. I thought, maybe she was scared of being hurt or abused mentally, too. She didn't have much experience, except with her husband. But, after what she said, I think there must have been some reservations there too; that even with him she'd held back. Maybe I was the first one she felt entirely comfortable with when it came to sex.

I slept well that night, and mom made me a large breakfast the next morning. We hadn't talked much for several days; just briefly in the evenings when she was muddled with booze. We didn't talk much that morning either as I had too much on my mind.

[I think one of the reasons she always insisted we go to bed early to get us out of sight so she could drink. My mother never considered herself an alcoholic. She never took a drink during the day and functioned in her business, but the bottle was the first thing she'd head for when she got home. When I would approach her with something on my mind, she'd say. "Just a minute, I need to relax and have a little pick me up." She would sit down with a bourbon and soda and a cigarette; then and only then could I feel free to ask her a question.]

After breakfast, I went to Mr. Johnson's to water his lawn and arrived at Carolyn's at around nine-thirty. I wanted to get her watering done, too before the sun got too hot and burned the grass. I had brought my guitar and put it in her garage. I was watering when Carolyn came out of the house and asked me to come in. I told her I would be ten or fifteen minutes; a short while later, finished, I went to the garage, got my guitar, and went inside through the back porch door.

Carolyn was at the kitchen table having coffee and toast. When she saw my guitar, she commented. "I saw that here the other night and wanted to ask you about it. Have you been playing long?"

"No," I replied, "just a few years. I brought it today because I've been writing a song for you."

"How long have you been writing it?"

"Well, about a month now, since I started to have such good feelings about you. You've always been so kind to me. I never had anyone who cared about me as much as you." This pleased her at first. But I could see the more she thought about it, the more it also disturbed her.

She said, "I do care about you, but you can be sure your parents care very much, too. Sometimes people are busy and just don't have the time to give it enough thought."

I wanted to change the subject, shifting it away from my

parents. I asked her if I could play her my song. I had spent a lot of time writing and practicing it for this performance. When I played it, I saw her eyes well up with tears, and her face filled with wonderment.

"That's a wonderful song. You never fail to amaze me; no one has ever sung a song to me, let alone write one for me."

"It's called, *Warm as the sun, Carolyn.*"

A bit overcome, she quickly asked me to play some other songs. I screnaded her for a while. Then she took me by the hand and led me to the bathroom.

"Would you like to wash my back?"

"Yes," I said, "and the front, too."

She laughed a little, and after we had taken our shower, I went to the bed and she stayed in the bathroom for a few minutes with the door closed. When she came out, I was on the bed with the sheet over me; still somewhat too embarrassed to lay stark nude. She came to the bed.

"I'd like to show you my body."

She sat on the edge of the bed and put a pillow on the floor in front of her.

"Kneel down..." she told me.

I got off the bed, knelt, and faced her looking up.

"Do you want to see my body?" I nodded, and she continued.

"This is my most sensitive place. Touch it with your tongue."

I did her as she instructed. She showed me what gave her the most pleasure, and I wasn't sure this was something I liked to do. That quickly changed when I realized how I could manipulate her sensations. She was very particular with her guiding me, holding my head.

"You'll know when what you're doing is right."

I did this for a long time, and as she came closer to a climax, I felt a great sensation of power over her passion.

From that point on, we were together three or four days a week. We experienced every imaginable act together. I was a good and willing student; I found she increasingly wanted me to make love to her. I wondered if all women had such strong desires. But I would learn in my life that women who matched my own were rare.

Near the end of our relationship, I brought my portfolio of drawings to show her, which by that time were excellent. Carolyn reacted very strongly to the drawings. Up until that time, she had just enjoyed our physical relationship, but at that moment, her perception of me started to change.

"You have something special within you; I don't know what it is. I only know you're not like other boys or men. It would make me tend to believe in reincarnation, which, of course, I don't. But your talents, sensitivity, and understanding aren't that of a fourteen-year-old. That I could fall in love desperately with someone that could only lead to something that could destroy us both; you scare me! Being with you, I risk my job... and how people think of me, but more seriously, I gamble with your life. You, who have some destiny I can't understand, I'm at a loss to explain my actions and confused about what to do."

I didn't know what to say, how to respond or what she wanted me to do. I took my portfolio from her and set it aside. She took me to her bed. We made love for a long time, and I felt a confidence I hadn't known before. I felt there was something special inside me. Her feelings and confirmation gave me a new drive to be something more.

We both knew it couldn't continue. The neighbor across the street had already commented that it wasn't proper that a young boy was in her house so much. Carolyn told her I was doing yard work in exchange for tutoring because I was having difficulties in school.

The woman said. "I thought you were a nurse."

"Nurses are educated people; I think I can handle helping a young boy with his studies!"

The neighbor was embarrassed and apologized. But it was the first time anyone had said anything and Carolyn knew the woman was counting the hours I was in the house. She told me about it. I covered myself with my mother by telling her I was sure I would do much better in school this year as Carolyn and her boyfriend, who was a school teacher, were helping me with mathematics. When I told Carolyn about the variation she said it was okay, but don't start making up too many stories. We looked at each other knowing it was time to end things between us. She and I agonized as we planned our last time together.

My mother and Charlie were going to Utah and then to Texas, driving Charlie's 1939 Ford coupe. My aunt lived nearby, and she was going to look after us. Win was 16, and dependable though reticent. I asked my aunt if I could spend the weekend with my friend Gary Smith. I made up a story for Gary too that Mr. and Mrs. Bennett had invited me to their new home in Arrowhead. Gary's grandmother lived with them, and she'd back up the story if asked. But, my mom didn't like Mrs. Bennett, so I had to make up another story. Somehow, I made it all work, so I was covered.

I had everything planned, and Carolyn had arranged to have others fill in so she could have the weekend free. We had never spent a full night together, and it was appropriate our last time would be something to remember forever. We had many laughs as we tried to make her look as matronly as possible for the coming charade. As mother and son, we rented a cabin, an old wood bungalow with a large bed and small cot, on the beach in Carpentaria. There were no real markets nearby, just a little grocery with limited choices, and a greasy spoon hamburger joint. Carolyn wasn't much of a cook, so the greasy spoon was the fare.

That Friday we arrived at four in the afternoon, and we made love for an hour. We were more relaxed than ever before. I had developed good control and the ability to manipulate her sensations to the fullest. We took a long walk on the beach, dipped in the water a few times and then went for a cheeseburger. We came out in time to sit on the deck chairs and watch the sunset. California doesn't have great sunsets very often, but this was a special one just for us. The glow went from deep yellow to crimsons and reds, spread across the sky with mare's tails and a dark cloud bank above the western horizon. The cloud bank had a bright white golden lining above the cobalt and ultramarines that were almost black. Carolyn's face took on the glow of the warm colors. It was perfect for someone whose inner reflection was a golden treasure. With the sundown, we went back into the cabin and turned on the water for the shower. It was cold, freezing; hard to believe on such a balmy warm evening.

"Don't be a coward." she said as she plunged in with a breath-sapping gasp.

We showered, but the water never got warm. We washed and laughed and shivered, then ran for the bed and got under the covers, pressing our bodies together for warmth. In minutes, we threw the covers off and knew nothing of temperatures. We teased each other until neither could stand it anymore. I kissed her body and worked my way to her soft mound where I lingered for a long time. Kissing her there had become my favorite lovemaking preliminary. She brought me to a point that was pure torture, and we made love more hours than we had ever done before. We had learned so many secrets about the others sexual hunger that it became an all-consuming physical and mental extravaganza. When we reached the extreme level of our passion and love, I knew this might never happen again for me. It was so incredible in intensity; it was almost insane. Carolyn had become insatiable; her desires had grown, and she seemed to want more all the time. It was fortunate that I could continue for long periods.

We held each other in depleted state of ecstasy and fell asleep. Somewhere in the darkness of the night, I felt her mouth on me, and we started once more. Then we slept again. Soon the morning light was streaming through a crack in the curtains. It slowly spread across the room like syrup of gold. I propped my head on my pillow to watch and to see if it would speak to me of sunlight and warmth and love. Carolyn rolled closer and grasped me. Her tongue went into my mouth and searched to find mine; it was sudden and furious. She wanted more. We made love harder this time, and she came and came. Finally, I reached it again also; a long pulsating then there was nothing left inside. I went soft, and she said, "What happened to the warrior? I guess he was defeated in battle." She looked comically grave as if this wasn't supposed to happen; it should be forever hard!

We had breakfast down the road, toward Santa Barbara, in a decent highway roadhouse and restaurant. We spent the day in Santa Barbara and returned to our cabin after having dinner in a Mexican restaurant in the city. The sun was setting, and we sat in front of the bungalow. We took a couple of cold Cokes out of the little refrigerator and drank them as we watched the final streaks of alizarin crimson fade in the sky before the darkness.

The man in the office had told me the hot water would take a long time as we were the furthest away from the boiler. The previous night we had jumped in and showered so quickly it never got there. This time, we let it run. When it got warm, we both jumped in and washed furiously, thinking it might not last long. Instead, it got boiling and nearly scalded us. We jumped out to adjust the cold and finally took a much more satisfying shower.

I knew this was our last night; at least that's what we were telling ourselves. I didn't know if I should believe it. It was hard to imagine us continuing the way we were going, but difficult to think of not having her there for me. And me for her. I didn't know what love was; maybe this was it. It couldn't be any better between two people. We had never had a disagreement or argument of any kind. What could be more compatible than that? But, we didn't have a life together either. The sexual thing was perfect, but being the only partner I had known, I had no idea if it got better. I thought of that many times, and I just couldn't figure out how that could be possible.

I turned to Carolyn and kissed the length of her body, and she kissed mine; we savored each other from head to toe. I could feel her going into that prolonged frenzy of passion, that driving need where she would repeatedly come. I knew she couldn't be a nymphomaniac because she had gone such long periods in her life without sex. Or maybe she didn't? Maybe she had many others like this before me, and this wasn't for real. No. I didn't believe that. No one was that good an actress all of the time.

Her passion was overwhelming. She sat on top of me throwing her head back and moving in all directions. She gained momentum and started to reach that level I thought was climaxing, but it must be just a state of exalted feeling because no one could come for that long and so many times. At least I didn't think so. I had heard women have much more stamina and feelings than men do. I loved that she could reach that level. She was grinding hard into my body when she exploded, taking fast deep breaths with a high-pitched squealing sound. We must be waking up the entire motel and campgrounds, I thought. She continued to move and pump up and down with no let up in pace. She stopped squealing and started to growl as she bore down on me. I was so excited that I came, letting out my cry of pleasure. But she never stopped, and I continued to feel hard and want more. She reached it again shortly after I did, and her body became rigid in a series of spasms. She kept moving. I whirled her over and was on top while she was at the peak of passion. I made love harder and faster than I had ever done before, and she responded in a frantic, almost demonic, gyration, her face contorted. She gasped, hissed and growled. Then we came together with such intensity I didn't know what or where we were. I was crazy out of my mind, and she was delirious. We laid there quivering together for a very long time. My body had become so limp I couldn't think or react to what had happened. As I regained my composure, I thought if we kept getting more intense as we went on we would surely die of the strain. She slept into the early hours and at times in the night, we were entwined, and I felt her nibbling at my ear and fiddling with my hair.

We returned home the next day to our ordinary world. The following Thursday I went to Carolyn's house and did the yard work. When she got up, I ate my lunch as usual while she had her breakfast. When she was done, we put our arms around each other and cried. I had thought long and hard about us and how it should end. I had my speech ready.

"I know it's time to end our relationship, I've learned about women because of you; you'll always be special in my life. I feel I'm a man now, because of you. I won't whimper and fuss because I don't want to spoil what has happened between us. I just hope one day, when the time comes, I can feel this way again. I think it's best that I don't work for you anymore. I don't know if I'll be able to do it without my emotions getting the best of me. I don't even know how I'll be able to be happy without you. You've given me more warmth and understanding than I've ever received in my life. I'll need that memory to see me through, as I don't know when I'll have someone so dear to me again."

Carolyn cried and told me she knew I was right. It was the reflection of what she felt. I gave her a drawing I had done, signed with love. I told her when I was 18, and society could accept us; I would come to see her again, and see if our love had endured.

The next year I found she had sold the house and moved to San Francisco.

[It's strange as I write this some sixty-eight years later that every moment is so clear to me. Things that happened in my 40s and 50s are never quite as distinct. The experience with Carolyn was so instrumental in my development and future relationships that I referred to it often. Some years later when I began singing with a band, I adopted Carolyn's last name. It made me feel like I was still a part of her life. It was many years before I had another relationship, and I was in my mid-30s before I would again feel the same level of love. I hoped and longed my whole life that I would see her again, even if just to tell her again what she had done for my life. But, it never happened. I realize now after a lifetime of experiences, we had a very special relationship; something rarely achieved between lovers.

Many years later when I returned from Europe, I made a concentrated effort to locate her. But, that was before the computer age of today and finding people has become so much easier. She had obviously remarried and hopefully had a family and was happy. I've thought about her thousands of times, each with such love in my heart. A few years ago, I read about a school teacher that had an affair with a student 16 years old. The television and newspapers made quite a scandal of it. She was depicted as some vile and evil woman that had corrupted this innocent youth. She was put on probation, and she violated it by seeing him again. When asked why she did this, she said, "Because I love him." She then served a year in prison. When the boy became 18, they married and now had children, and from what I've read are happy.

I have a friend who is 58 years old; his wife is 23. They married when she was 19 years old. But, that's accepted in our society. My relationship with Carolyn, even now would likely not be. But I never in my life, until I met Joyce, ever felt more love and satisfaction as I found with Carolyn. Through the years, I have a much clearer understanding of how singular she was to have handled everything the way she did. Now with a lifetime to evaluate those memories, I realize we truly had something extraordinary, somehow we were matched in a way that seldom happens, and I was so fortunate it happened to me.]

* * *

A year later, after giving Carolyn that drawing, I entered high school and majored in art. My first day in class, we were asked to do a drawing of a still life that had been set up. The teacher, Mr. Wright, walked around the room watching each student as he attempted to reproduce what he saw. "We must clean up now. Please put your names on your artwork and leave it on my desk." As the class adjourned, he approached and asked me to stay for a minute after the bell. "Where did you learn to draw like that?" he asked. I told him how I became interested in art and related the story of the copying board, my brother's drawing gizmo. He asked me to bring some of my work to the class. The next day I brought in a portfolio of drawings and Mr. Wright kept them for a week. After that, it was as if I was the only one in his class. He gave me his full attention except for one other boy, Bob McClay. [I have through the years seen Bob at various reunions. He alone was the only other student to follow an art career seriously.] I went to Mr. Wright's house on Saturdays when I wasn't working too early. He would loan me books and encourage me to learn about the Impressionists. It was his encouragement that fostered my move to study in Paris.

Pencil drawing, 1947, from a photograph of my great grandfather.

3

WHEELS & A JOB

When I learned to drive, my world changed. I had been working very hard for several years with my yard work services. I knew I would want a car when I learned to drive, so I had saved four hundred dollars in the bank. That was a good sum of money in those days.

When I was 16, my mother said, I should ask my father to help me pick out a car. On a weekend, he came out and he, my brother and I went out to look at cars. My dad saw an ad in the newspaper for a 1937 Plymouth sedan. It claimed to have only 60,000 miles on it and be in perfect condition. The story made sense since fuel was rationed during the war years so you couldn't put many miles on a personal car. It was a dark blue color and in pristine condition. It didn't have a scratch anywhere, and it was hard to believe it was ten years old. They hadn't produced any cars from 1941 until 1946, so the styles had not changed much. The woman wanted $550. My father haggled with her for a while, and they settled for $500. My dad came up with the extra hundred and made the deal.

In retrospect, the psychological effects were fantastic. With my car, I thought of myself as a man, as someone who would accomplish great things and succeed without question. Carolyn had given me confidence and maturity, and wheels gave me independence and mobility. I had a new job and was making more money than any of my friends. Working for Mr. Price and Mr. Boyle at a Whelan Drug Store at Ninth and Alvarado, I had become a necessary part of the business, and I started doing all of the inventory and ordering. Boyle and Price were good about giving me time off for other activities, I always got the job done, and they knew it.

I had been working for the Whelan Drug Store for about two years when one evening a man approached me at the closed lunch counter where I was taking a break. He gave me a card and said he knew of my work and was interested in offering me a better job, earning more money. I met with him a day or two later. He said the owners of another Whelan Drug Store, on Main Street downtown, were having a lot of inventory control problems, and they'd be interested in talking to me about their problems. I took the following Saturday off and went to meet with them at their store. I looked at the systems they had in place. I realized what I had done for Mr. Price and Mr. Boyle at my store was inventive and extraordinary. I had created forms and inventory methods that cut the time down for keeping track and ordering. When I saw the size of the downtown store, I knew that with their system they must be losing a lot of merchandise without knowing it. I was very surprised they had no real handle on the way the stock room was set up, small items on large shelves, large items squeezed in a small area. It was a mess, with no idea of how to solve the problems. But it was one of Whelan's most successful stores, and they just kept things going the best they could. The inventory manager was also a clerk and had a brain the size of a pea. When I started asking him questions about how certain things were done he became defensive, and another clerk who worked with him on inventory control joined in with an open attack on me.

I was 17 and looked 15. These men in their 30s and 40s were not going to put up with this teenager. The owners watched what was taking place, and just sat there bewildered. I said I could solve their problem, but I didn't want to work at that location as a permanent

44

job, that I had an obligation to my current employers. I would see if they'd let me work part time in the summer months, and I would make them a proposal. They agreed.

When I talked to Mr. Boyle and Mr. Price, Mr. Boyle was his usual stiff-lipped self. He said the system was theirs, and he wouldn't share it. I reminded him the system had been developed by me with no input from anyone else. And I had worked it out in my head while driving to and from work, which was three hours a day I wasn't paid. I designed most of the forms away from the store as well. Mr. Price took over and asked Mr. Boyle to let him handle the situation. At this point, I was angry and frustrated. Mr. Price was a gracious man, and he showed great appreciation for my ingenuity and methods. He said he would talk to the people and tell them what could be done. That Mr. Boyle was wrong, that I had saved them considerable money, and he was going to see if he could make me a deal. And he and Mr. Boyle would be giving me a raise as well. Several days later, he told me he had talked to the owners and had gone to their Main Street store. He said it was in such a mess; he wouldn't know where to start. But he had told them I would come up with a plan. He had evaluated their situation and the store, and he would help me put something together that was beyond just a new inventory policy.

I learned, from this, a critical lesson about people, business and myself. When I saw the store at 6th and Main Street, I didn't like the area. It was a rough part of town, and parking there at night and working until midnight, then going out to my car, was a scary thought. Because of that, I used the excuse that I must evaluate it with my employers. I learned that was the proper thing to do. I couldn't have made a deal such as I did without the help of Mr. Price.

I worked the entire summer, six hours each day during the

week, at the Main Street and another six in the evening at the Alvarado store. My proposal for the Main Street store was that a new and more efficient staff should be hired. One of the major problems as I perceived it was the employees themselves. The physical change was easy, but the personnel problem was the most difficult. The owners were making significant money, the liquor department and the cheap merchandise was a gold mine, so the owners just didn't pay much attention to the details. And the employees were stealing from them. They needed an entirely new system that tracked everything and kept it in order so missing items would be evident. When I realized what was taking place, I became aware of how much was missing. I then realized the forms that I was filling out were being altered. Again, I consulted with Mr. Price, and we made a plan. He gave of his time freely and I was making nearly double what I was making at the Alvarado store.

By the end of the summer, the store was on a whole new level, and the owners had realized how poorly they had been running things. Their attorney, who was the original man that came to see me came in on my last day. He expressed how grateful they were and gave me a bonus check for one thousand dollars. He said when I was out of school in another year he would be interested in having me work for the Whelan Drug Company. In what capacity he didn't know but he would assure they'd find a significant position for me.

Even with work, I was participating in musical programs, sports, and the Keenan Wynn Camp troupe obligations. I was gaining ground socially. I knew what I could do, and my confidence soared. I made it a point not to tell anyone about my long drives to Los Angeles and the hours I was working. I felt it was better just to play the role of a very busy person who didn't have a lot of spare time. A few close friends knew and were sworn to secrecy, not only because of where I

46

worked but because I felt it was important to maintain a particular image. I knew if classmates knew I was commuting downtown, no matter what the job, it would be interpreted as a negative. It was also illegal for me to work thirty-two hours per week.

I worked for Mr. Price until I graduated from high school, and he came to my graduation. The experience working for him would factor in the rest of my life. I learned there were many people in the business world who make money by blind luck. Few evaluate the details and the results on any critical level. I also learned that people are affected by their surroundings, their past and the people they associate with; I realized the environment I was working in was one I must escape. I needed to align myself with people of higher intelligence, greater creative prowess, and more success. The contrast and divide, between the level of the more elite students at school and the people of the Whelan Drug companies, was the size of the Grand Canyon.

My mother came to my high school graduation. My father never showed up. I was disappointed. But it confirmed there wasn't any relationship with him I could depend on. [My dad died at 78 of lung cancer and I felt very little. I don't think we, in all of our adult years, ever communicated on any satisfactory level. In his 50s, he married again to a sweet lady. She liked to cook and clean and take care of him, and I guess he had a satisfactory life. She was five years his senior, and he was a little embarrassed about it, but as it turned out she lived to one hundred and eight years old, so who was the youngest? I have certain regrets that I didn't have the people skills to get through to him, as I know he was a very intelligent and talented man. I wish now I had worked harder to develop a bond and friendship.]

* * *

When I quit the Keenan Wynn Camp troupe, I regretted it as I had had a lot of fun with the many talented dancers and singers I had worked with. Barbara Ruick, who brought me into the group, had other interests now, and Debbie Reynolds had become very much in demand in the movie industry. Doing the camp shows was a fun part of my high school years. Every time we rehearsed those shows I would fall more in love with Debbie, she was always so nice and loving to everyone. We never had any time together, and she didn't know my feelings. I was lucky Mr. Price, and Mr. Boyle, my bosses at the Whelan Drug Store felt the shows were important for the men in uniform, so they were always very accommodating with my work schedule.

[Some thirty years later, Debbie and I had a chance encounter when she came into the De Ville Galleries. When I approached her, she didn't recognize me. I asked her if she remembered me. She looked carefully, and then her face became animated, and she seemed so happy to see me. I had followed her career with great interest, and I wasn't surprised at her success. She was an outstanding talent even as a very young girl. She was living in Malibu and asked if I would like to come to dinner at her home. I told her I was going out to my house in Malibu which was under construction, to see how it was progressing, and she said she would like to join me. I picked her up, and we went out to the building site together. It had been raining, and the surrounding terrain was quite muddy. She walked through the mud, not minding it, and admired the house with me. She was so enthusiastic about what I was doing. We went to her home and after eating an unusual dinner of caviar, champagne, and toast, we settled down for a fun ride down memory lane. She had a superb recollection, and we laughed at the antics of the troupe.

Keenan Wynn was a fantastic character, and he brought out the best in everyone.

I told Debbie how in love I was with her in those years, and she seemed very touched. She then said the years with Eddie Fisher and Harry Karl had been difficult and stressful. Harry Karl, who she thought was the master entrepreneur, invested all the considerable monies she had made, in his failing business and lost it all. I told her about my life and two failed marriages that gave us a mutual bond.

I told her about Joyce. That I had finally met the girl of my dreams, and how happy I was with her. She smiled and said she was happy for me, but I could see she was disappointed. I guess she thought I was a single guy, and I think she needed someone. I told her I wanted to be friends again, and I wanted her to meet Joyce. Being with her brought many feelings back, and I realized with all the fame and fortune she was still the same beautiful person.]

***

I played a lot of tennis and basketball in those years and became one of the better tennis players in the 14 and under level. Then in high school I was able to play on the tennis team. High school was fun, and I was popular with my talent for singing, guitar, and art. My primary objective, however, was romancing and pursuing women. I got close sometimes, but after my affair with Carolyn, nothing materialized until my senior year. Sue Atkins was about a year younger than I was. She was in a way a bit of a trollop; she had a reputation for being easy if you had a condom! Many of the guys claimed they had had her. I liked Sue; she was cute, fun and had a great personality.

I moved to live with my father when I was 17 years old. My mother and I had difficulties getting along, as I couldn't deal with her alcoholic personality. I couldn't understand why she had to drink and smoke so much, but she always said it was her only pleasure. It got to me, and I asked my father if I could live with him. He lived in the Silver Lake district, and I took the Riverside Drive route to go to his house and on to the downtown area to work at the Whelan Drug Store. The trip in those days was a long slow journey as it was before the multi-lane motorways were built. It took me a full forty-five minutes to get home and another half an hour to go on to the store. It added up to nearly to three hours each day driving.

On a Saturday night, Sue told me she was going to be with her father in the Quonset village in Griffith Park, a real estate development completed during World War Two for housing soldiers. It wasn't far from my dad's house. She said she could go out with me from there. I picked her up, and we went out for something to eat. But she had to be home by ten o'clock. I took her home, and she said, she could sneak out and meet me after eleven when her father and his wife went to bed. I waited in my car in the parking lot and finally fell asleep. About 12:30, she knocked on the window, and we got in the back seat and started necking. We got hot into it; I put on a condom, and we made it like rabbits in heat. We were both so horny; I hadn't been laid since Carolyn, which had been almost three years before. Sue was a hot number; she enjoyed it even though I didn't last very long. I continued to play with her, and she couldn't get enough. After a while, I put on another condom, and we had a long and very satisfying session. I was so excited about having a new relationship and having a sexual partner again; I thought I must establish a trust with her. I told her I had great feelings for her, and I would never discuss our relationship with anyone. It could be known we were just friends. She liked this as she was aware many of the guys had talked about her promiscuity. But, between sports and my many hours of working, I didn't have a lot of time to devote to her. We managed to have some exciting episodes over the next couple of months, but I think it just wasn't enough for her. She was looking for some permanent relationship. It wasn't long after that she left school, and I heard she was living with an older guy.

* * *

When I was working that summer helping to pull together the inventory for the Whelan Drug Company, I worked with a young black man by the name of Andy. One day after Andy and I had become friends, he asked me to go to with him to a jazz club a few blocks from the store. He said he was singing and dancing that night in a contest. He knew of my background, and he wanted me to see him perform. I called Mr. Price to see if it was okay to take the night off from my evening job. He said it would be good for me to take a break.

Andy and I went to Philippe's for dinner. It was a traditional place near the train station and famous for the French Dip sandwiches. That was in 1949, and the restaurant is still a favorite place sixty-six years later. When we entered the nightclub, it was after eight o'clock, and it was already quite crowded. The five-piece band hadn't arrived, but the people were preparing for the competition. When we entered, they looked at me with suspicion as I was the only white person there. Andy put his arm around me and introduced me to all of his friends. They must have been a tight group as he knew everyone by name. We settled in and by nine o'clock, the place was in full swing. I had a lot of exposure to incredible talents in the Keenan Wynn Camp troupe and the military shows, but what was displayed that evening floored me.

The first one up was a short fat lady, wearing what looked like a factory worker dress. Andy leaned over to me and said she was great. The group started to play. They were professional and had a great sound. The lady began to bounce and gyrate until every ounce of flesh on her body was moving with the beat. I was thinking to myself what flexibility she had as her body seemed to be made of soft rubber. She sang *'Just one of those things'* and it was the best rendition I had ever heard. Where did this dowdy fat lady learn to sing like that? [Later, in Europe, that song became one of my standard songs, and every time I sang it I thought of her, but I knew I could never match her performance.]

A series of very talented people appeared one after the other in rapid succession, but I didn't react quite like with the fat lady. When Andy got up, there was a tremendous ovation before he even started, and it was obvious he was the favorite of the crowd.

The group played a fast-paced jazz version of, *'Night and Day,'* and Andy started to slide from side to side. [Years later I saw a show by Michael Jackson. His dancing reminded me of Andy.] After some of the most original dance moves I had ever seen, Andy started to tap-dance around the tiny floor. I was amazed; he was good. Then he began to sing. The second chorus of the song went into a regular beat, and Andy had a strong and beautiful voice. It was a fabulous performance, one of the most memorable in my life. He won the award, and the acceptance and warmth of the people were my perfect introduction to the black community. I developed a love and respect for the hardships they had endured, and later in Paris, I began to work with so many great talents that escaped the prejudice and restrictions they had felt in our country. Andy was a Sammy Davis

Jr., with equal talent, but I never heard about him again after I left the store. I told my friend and agent Wendell Niles about him, and he was going to get him an audition. I called the store to see if I could talk to him, but he had left. They gave me a phone number, but it had been disconnected. I remembered he had said his mother wasn't well; she lived somewhere in the south, so I assumed he had gone back home to be with her.]

* * *

After high school, I was singing a couple of times a week with Mel Baker's orchestra and quit working at the Whelan Drug Company. When I started classes at the Art Center School majoring in commercial art, I got a job at the Times-Mirror newspaper working in the Art Department, thinking I would gain some real experience. It was mostly painting out backgrounds on photographs. I wanted to do something that was art related even if it was only retouching photos. That was essentially blocking out things they didn't want to be shown in some article, or some person that wasn't significant to the story. It was tedious work, and the parking was a real headache. I not only didn't like the work, but I wasn't making nearly the money I had made previously. After a few months, I told my boss I wanted to do ad layouts and something more artistic. He said he had several people ahead of me that would get those jobs first. I quit, but I had gained an understanding of a newspaper operation. I had wandered around endlessly and talked to everyone I could, watching all the various departments and how they operated to find out more. But I found the people there were a hyperactive bunch; brusque and not people I wanted to associate with.

I was living with my father at that point. He had an extra bedroom, and I was so busy it was just a place to sleep. My step-sister was a Hollywood social climber. She was having an affair with Lauritz Melchior, the famous singer and later married him. Gene Autry was often at the house; he had something going on with her, too, but I was never sure if they were having an affair. She was also dating Trini Lopez, who was becoming quite the rage at that time. [She eventually became a successful agent with her own agency, and later retired to Hawaii.]

The Art Center School I attended had a fine reputation. But many of the teachers were burned out. They went through the motions but didn't have the kind of dedication I had experienced with Mr. Wright, my mentor in high school. After the first semester, I changed schools and went to Woodbury College, which was on Wilshire Boulevard at the time. I had several good teachers there, and the professors and the students admired my work. I won nearly every poster and commercial art contest at the school.

When I was attending Woodbury College, I was introduced to a woman by the name of Bertha Marksman. She had a small shop and gallery on Rodeo Dr. in Beverly Hills. When I showed her some of my work, mostly paintings done at the home of Mr. Wright, she was openly enthusiastic. I framed about ten paintings and several drawings for what she called a one-man show. I was working for the Times-Mirror newspaper at the time, and as I mentioned, I was discouraged with all aspects of that job. The idea of a one-man exhibit, my first one, was very exciting. She had the show on a Saturday afternoon and served tea and crackers. About fifteen of her friends were there, and passerby's that happened in because they were shopping on the street. I was there for about three hours and everyone complimented me on my skill at such a young age. I had heard that often over the last few years, and it meant little to me. I knew I was good at drawing, but my paintings were mediocre.

54

Nothing was sold that Saturday. About four days later, I came by when I didn't have any classes, to see how things were going. Only two drawings were on the walls, and the remainder had been taken down. Fat Bertha said they were not selling, and she couldn't afford to keep them up. She had sold one drawing for sixty dollars of which she took half. The frame cost me nearly twenty dollars. By the time, I took into consideration the time and expenses overall the show was a big loss. A week later I brought everything home, discouraged, but with the resolve, I would never put out the effort unless it was for a legitimate operating gallery with an established clientele. I had learned a valuable lesson about business.

II

ART, MUSIC & LOVE

4

PLANS FOR PARIS

I realized that commercial art wasn't what I wanted; it was too confining. But those efforts would teach me to be very independent. My whole life seemed a training ground for my fierce independence. If I was to make it as an artist, I needed to study and surround myself with those with whom I could learn and benefit. I began to plan how I would go to Paris and attend the famous Beaux Arts Académie. In my last year at Woodbury, I sent off a portfolio of eight by ten glossy photographs of my drawings and my paintings. I didn't send any of the commercial art, just the work I had done at George Wright's home. I continued to see George, and we planned together much of what I was attempting. He had been in Paris but had never had the chance to work there; he had married early and needed to support a family.

My dream of studying the Impressionist painters of Paris was a fantasy fostered by the many books I had read on those artists and their lives. I had saved considerable money, but I was unsure about my ability to stay the course for years of study. I contacted my agent at the William Morris Agency, to see if there was a possibility of work in Paris if I was accepted. I had been singing and entertaining for several years with local orchestras and bands, mostly just here and there and on weekends. I had a beautiful voice, and I was a good dancer, but I had no experience in nightclubs or any steady appearances. That would be a new experience for me, too.

Then I received a reply; the Académie had accepted me, and I was overjoyed. It was no longer just dreams. I was going to study and live Paris! When word got around Woodbury that I was accepted to study in Paris several of the students that were graduating came to me to find out what the plan was. Three of the guys going to school on the GI Bill decided to join me. We had several meetings, and they all enrolled at the Académie Julian, which was approved by the GI Bill for support. The amount they received would be enough. The exchange rate for the dollar was quite high and prices were low compared to the U.S. I didn't have any support, but after selling my car, and with the savings I had accumulated, it would be enough. In a pinch I knew I could live on a hundred dollars a month, so this was a substantial cushion in case I couldn't find work. But my agents found me a singing engagement in Paris. They had sent several of my recordings to their contacts in London and had a potential for a spot at the Lido nightclub in Paris. I didn't know the Lido or what kind of club it was, but they said it paid well and was a big show. It wasn't a done deal, however; they wanted me to come and audition before they would sign a final contract. I was confident I would do well in the audition, but there was a significant problem. They wanted me the end of May, as rehearsals were to start the beginning of June. I went to the faculty of the college and explained my problem, and it was arranged that all four of us would graduate regardless of leaving early.

The three men joining me were just that; grown men. Each was quite interesting in their way. Walt Kell was a burly guy, about six feet tall, and good looking. He was a little withdrawn but had a good sense of humor. Walt had served in the Navy for four years in the Pacific during the war, and that gave him certain camaraderie with Jack Fries. Jack was a giant of a man of Danish descent. Bald but very handsome, he had also been in the Navy in the Pacific. Frank Salazar was of Spanish heritage and had served in the Marines in the Pacific. Frank had seen a lot of action and had twice received the Purple Heart. Frank was good looking as well and a real ladies man. This group was a tough bunch, who had been through the war and wanted to have the education and adventure that Paris could provide.

We all wanted to save every penny possible, so we took a Greyhound bus to New York. We were excited about the trip and studied French and books and maps of Paris on the two and a half-day bus ride. Frank was the most outgoing of the group, and he, and I seemed to have more in common. We teamed up and sat together most of the trip. He was ten years older than I and had been married. He had a son named Perry after Perry Como, a famous singer Frank admired. He and his wife had lived in several apartments and finally bought a house with his GI Loan. The marriage didn't work out, and Frank went back to school at Woodbury College. Walt and Jack had their Navy experiences in common, and they got along well. We didn't sleep except on the bus so by the time we got there we were beat. Walt had friends who lived in Greenwich Village; they were entertainers and a couple of wild characters. They had agreed to put us up for a few days until we rested and could make the trip to Montreal where we would board the Greek Line ship, *The Columbia*. It was a round bottomed old passenger vessel, built in the 1930s. It was also slow. It would take us ten days to get to Le Havre, and then we would take a train to Paris where I would arrive the day before my scheduled audition.

[In fact, Walt, Jack, Frank and I got along well for the rest of our lives. As I write this, I'm 82 years old, and Jack is 90. Walt and Frank have passed. Because I was much younger than the others, they treated me like a recruit in the service. It was all in good spirits, and I know they all had great respect for my talent as an artist. They didn't know much about me other than the recognition I received at school and as a familiar face at Woodbury until the Paris plans started.]

When we arrived in New York, we took a taxi to the village. Walt's friends were waiting for us and had a nice lunch prepared. Their names were Carla and Fernando; a very well-known Flamenco dance team at that time. Carla was a very sexy dark-haired beauty. She wore a sheer silky one-piece loose jumpsuit. Her breasts and nipples moved lusciously under the thin garment, and her black bush was evident. She knew what she displayed and enjoyed turning us on. When we arrived, she hugged and kissed each one of us and welcomed us to their apartment. It was a rather run down, old, red brick building; the kind you would often see in the New York suburbs. The apartment was half of an entire floor. It had an extra bedroom with twin beds and a dance studio with wood floors. The studio had a sofa-bed, and Carla had put an extra portable bed there as well. As the youngest, I got the portable bed. It didn't matter; I could sleep on anything and be happy.

The three days we spent with them was wonderful. The rather shabby apartment meant nothing when you had such fun and exciting people to share it. It was a new experience for me, and they were a type of carefree people I never knew existed. One night they took us out to a local Spanish restaurant where they were well-known. The woman greeted all of us as if we were long-lost relatives. We sat down, and she proceeded to feed us family style with more helpings of whatever we wanted. It wasn't like any restaurant I had known. It was as if eating at someone's home it was so informal. The main dish was like a colossal enchilada filled with rice, pork, peppers, onions and who knows what. I still remember the evening and the tastes vividly.

I had watched the dance team rehearse in the studio several times while I was there. They spent hours each day, working out routines and physically pounding away on the floor. They were fortunate the couple that lived downstairs both worked, so the noise wasn't a problem, and they never rehearsed on the weekends. [I had never experienced Flamenco dancing up close but later in life, I saw many dance teams perform in Spain. But I never saw it performed as well as Carla and Fernando.]

When I had arrived, Fernando saw my guitar case and asked me to play and sing. When I did, it was the first time my friends had ever heard me. I had told them I had work lined up in Paris if everything worked out okay. But I don't think they took me very seriously. Only Frank had a grip on what my job plans were, as we had talked about it at length on the bus ride. Fernando brought out his guitar, and we tried to play together, but he was a Flamenco guitarist and much better than me. I played a finger picking technique that was strictly to accompany my singing. When I watched him play and saw him dance, it was a clue as to the kind of future there was in the entertainment business. Here was one of the best Flamenco teams in the country, performing in and around New York, with a man who played guitar just like the best in the world, but they didn't have anything. Carla said if they didn't have a gig within a month or two, she'd be waiting on tables. Carla was in her late 30s, and Fernando was in his early 40s. But they seemed happy and full of life.

Greenwich Rooftop, Carla, Christian and her mother, May 1952.

[Who is to say what is worthwhile, or what the future will bring for any of us. But, I have thought a lot about them over the years; how little they had and how long they had been living that life. Walt and I kept in touch when we returned to Los Angeles. He went into the antique business, mostly just selling odds and ends in his little shop in El Segundo, California, in the beach suburbs of Los Angeles. He taught painting to little old ladies, and some of them bought his artwork. He was the least talented of our group, even though he was a very hard worker. There was just something missing in his vision, he didn't know what was good so that he couldn't grasp the essentials of his craft. He was with a woman he loved, and I never knew if they were married, he always referred to her by name and never as his wife. Walt was always a smoker, and he died of lung cancer at 70. I had asked him about Carla and Fernando over the years, and he said he had lost touch. I didn't have to ask, I

62

instinctively knew they hadn't fared well.]

 They were great hosts, and it was my first trip to New York. The four of us tramped all over the city and saw the museums, galleries, and points of interest. By the time we left, I think we were as tired as when we arrived. We boarded another bus and headed for Montreal where Walt had booked us in a little hotel for one night. We didn't even go out on the town; just ate and collapsed. We had to board the boat by four in the afternoon, so we just had one day in the city. It was a great place, and I was sorry we didn't leave a day or two to see more of it. But it was a French atmosphere and a taste of what was to come.

5

THE ART ACADEMIES

The first few days of the voyage were quite rough, and the old round bottomed ship rolled from gunnel to gunnel. Jack and Walt were both ex-Navy, and the motion of the boat didn't faze them at all. Frank, a former Marine Corps sergeant, had been on transport ships during the war and was a seasoned voyager. I didn't seem to have a problem with the motion either, although I wasn't in the least accustomed to it.

Our waiter was miffed as our table was the only one for several days that had anyone showing up to eat. He had to work hard as we were a hungry bunch. Since I was so much younger than my friends, they considered me a novice at sea travel and just about everything else. Walt would talk about the most disgusting subjects he could think of at every meal and then others would chime in with their additions to complete the imagery. Their attempts failed as I ate with gusto the entire trip.

Onboard Walt was trying to romance a German girl named Clara. She had unusually large eyes and was quite fascinating to look at. Walt pursued her until she became sick and started barfing at the rail for hours. With that, she had lost her allure, and he abandoned his quest. I, however, realizing the choices aboard for female companionship were indeed slim, began to bring her wet towels and attended to her in her hours of distress. Jack was pursuing an older married woman with little success. Frank had picked out a real little dolly but he had a small prospect of conquering. I had learned the old saying, 'go ugly early,' and although Clara was quite pleasant looking it was hard to get past those abnormally large eyes.

The third day things started to calm down, and Walt was back on the trail of Clara. She cuddled next to me and made it quite clear he was no longer in the running. Clara and I got into some serious kissing and petting that evening. We were sitting in a deck lounge with other couples on both sides. Lying on our sides facing each other with a blanket covering us I felt her tongue darting in my mouth, and it made me crazy with passion. She sucked on my mouth and tongue until it almost hurt. I felt her hand go down to my groin, and she deftly unbuttoned my pants, unzipped my fly and pulled me out. She played with me for what seemed like hours, all the time pushing my hand away from her pussy but allowing me to fondle her breasts. Her breasts were quite small, but she had nipples to match her eyes.

The couple on one side left, and the other was as engrossed as we were. Clara made a very smooth move and suddenly was on top of me and before I knew it, she had slipped my member inside of her. I couldn't believe she had done it so adroitly. It surprised me as I didn't expect to start right there. She slowly moved as to not draw attention to us, but there were people coming and going, and I'm sure it wasn't too difficult to figure out what was going on. She asked several times that I not come inside her; she had no protection. I felt her quiver several times and knew she was reaching her apex. It didn't seem to affect me, and whenever I felt I was getting close, I would stop her. After a close call, she said we should stop. We arranged ourselves and went upstairs to the poop deck. No one was there, and we cuddled under a stairwell. She started playing with me again, and I admitted I was getting frustrated. I felt as if I had a perpetual erection. "Don't worry," she said, "I'll make you happy!"

And indeed, she did! I never in my nineteen years had had a more dramatic climax. Clara was only my age, but she was as expert as any woman I had met before or since then. During the next five days, Clara never took her diaphragm out but she gave me a multitude of blowjobs in between some very unusual fucking episodes. Once we did it at the stern at two in the morning; the boat would shudder dramatically as the prop would cavitate on the big swells. We sat there on a bench with her straddling me and took advantage of the boats intense vibration. Several times we did it in bathtubs in the separate small rooms that accommodated the cabin class passengers.

Christian, Clara and Frank on deck.

Christian Title

The guys and I made a deal to allow anyone of us to use our cabin for an hour at a time. We would put the Do Not Disturb card out; it had Beware scrawled across it in large red letters. If it was an emergency to get in the cabin, the code was to whistle '*Old McDonald Had A Farm*' while walking down the corridor. Then the occupant could vacate as soon as possible. My mates were obviously jealous as the youngest member, the one considered inexperienced; I was the only one to use the cabin. One day when they were listening at the door for the right moment, they sang the code in unison as loud as possible right outside. I was at a crucial peak, Clara and I gasping and crying out. They thought that was the funniest thing in the world.

Clara and I stayed in the cabin for hours and wouldn't unlock the door. When we thought we heard them, we would fake all the sounds of passion and climax. We exited some three hours later, and I had gained new respect from my colleagues. She made the trip something special; we hit it off so well and never had a cross word. She told me she was returning home to get married; she had been in Canada for two years as an au pair. A job she said she didn't have full knowledge of when she went there. She thought it was to be working for a married couple, but it was to care for the children of a single man. She said she had fallen in love with him, but he wouldn't marry her. On the rebound, she had heard from a school friend that had always wanted to marry her. She was returning for that purpose but wasn't sure it would work out. She had no place else to go. When the launch took us ashore in Le Havre, Clara stood at the rail as she was continuing to Bremerhaven. She waved goodbye and blew kisses at me.

"Thank you for the gift," she called to me. She was holding a small box in her hand.

67

On the train to Paris, I told Frank I hadn't given her a gift. Frank said Walt had wrapped it for her and said it was from me. "What was it?" I asked all the way to Paris, but only got answers like: "It's something she'll always cherish. She'll sleep with it under her pillow! Of course there is the chance it could ruin her life; I guess even suicide is a possibility if she contemplates it for too long. It was certainly a once in a lifetime memento." They went on like that until they had drained every last joke and laugh out of it.

When we arrived in Paris, we went directly to the Hotel de Seine. The hotel was a well-known student hotel in the Mabillion arrondissement of the Left Bank and central to the Beaux Arts Académie, the Sorbonne, and the Julian Académie. We had settled into the hotel when Frank told me what the gift to Clara was. It was the Do Not Disturb—Beware, sign. That Walt had given Clara the sign bothered me. She and I had had a special relationship, and I had shown concern for her future. We had spent nearly every waking hour together on the voyage for eight of the days. I left with a feeling of love and respect for Clara. What they had given her was a locker-boy-mentality trophy of conquest, not a reflection of my feelings.

The Hotel de Seine was the first home to Frank, Jack, and I while in Paris. Walt had after a few days found a seventh-floor walk-up a few blocks from the Académie Julian. He was proud of the place. It was within his budget and had an excellent view of the rooftops and the street below. We visited him the following week after he had spruced it up. The place had a wash basin, a portable bidet and a table that sat two people by the window. The room was only about eight feet wide and twenty feet long. The bed was about as wide as an American single bed. It had two old stuffed chairs that looked like remnants from the Napoleonic era. The ceiling sloped toward the window on the street side and barely had room for Walt to walk down

68

the center of the window cubicle. Walt was six feet and had a large frame, making him appear to be much bigger. I was six feet as well, but slender, about fifty pounds less than Walt. Frank was a similar height and had a medium build, but he had an aura about him that commanded respect. Jack was a giant; the big Dane we called him. He was six-foot-six inches with a massive build. He carried two hundred and thirty-five pounds and still appeared slim. Compared to the French, who were mostly small people, this foursome always attracted attention, mostly because of Jack. He had been a heavyweight champion in the Pacific Fleet in the Navy, and his size and quick reflexes made him an impressive individual. He had gone bald young; only a few strands of hair remained on his nicely shaped head. Regardless, he was very handsome, with beautiful features and well-proportioned body. He wasn't quite comfortable in Walt's new place as it made him claustrophobic; he couldn't stand without bowing his head. And for all of us climbing seven floors of steep stairs was exhausting.

The hotel room in Rue de Seine had nine-foot ceilings and two large windows overlooking the street. It was a four-story climb, but nothing like the nearly vertical stairs that Walt had to contend with every day. The room had three beds and a sink, but the bathroom and showers were down the hall. You paid extra for showers, and the water was monitored from the concierge's desk and quarters. Walt had no shower facilities, and the toilet was one and a half floors below. He rigged up a pee bottle to save him trips during the night. He heated water and took baths in the portable bidet. There were several bath houses in the Saint Germain-des-Prés area, and we used them when we wanted a long hot shower, free of complaints from the concierge.

I spent the first week getting registered at the Beaux Arts

Académie and the Sorbonne. The others were enrolled in the Julian Académie on the Rue du Dragon also in Saint Germain-des-Prés. I went there often for the croquille classes. Jack and Walt never went to those, but Frank would meet me, and we would have fun with the quick sketches. As it turned out, I went there often when I didn't have classes at the Sorbonne which was only two per week in the beginning. Often the overly regimented routine at the Beaux Arts caused me to attend classes at the Julian Académie instead. Many of the professors taught at both ateliers, but the Julian was much less structured, and we could pursue subjects of our choosing. The day after our arrival, I met with the director of the Lido nightclub on the Champs-Élysées. I started rehearsal the following Saturday. Although I was a very confident young man at 19, the experiences were coming so fast and furious I felt unbalanced.

Every moment I wasn't occupied I haunted the halls of the Jeu de Palme to visit the Impressionist masterpieces I had so long admired in books. I made a special trip to spend the day at the Louvre, specifically to see the famous *Mona Lisa*. What a terrible letdown it was! I don't know what I was expecting, but the painting didn't excite me at all. I guess I thought there must be something special to come from viewing it in person. Not at all. It was beautifully executed but dull.

The Italian masters of the Grand Salon didn't get me going like the Impressionists. My passion for the Impressionists increased with my daily visits to the famous museum in the Tuileries Gardens, which bordered the Place du Concorde. I found myself attending only the required classes at the Beaux Arts Academic and spending every minute I could at the Académie Julian where I could pursue the Impressionist style. The daily hours at the museum started to make a real difference in my work.

I purchased one of those excellent French portable easels and soon I could be found working outdoors along the banks of the Seine. I was working hard each night and painting every moment I could find. My sex life was concentrated on the Bluebell girls of the Lido. Although I had to be careful as Madame Bluebell kept a very watchful eye on her ladies, especially the young ones brought over from England.

I played the field when it came to the girls of the Lido. The French girls were unusually free-spirited, and a few were just game for a fun time after the show. Later on when I moved from the Hotel de Seine, the new Rue Lauriston apartment was a special place for them to come. Its walls were decorated with my paintings, and it had the atmosphere of a Left Bank artist's enclave. I always had some fears of getting a venereal disease, but penicillin was available, and there wasn't anything in those days it wouldn't take care of quickly.

I had a special relationship with one of the most beautiful of the costume topless dancers, Ginette. She was always laughing and came to my place often. She had a steady boyfriend who was about twenty-five years older. He rented a fancy apartment for her, bought her the best clothes and jewelry, and lavished her with constant gifts. He was evidently married in England where he owned a brewery. He visited her every couple of weeks for a day or two. Ginette was bored waiting for him, so we made a perfect match. Often on the weekend, she'd come and pose for me. She was not shy and loved to display her spectacular body. She was the most uninhibited, free spirit I had ever known. Ginette liked sex, but she was a lazy lover. She wanted to be played with and used without too much effort. In a way, it was perfect for me as I was tired during the week when I didn't get much sleep.

Lido Cabaret 1952

Ginette was instrumental in my moving into the showgirls' dressing room when I had problems with the gay men in the men's dressing rooms. I had a semi-private room, but the flamboyant swish group constantly invaded it. Terry Garth, (stage name Terry Brent) was an ice skater in the show. His partner Phil, who was also gay, had the dressing room next to mine. He was a Canadian and a very nice man. He saw what was developing before I did, and warned me to keep clear of some of the male dancers. I had to fight to make them keep their distance. I made it very clear I wasn't interested. They wouldn't accept I was straight and didn't want to try the homosexual path. One night after the show when I was changing and standing in my undershorts, I was grabbed from behind, between my legs. I shot around, gave a couple of quick jabs with my left fist into the right side of his face, then I hit him dead center on the nose with a right hook. Blood splattered all over the place. The entire cast ran in, and the gay stage manager started screaming at me. The dancer lay prone on the floor and wouldn't get up because for sure I would hit him again. Since I was the only straight male in the show, it presented a real problem, but even the female impersonator, George Matson, sided with me. Thankfully, there was a solution. There was a small half-dressing room open at the entrance to the women's dressing area. Ginette spoke up, and all the girl's confirmed I was welcome to use it. So it was a done deal, and I spent the next nine months there. The girls liked me and we had a lot of fun together. I think that also I learned from this exposure.

6

PARIS

St. Germain-de-Pres, Christian just arrives

Frank and I had been living in the Hotel de Seine for several months. It was comfortable and worked out as a good orientation stop before looking for a permanent residence. The area in Mabillion was close to the schools, and it had an exciting atmosphere; many food take-out stalls, charcuteries, and an array of markets and restaurants.

We often took food to our room and sat at the window overlooking the street. The table would seat four and at times we had dinner parties with girlfriends. Frank was tall, dark, and handsome; women were immediately attracted to him. Frank had a great smile and loved to laugh. He was a good friend and companion, honest and sincere, but he was the kind of guy you made sure that you shared everything with him. He didn't like surprises. I think it was his years in the Marines, with men who hit the beaches of the islands of the Pacific and slept in the jungles, fighting day and night. They developed a way of bonding with their mates; a quality that taught me a lot about friendship. The more information you give to a friend the better friend they will be. You don't know someone until they share their emotions and experiences.

1952 St. Germain-de-Prés group: Christian, Don Stewart, Walt Kell, Jack Fries, Frank Salazar, Mrs. Stewart in front

One day, Frank asked me, "What do you think of getting an apartment; one where we have a kitchen and a bathroom?"

I hadn't given it much thought, as I had been so busy with school, rehearsals, and shows at the Lido. But it seemed like the logical thing to do. Frank said he would go out and look, and we discussed the budget. I let him decide, as I was making good money with my new contract and could afford much more than he was able to spend. About a week later, he said he had rented a place, and we would move the next Saturday. I felt Frank had the experience to find the right situation, and I trusted his judgment.

The apartment was on the Rue Lauriston, one block from the Kleber metro station, and only about two blocks from the Etoile, which was a direct line to Saint Germain-des-Prés. The area around the Arc de Triomphe (Etoile) was a much higher-end neighborhood than the Latin Quarter where we had lived in the Hotel de Seine. The Trocadero and the river were nearby, and it was an easy jaunt down the Champs-Élysées to the Lido. It seemed a good choice, and it was only sixty dollars a month; the hotel was costing us ninety. I hadn't realized we could get a place so nice for so little. It was on the second etage, three flights up a broad and comfortable staircase. It had a small entry with a modest bedroom on the left. Then a hallway which had a tiny kitchen on the right and a bathroom directly across and a door to a large combination living room bedroom with a sofa-bed. The big room had three enormous windows overlooking the street. I chose the smaller bedroom as I felt I would have more privacy, and it would be quieter away from the windows. We had had considerable street noise at the hotel, and I wasn't sure how much traffic we had on the Rue Lauriston. I was also conscious of waking Frank coming in so late after the show.

But the front room was by far the lighter and more pleasant place, certainly better for entertaining guests. It had a large round table and a coal burning fireplace. Two large upholstered chairs by the windows were ideal for reading and relaxing. The drawback was the sofa-bed, not comfortable when a girl spent the night. But compared to the hotel, which had only single beds, it was a step up.

During the next week, we brought paintings and started to make it more personal. In a couple of weeks, it began to look like a real cozy nest. There was a café in the building two floors below our apartment; the concierge and her husband ran the restaurant and lived in the back, through a cobblestone courtyard. They had a six-year-old son and in the late afternoons, he was always running about. At first, I was happy to have a place to bathe and cook, but I soon missed all the convenient markets and take-out food places to which we had become accustomed.

Lucky Trenet, Christian, and Barbara Skoss on the banks of the Seine.

They were mostly run by mom and pop operators, who provided reasonable food to the working people of the market area. The quality and taste of food in these little places was truly amazing. We had a small market on the corner of the Rue Lauriston, but there was no real food shop area for quite a long walk. I often brought food back from Mabillion after school. Taking it on the metro was a pain but easier than trying to find the same things in the Etoile area.

Frank missed the gang that would hang around the El Royal in the heart of Saint Germain-des-Prés. The Académie Julian was only down the Rue du Dragon, one block from the bustle of this busy corner. After school, we would meet at the El Royal and have a café au lait. The gang would sit there for hours, talking and reading the latest news from home by passing around the afternoon Paris Herald Tribune edition. Art Buchwald was a hilarious writer and character that wrote most of his articles in the El Royal. He was a famous writer for this paper, and if he were around, we would all compliment him on his observations of the Paris life. [He went on to be a national favorite back in the U.S. in later years and wrote many books.]

I would always leave early so I could get a nap or at least a little rest before my gig at the Lido. The first evening show was at 8:30 and the second show at 10:30. I only did two songs in each show, so I had a lot of time between, but I had to be there to join the others in the finale. I could go out on the street and sit in a café or take a short walk, but that was the limit. In the foyer of the building, there was a little hole in the wall sandwich shop and a very pleasant girl by the name of Chantal. She was very young and the daughter of the owner. She went to school during the day and was in the shop until eleven each night. I would spend my time sitting there reading and when she wasn't busy she'd help me with my French. I was attracted to her, but she was very young and naive, and the girls at the Lido preoccupied me.

Christian Title

"Americans in Paris" 1952, Christian, right center with hand to mouth. Photo by Martin Dain.

[Four years later, I was sitting on the stern of my yacht *Patience* in Cannes harbor when Chantal walked past me on the dock. She was there for the last night of her vacation, and we spent it together at her hotel. She told me how she much she had wanted me to ask her out and that she had sneaked into the Lido to see my performances on several occasions. We had a perfect evening, and we continued our affair in Paris many months later. She was the last woman I had seen in the Paris years before I boarded the SS *Ile de France* for the trip home.]

Nude study at the Ecole de Beaux Arts, 1952, Oil on canvas

Noddy

One night, on a short walk during a break between shows at the Lido, I saw someone for the first time, up close and in the full light, she moved me in a way I had never felt before. We had been introduced at a rehearsal some days before; she was with the famous songwriter George Auric. She was so stunningly beautiful I couldn't pull my gaze away from her face, even to see where I was going. I only had twenty minutes until I had to be back for the next show.

I was as forceful as my limited French would allow, and we arranged that I would come to hear her sing at the Cave du Roy. Her name was Noddy Daniel; the first and only time I've ever heard that unique first name. [Years later she achieved a significant following using the name of Virginie Reno, which had more to do with her real name, Virginie Anavasi.]

I went to hear her sing the next Monday when the Lido was dark. At the Cave du Roy, I was able to convey to the bullish woman hostess that Noddy and I were friends. She excused herself for a moment. When she returned, I was shown to a front row seat. That wasn't so special since there were only about six rows of tables in the narrow tunnel-like cave. Paris in those early after the war had many underground caves converted from basements into meeting places beyond the eyes of the Germans. Eventually, they became bars and nightclubs because they held such fascination for the tourists.

Noddy had a great stage presence, Edith Piaf-like with her diminutive five-foot frame. I could see she had patterned herself and her style after that great and tragic French star, but Noddy had the great advantage of incredible beauty. When I said my goodbyes that evening, I walked the streets of St. Michael and Mabillion for a long time. I fell more in love with every step. By the time, I reached my apartment and climbed the stairs to our room I knew she would be part of my future.

I hadn't seriously considered any relationship in my life to that point as anything more than temporary. I didn't view women in terms of permanent relationships because of my age. I was 20 years old and had a bright future. I knew many of my friends in high school and college that were involved too soon and had fallen in love. Being in love is a burden when a life is to be mapped out; it seemed it led many I know to the end of their real growth.

I had avoided deep entanglements these last years, but I felt if I could only have Noddy I could still make my mark and also have the jewel of my dreams. When I arrived in my room, Frank saw my look of total captivation. I told him about Noddy, and he offered a quip of GI jargon. "You show me the most beautiful woman in the world, and I'll show you some guy out there that's tired of fucking her."

Noddy and I met for lunch the following Saturday. We were both in lust, and I didn't want to spoil it by being overly aggressive. We talked all afternoon into the early evening until we both had to return home and change for our nightclub performances. The next afternoon we met for lunch and spent the day walking the Seine and talking. My French was improving fast with the desperate need to communicate. We held hands and squeezed each other a little in a casual way. We stopped under the *Alexander*, the third bridge, and I hugged her. Something I had seen other couples do so many times while walking the quay. I was a full head taller, so my head rested on the top of her head. I became very aware of the size difference between us. I was a foot taller and close to seventy pounds heavier.

Her hair was jet black and mine was a golden blonde. As we hugged, I ran my hands over her slim body, and it almost made me crazy with desire. She had the cutest little bubble butt and very shapely legs like a ballet dancer. Her breasts were quite small but well-rounded; she didn't wear a bra, and as we hugged, I could feel their firmness. She was 16 years old with the fresh look of a child. It was for this reason I moved slowly and thought she might even be a virgin. I'd never had one before and even though I'd been told many stories about the supreme prize I wasn't going to put myself in the position, I would embarrass her or myself. I thought even of the statutory rape laws in the United States and wondered if they applied in France. I had to find out before any serious moves took place.

We had the next evening free; Monday was a traditional dark night in the Paris clubs. In the afternoon, we met at the Beaux Arts Académie where I showed her many of my more recent drawings and charcoals. The professors had been impressed, and many were hanging on the walls of the working studios. She approached a nude study and evaluated it for a moment then asked if I would do something like that of her. I immediately forgot my French vocabulary. I nodded and smiled that I would indeed be happy to do such a study. I explained she couldn't pose at the Académie since the school selected and paid for, the models.

She asked. "Could we do it in your place? It would be more comfortable."

"Oh yes," I replied somewhat amazed by her question. "We can go there now. We have lots of time before dinner." But I was quite nervous at the straightforward approach. I wasn't sure how I would handle her nudity before we were intimate. The apartment was fifteen minutes by metro. I tried to put together some semblance of a plan of action. I commented on the third etage climb, and she said she had lived most of her life climbing stairs; many more than those to my apartment. That, I said to myself, is why she has such great legs.

We arrived at the apartment. I knocked before entering and to my surprise Frank was there. He was with an American girl that was going to the Julian Académie with us. When Frank saw Noddy, he was almost speechless. I had talked so much about her in the preceding days he should have known how beautiful she was. But I guess he thought it was love talking and took it with a grain of salt. When the reality was looking him in the eye, he had a reaction very much like my first one. His girlfriend also took note of his response and quickly turned to Frank.

"Why don't we go to my place and let these two lovebirds be alone."

I gave her a few, hidden from Frank, facial expressions encouraging her suggestion, and they made a hasty exit. On his way out Frank said. "I'll take my heavy jacket because I won't be back until after midnight." He had the expression of a cat eating ice cream, but I appreciated the courtesy. As soon as they left, Noddy asked when Frank would be back. I told her and she seemed pleased. We looked at some of my paintings.

She turned to me. "Will you paint my portrait?"

"I'd love to paint you; you're the most wonderful girl I've met in Paris."

She pushed her body against mine and turned her face up to me presenting her mouth for me. I kissed her softly. My lips just parted enough to be relaxed. I felt her tongue slip between and tease mine. She rubbed her body against mine and clasped both her hands on my ass. In a few moments we were embracing passionately; the tenderness had given way to something far more urgent. After a few minutes, we broke apart. I needed to slow down a little and get my bearings. I had often escaped into my magic world of dreams and fantasies of women, but this one was happening.

She started to undress. I didn't know if I was to draw her and she was making this move to not go further in the heat of the moment or should I start taking my clothes off. Silly, I thought. In any other case, I would just undress and see where it went. I started unbuttoning my shirt.

She was naked now and asked. "Do you like my body?" Before I could answer she commented, "My breasts are too small."

"No! Not at all. I'm an artist, and your body is perfect."

While I was talking, I finished taking my clothes off. She went to the corner of the large room and turned down the bed, so only the sheets were exposed. Then she went to the windows and closed the curtains. She walked to the bed and stretched across it in a provocative pose. The usual routine with a girl I was pursuing would be to get started on the bed; slowly undressing with the rising passion. She was moving much faster than that. Perhaps she was a virgin and knew she was about to make love with me and didn't want the clumsy preliminaries. I slipped into her arms, and we were in the heat of passion again quickly.

Her body was small and delicate yet hard and firm; a hundred pounds of whirling passion. She wanted me inside her like a starving animal. Her screams were that of a woman who knew how to respond and enjoyed riding the crests of pleasure. I asked her to wait as I was so close, and I wanted it to last forever inside her. As we hesitated, I asked if she was safe. I knew all the right words for this information as I had learned from several meaningless encounters.

"It's good... It's good," she repeated.

I didn't know if she meant she was safe or that it was just good. For two hours, I remained on top and functioned as a pleasure machine. It wasn't necessary to try many positions as it was perfect this first time just as it was. She reached a climax so many times I lost count. My second climax was well over an hour and every second felt better than it had ever before. I didn't know I could be so in love, so involved, so soon. I was floating on a cloud, a euphoric haze of forever pleasure. I felt like Superman because I held back for so long concentrating on her, thinking she'd tire. But she never seemed to. There had been few times in my life I could reach that level and hold it for so long, yet still enjoy every second.

During the months that followed, we spent every available minute together. The sex, only in her safe periods, was always good. The other times we wore condoms which were never the same. I would go down; eating her delicious little muff with supreme desire. She was embarrassed the first time I put my tongue on her clit, but her excitement soon overcame any thought of anything else. She became quite selfish and preferred to be satisfied that way as she had a fear of pregnancy. I loved her, so it was my pleasure as well.

Noddy usually worked at a club for a week but rarely longer, and then moved on to another. Her agent kept her very busy because although she wasn't known she was an exquisite and a growing talent. Often her engagements were in another city, which concerned me because we were then apart for a week at a time. Living in hotels in strange cities, there was no question in my mind there were constant streams of men pursuing her at every stop. When she played gigs very close to Paris, I would sometimes catch a train to see her, and we would spend an afternoon together. We both professed our love for each other, and I was confident she didn't need or want another man.

Our close relationship and my French studies were bringing my language skills to the point we could actually express ourselves. As my understanding increased, I began to realize Noddy was a very self-confident girl. She was now 17, and I started to see a difference in the way she used her beauty to entrance both men and women. She had matured quickly in the few months we'd been together. There was suddenly a full-blown woman in my life, one who now put her life and career before mine. As time went by I found our conversation was now usually about her travel, singing and how she could get bigger engagements. When I talked about my art career and my passion for the Impressionists or wanted her to accompany me to one of the beautiful exhibits and displays, she would show little interest. One Saturday I took Noddy to one of my favorite museums and showed her what I wanted to be my future.

She said, "Didn't they all have terrible lives?"

"Times have changed; there are opportunities now that never existed for them," I explained to her. She looked at the different artists' work, and at me, with mild interest. I could see in her look it was the beginning of the end.

A month later, she got a club date at a show in Nice. She came home for just one night, and we spent it with her younger sister and mother at their flat in Neuilly. When I saw the meager place she had lived in with her mother, I understood more fully her driving ambition and desire for recognition and money. I wanted her to come with me that night so we could be alone. She said she couldn't leave her mother after being away for so long. She promised to call me the next morning before she left so we could plan to meet. I was already missing her and my heart felt empty. I was very much in love with her. Although I knew it wasn't to be; it had been such a passionate and great physical love, I didn't know if I could ever find someone again that would make me so crazy.

She never called that morning. I expected a letter explaining but by the following week, nothing had arrived. I called her hotel, and they said she'd left without leaving a forwarding number. I called the club that evening. They put me on hold for a long time; then someone hung up. I called again and explained it was important that Noddy call me that evening during the break. She never called. That night I slept with Ginette.

[I didn't see Noddy Daniel again for ten years; until I was in Paris with my second wife, Marie. I saw a concert poster with her picture. I got tickets, and it was an enjoyable experience, she had become truly a great performer. After the show, I saw her backstage. She looked worn and ten years older than she should. She was still beautiful, but I could feel the stress she was having with our meeting. Marie noticed it as well. Noddy said she was married, and we made a few minutes of polite conversation. I congratulated her on her success, and we parted. Over the years when I was in Paris, I checked what I could to see how her career was going but that was only curiosity as I felt nothing when we met again.]

Shar (Lessons Learned)

This period in my life was the entry level of my exploits and the experience provided many lessons that governed many aspects of my future.

When a girlfriend would spend the night, we would always get up in the morning and have coffee, bread, and croissants at the café. The concierge, Shar, and her husband, Pierre, worked there from 7:00 am until 4:00 pm and their son Binney was always there before he went off to school. Shar was quite dark in complexion and had jet black hair, about thirty-five years old, five-foot-four inches tall with a mature and full figure. She always wore low-cut tops that emphasized her large breasts. Pierre was only an inch or two taller, and he was bald as a billiard ball. He had a big gut and an oversized mustache that was quite comical looking, but it fit his personality. He was outgoing and quite popular.

I began to notice that mornings when I was with someone, Shar would seem to take an unusual interest in me and my companions. When I was alone, she'd give me special attention and flaunt her big tits by leaning over the table when she served me. Frank and I discussed Shar as he, too, had noticed the intense way she looked at me. I asked him if she had come on to him at all. "No. But I think she has a thing for you; she'd jump you in a flash." Frank always used the word jump which must have been an expression from his Marine Corps days.

One day Frank said Shar had asked him about me. "What did you tell her?" I asked.

"I just told her you were known as the super stud."

"Oh great. Are you setting me up? She's the concierge of the building, and I understand she was the concierge during the German occupation. And she was in the underground. I think she's a very tough cookie. Besides that, even though Pierre is impassive, I think he must have noticed how she dotes on me. What if he does something to me about it?" Frank just shook his head.

One morning another bartender that filled in on occasion was there instead of Pierre. Binney wasn't there either. Shar came and sat with me while I had my coffee. She told me she wanted to see my paintings and asked if I would I show them to her. I agreed as I didn't mean to offend her. She asked me if she could come up that afternoon when she closed the bar. I said I would be home around five or so if she wanted to drop by. She came within minutes of when I returned. Once I closed the door behind her, she was all over me pinning me against the wall. She told me she'd wanted to fuck me so bad, for so long, she could hardly wait. She pushed her mouth on mine, and her tongue pressed deep into it. She was as hot as a firecracker; with a frantic look on her face, she rubbed my crotch. I had never had a woman go after me in such a violent manner. I sensed she was real trouble, but her passion was contagious. In minutes, we were in bed, and her mouth moved lower on me.

"It is magnificent," she groaned. She jumped on top of me and guided me inside. For a half hour, she went madly about her intensive quest. "Let me make you happy..." she kept saying. "I'll be the best fuck of your life."

She moved like a woman possessed, and after some fifteen minutes, she stopped, paralyzed, with eyes wide open and glazed to the point that she saw nothing. She moved a little but kept instructing me to stay still. In a few minutes, she pulled away and started using her mouth again, in such a frantic way that it scared me.

Finished, she pulled off, looked at my watch on the stand, rushed into the bathroom and said, "I must clean up." I still was bringing myself back to gathering all the facts and emotions of what had just happened when she came out fully dressed. She kissed me, said goodbye and rushed out the door.

Shar was a woman so extreme I thought she might be bordering on insanity. I had never known anyone that physically aggressive, but it was exciting. I decided she was a nymphomaniac with a compulsive character, and she could only be trouble in my life. But, at the same time, I wanted more. I could imagine what it would be like to have some real time with her. What would she do if I was equally forceful and gave her the full treatment?

The next morning, I avoided the café and took the metro directly to Saint Germain-des-Prés with Frank. We sat in the Royal, I told him about the episode, and that I hadn't wanted it to happen; I joked... but I was weak and couldn't help myself. He thought it was quite entertaining.

A few days later, I was heading down the corridor to the staircase. Shar passed me and said. "I'll be there in fifteen minutes." She didn't ask if I was busy; she had no idea if I had plans, but I guessed it would be a quickie so she wouldn't be missed. I went back to the apartment. I heard a knock, and when I opened the door, she was already taking her clothes off. She rushed into the bedroom; ripped the rest of her clothes off and started frenziedly helping me undress. In seconds, she had me on the bed the same as before. When she climaxed, she finished me off, again, with her mouth and before I could say three words she had swallowed, got dressed and was out the door. I wished I had had a stopwatch; I think the whole deal was about twelve minutes flat. I began to think about the prospects of such a relationship; no one would suspect we had made it in that length of time. In a way it was somewhat convenient, she'd expect nothing but a stiff rod, work it a bit and satisfy herself, finish me off and be on her way. No expense, no conversation, just pure and simple fucking to get it over with in a hurry. It was an unusual situation, but the long-term possibilities were not attractive.

A few nights later, I was coming home from work. It was one-thirty in the morning, and I was tired, having been out with some of the gang to have a late bite to eat. I had had several days of concentrated work at school and hadn't had a lot of sleep. It was a Friday night, so I was looking forward to sleeping in for a long time in the morning. When I got home, I undressed quickly and was just getting into bed when there was a light knock on the door. I knew it was Shar, yet I still opened the door. She was in a nightgown with nothing on underneath. There was no conversation, she just pushed me on the bed and started telling me how she missed me and how horny she was. She bent over the bed, sticking her vast butt up in the air. I got her from behind, and for the first time I was in control. It was a long and pleasurable episode. She reached her peak several times and then she started to cry. I stopped.

"What's wrong?" I asked.

"Nothing," she said, "I'll tell you later."

I stood before her, and she finished me off with a hand and mouth technique that was admirable. She had brought a paper bag with her, took out the douchebag and nozzle and went into the bathroom. She came out and said, "I must go."

"Why were you crying?" I asked.

"I have never known such pleasure; I was crying for happiness."

She left with her douchebag still hanging on the door. I had been told before I was good in bed, and all the lies women make to their lovers. But this time I really believed it. I realized she had always been used, and that was why she was so abrupt in the act. Just moments ago she had been quieter in her body motions, not as desperate as before, and that was a different experience for her. I was exhausted so I didn't give it much thought that night, and I slept until two in the afternoon the next day.

When I did have time to evaluate the situation, I started to feel remorse. Why was I letting this woman get into my life? I decided to cool it. That afternoon I went into the bar to see if I could talk to her, but the other barman was there handling the place by himself, which was often the case on Saturdays. I decided to let things calm down by just avoiding her. The next few days were quiet, and I asked one of the girls of the Lido to come home with me. We spent an enjoyable evening, and it was nice to be with someone who wasn't so intense.

In the morning, we exited to the right, avoiding even walking past the front of the café. The café on the next corner was nearly a full block away. When we were three-quarters of the way along, I glanced back and Shar was standing on the sidewalk watching me. I waved in a friendly manner, but I could feel the chill of her jealousy.

That night I again came home very late and put a sign on the door with a picture of a man and woman together kissing, and DO NOT DISTURB! I wasn't in the mood for her. The next morning was

Sunday, and the café was closed. I walked to the Trocadero and sat in the Grand Café. I was just dipping a croissant into my coffee when Shar sat down next to me.

"Why did you put the sign on the door? I wanted to see you, and I know you were not with someone."

"I was tired and I don't care for what we are doing. I like Pierre, and it isn't fair to him."

"He never fucks me, and he has a woman he goes off to see, and I need someone too," she said. "Even if he knew he wouldn't care."

"That's fine for you, but I'm a young man, and I like being with other women, too. You knew that because you've seen many of them. I don't want to be obligated."

"Okay," she said. "When you want me, you just tell me and I'll come. I'll be the best fuck and most exciting woman you'll ever know. Come with me now, we'll go back and I'll make you a special day."

"No," I said. "I don't like this... to see how fast we can get it over with just isn't my style."

"Pierre is gone to his mothers with Binney, and I have the full afternoon."

I had wanted to know what she was like with some real time, so I went. It was an afternoon to remember. She was completely wild, and it was madness for several hours. I was completely fascinated with her physically, but I was also aware she was probably crazy. Who knew when she'd stab or shoot me or who knows what?

For the next three months, I brought other women home. Despite what she'd told me that Sunday morning in the Grand Café, Shar became increasingly obsessive and started to show her jealousy more openly. Finally, I had had enough; I was just not comfortable coming home. I told her she had to be reasonable and that we couldn't continue. We must just be friends. I was with Noddy by this time, and she had come to the apartment with me several times; the last thing I wanted was Noddy to encounter her in some crazy rage. Shar said she understood. But I had to quit going to the café, as she continued to glare at me with hatred in her eyes. She cornered me one day and said she had to be with me one more time. She wanted my baby and then she'd ask for nothing more. I told Frank I feared she'd do something horrible.

A week or two later, a friend at the Beaux Arts said he was going back to England and was giving up his apartment. It was just across from the school on the third etage. It was front facing and had a good kitchen and bathroom, and a small bedroom in the back. It was a similar arrangement as Rue Lauriston. It was very run down, and plaster was coming off the walls, but the stairwell was very presentable, and I could see most of the apartments had been refurbished. This was my out; my chance to elude Shar. I got some of my friends that needed money; Bob Hill was a good friend, and he was handy with repairs. And after making a deal with the owner for fifty dollars per month, we proceeded to fix the place up. We worked on it for three weeks, and I spent six hundred dollars on new doors, paint and wallpaper. I put in a new refrigerator, stove and got the landlord to give me three months' free rent on a two-year lease.

Back at my old apartment Frank told Shar I had to fly home, my father was sick, and I would be back in a few weeks or a month. Frank couldn't afford the rent by himself so I paid my half for three months until he could find another partner, which turned out to be a Swedish girl. I was afraid Shar would go to the Lido and check to see if I was there. For weeks, I checked with the stage door attendant to see if anyone fitting her description came around. She hadn't and thankfully, I never saw her again, but I had learned a crucial lesson. If you even suspect someone isn't exactly right in the head, don't take chances, cut the relationship off quickly and hit the road.

* * *

Frank Salazar was the most creative and had the most developed imagination of the group of us. Unfortunately, Frank didn't work as hard as he could have to make the transition of his great imagination to images on canvas. But, his ability to draw quick sketches and characterizations was one of the best I've ever encountered. He could capture the people, the mood and atmosphere of a nightclub or café in a few minutes with such ease. I admired his natural talent.

Another companion was Alex, one of the great characters of Saint Germain-des-Prés and Montparnasse. He was a fun personality; always out and about, making the rounds and talking about his writing and poetry. Whenever he would see Frank and me in a café, he would jump at the chance to sponge a coffee from us. I never knew how he supported himself or where he lived. He always carried a notebook and briefcase with his writings that he insisted you read. Alex was also a sloppy and unkempt soul; he had a massive head of hair and a nose like Cyrano de Bergerac. His small black eyes would peer down this long extension on his face, which made him very interesting looking. He always needed to borrow money, and a few times, I loaned him small sums. He borrowed from everyone, and I think that's how he survived. Art Buchwald did a piece on him in the Herald Tribune, called the *Poet of Saint Germain-des-Prés*.

There were many characters in the Latin Quarter like Alex. They were always reading Sartre, Heidegger, and Barth and preaching the existential philosophy. I wrote a piece about them called the *Hot Tub*. It was a fantasy about taking the grubby community of the Left Bank and putting them in a giant tub and scrubbing them until they no longer smelled so bad. I passed it around, and it got many laughs.

One of the gigs I did in St. Michael was at a wild looking cave called the Metro Jazz, also known as the Trois Mailletz. I worked there with an incredible black trumpet player and his small band. Peanuts Holland was from the south, and he was a significant artist in the history of jazz. It was unusual to have two male singers at a club, but we were very different. Al Fats Edwards was a big, rotund, black singer that did wild comedy songs; he was a character and a half. My favorite was a song called, *Beans*. When he sang that word, long and drawn out, he would finish by letting out a loud fart. It was even in the newspapers, and Art Buchwald came at my request and did some funny lines about it.

My American friends loved this place. It was in a corner building, timeworn and stained gray by the years of dirt and pollution. One side of the building leaned toward the street and was held in place by large poles that looked like the kind used to string telephone wires. The entry was just a small door leading down a narrow stairway with worn stone steps. It opened up to a small room about twenty feet long. Behind the bar was Jacque, a very short man who looked like he was standing in a trough. He was quite comical looking, but fast and a good bartender. He added a lot to the character of the place. This bar room was about fifteen feet wide and had at the far end an entry to the larger space. This room was about thirty-five feet long but the same twenty-foot width dimension as the bar. The entire place was stone, and it made you feel like you were in a dungeon, which it probably had been a few hundred years before. It had only one air shaft with a fan, so the place got thick with smoke and the smell of beer and booze.

I loved the atmosphere, and Peanuts, his Swedish wife and I were to become good friends. Al and I worked together several times also, and we did a lot of after-hours carousing together. I made a trip once with Peanuts and his orchestra for a one-week engagement in Stockholm at the auditorium at Skansen. It was my first trip there, and his wife showed me all the sights. She introduced me to one of her girlfriends, and I fell in love for a week. I always wanted to go back and see her, but too much time passed and like so many other encounters it faded away.

Christian Title

"The Red Bottle" 1955 Académie Julian

7

CLUB LIFE

The Mars Club

There was a particular little piano club off the Rue Marbeuf near the Champs-Élysées at the end of a one block dead end street. The street was dark and distinguished by a blue neon script sign, 'Mars Club.' The location was a definite asset and it possessed a certain mystery.

When entering the dark interior, a soft pink spotlight on the keyboard highlighted that it was a club focused on the piano. Even the layout emphasized this. When you entered the club on the left side of the thirty-five-foot wide space, you faced a long bar. Maybe twenty people lined up facing the arrangement of liquor and the mirrors reflecting the piano that sat opposite the bar. The norm was for the people seated there to turn on their stools and face the stage when someone was performing.

At the front of the bar, Madame Benjamin, the wife of the owner usually sat with her desk light as she watched every transaction. Her husband, Big Ben (I'm not even sure they were married), was at the other end of the bar watching the overall scene and activity in the club. His fat body overhung the stool; his swollen lower lip drooped, quivering, over his chin. The debauched look one can only see in the face of an over indulgent gay American in Paris in the early 1950s. Madame, at the cash drawer, usually had her little girlfriend by her side. Geli was a poor little waif whose whole life depended on the whims of her stone-faced lesbian lover.

A wrought iron railing and double step separated the right side of the club making the entire area like a stage. Tables shared it for the more serious listening clients. The steps were at the front, opposite the piano, and limited anyone from taking a seat unless they passed the bar and around the rear of the room and its fifty feet of railing.

I had been to the club a couple of times after hours when the Lido show closed, and I didn't have any early classes. George Matson, an entertainer who did some hysterical female impersonations, knew Big Ben. George was gay, too, but he had no interest in the fat slob. George was good looking, and one of the few in the Lido show that respected my preference for women. On another occasion, I visited the club with Terry and Herman Garst, Terry was the ice skating star of our show, and her husband was a musician and arranger. They became my first real friends in Paris and were delightful people.

After an interview, Big Ben hired me for a one-day, Saturday night tryout. I had finished at the Lido and Ben hadn't had a singer for a while. He made me an offer. It wasn't much, but it was cash, and unless you worked for a larger club or someone with some influence, you couldn't get the work permit. I was tired of every night work on top of a busy school schedule I had done while at the Lido. To work at a new place for only a couple of nights, a week was appealing. I loved The Mars Club and felt it held something special for me. It was intimate and close. I had never worked in such close quarters. I soon learned the owners had no taste or class. She was the money counter, and he bought all the booze through his military contacts at SHAPE, Supreme Headquarters Allied Powers Europe. Despite Ben and his wife, the atmosphere was unique. I'm convinced it was more of just everything coming together the right way at the right time.

* * *

Sidney Bechet came into The Mars Club one evening. Ben knew him and introduced me. I knew the name, as he was, next to Louie Armstrong, probably the most famous of the early jazz musicians. A little later, after I had done a set with Art Simmons, Sidney came over and asked me to visit him at the Veau Colombier, his legendary jazz club on the Left Bank.

I went there the next week, and Sidney asked me to get up and sing. I declined as I had never sung jazz and the tempo and volume was intimidating. Sidney asked me to come the next Saturday and rehearse with them. He said, "We can see if you'll make a good jazz singer." I went and had a good time. It was more of a romp than singing; I don't think people could hear that much of me. Sidney did a solo with every number, and he was the consummate talent. I started singing there three nights a week, and I got the feeling and mood of jazz which I had never done before.

I worked with Sidney on and off for a year. He was an interesting man. His wife was German, but she never came to the club. They lived outside of Paris. His mistress lived in Paris, and she came to the club on several occasions. I was told the wife knew of her, and there was no friction. Sidney was an excitable man and could get himself in a tizzy over the slightest altercation. Claude Lutere had been with Sidney since he had returned to France, and he was a calming and stable influence. There was a constant parade of movie and music entertainers to the club, and it was exciting and intimidating to sing in front of a famous singer.

Billie Holiday

I met some of the greatest talents in music while I was with Sidney. One evening Billie Holiday came in with her husband. She sat down in the back, but he left after they arrived. I tried to talk to her, but she was high as a kite. I never knew on what.

Sidney told me. "After you finish your set, introduce Billie and get her up to sing."

I looked at him. "She can't even walk or talk, let alone sing."

"Just introduce her and help her to sit on your stool, give her the mic. Then watch and listen."

I did just that. I introduced her, and she seemed to kind of wake up, a little gleam in the eye. I helped her to the stage, joking with the audience as I did. Sitting her down on the stool, I handed her the mic. She turned to Sidney and asked. "How about *Gloomy Sunday*?"

I thought it was going to be a gloomy Friday night; I doubted she was going to able to perform, and it would end up an embarrassing moment. The band started, and they were mellower than I had ever heard them; soft and graceful. Billie began to sing, and the room went quiet. Her eyes closed. She sang like nothing I had ever heard before. I had listened to her recordings like thousands, maybe millions, of other people. But it wasn't the same as seeing and feeling her in this so intimate setting. She sang several songs and never missed a beat, and as the music and her singing moved me, I became one of her great fans. It was very much like Lena Horne, who I never had a great admiration for, but after watching her perform in close quarters; I knew she was the ultimate entertainer.

Hearing talents such as Billie and others, I had the privilege to see up close, in such personal venues as the small clubs in Paris, convinced me I could never be that good. Nor did I want that life. Although I knew, I had an outstanding voice the experience with beautiful, talented and often tragic celebrities, made me confirm my commitment to the world of art.

Eartha Kitt

I was working one Saturday night at the Veau Colombier with Claude Lutere. Sidney was home with his mistress Jacqueline and their new baby. It was a crowded night with many people there who expected to see Sidney. We were doing our best to keep everyone happy. A bright-eyed, exotic looking woman sat with another woman near the back of the cave. Al 'Fats' Edwards was with them; he was a new friend I had met with Peanuts Holland at the Metro Jazz, some weeks before. Al had an interest in art, and I had brought him to the Julian Académie to meet some of my friends and see their work. He introduced me to the bright-eyed woman, and I immediately recognized Eartha Kitt. She was gaining a big reputation for her unusual style and fanciful repertoire.

I asked Claude to do few ballads, as I was never quite as confident with the jazz numbers. Since Sidney wasn't there to do his solo interpretations with every tune, he obliged. When I finished, Al asked me to join them. He had told Eartha I was a very fine artist and singing was only a means of support to satisfy my ultimate ambitions. She asked if she could see my work and that she had never been in an art Académie; she wanted to do the same thing as Al had described to her.

The next day was Sunday, and I had the day free. I asked her if she'd like me to take her to the Jeu de Palme, where I could show her all of my favorite Impressionist masterpieces. I offered to pick her up at her hotel, but she said she'd like to meet me. We arranged to meet at the entrance to the museum, which was easy to find, as it was right at the entry of the Jardin de Tuileries on the Place du Concord. She was a half hour late, and I had all but given up hope when she arrived. She looked spunky and exotic at the same time and carried herself with grace and flair.

Her outgoing and exaggerated personality seemed to set the pace. I don't think people knew who she was, but she was such a strong presence that everyone appeared to be watching us. She was silent on our tour and listened to my evaluations with intense concentration. It was different with her. I had made this visit many times showing friends the paintings that were my passion. I truly had a love affair with many of them as I walked through this museum nearly every day after school my first year. No one I had ever taken on the tour had showed the level of curiosity as Eartha did.

We had an excellent lunch at the El Royal café and bistro in Saint Germain-des-Prés and discussed the paintings at length. That evening we went to the Auberge Basque for dinner; she had previous plans but canceled them. We had a mutual attraction so strong we both knew it but said nothing. We went to the Calavados, after dinner, where Blossom Dearie was appearing. She was an unusual pianist and singer I thought Eartha would appreciate. It was also across the street from the George V Hotel, where she was staying.

The next day I met her at the El Royal and took her to Chez Moligne the restaurant just a few doors away from my apartment, and a hundred meters from the Beaux Arts Académie. Classes were in session so that we couldn't go in, but other ateliers were used by artists just doing assignments or personal projects. We toured these rooms, seeing the work in progress and some talented sculptors at work. She couldn't join me for dinner, but we arranged to meet at ten o'clock at The Mars Club, which was also quite close to her hotel.

That evening she met Art Simmons at the club and he asked her if she'd like to sing. She declined, and I found out later she only performed with her pianist and arranger, and her renditions were so personal she didn't like to work with other accompanists. At midnight, I told her I had early classes at the Sorbonne and needed to get some sleep. I dropped her off by cab and then went directly to my apartment. She was busy on Tuesday, and we made plans for her to come to dinner at my apartment on Wednesday. I was working only on Friday and Saturday nights with Sidney, so I had more free time than usual.

That evening I picked up veal shanks braised in red wine with all the trimmings from my favorite little shop in Mabillion. I stopped at my favorite bakery for bread and apple tarts. I seldom ate sweets, but on special occasions, I ate this specialty with high expectations. Eartha arrived and loved the apartment. I had it looking artistic and fun, and it was a major transformation from when I first saw it. She wore very casual and just tight slacks and a work-like shirt. It was very stylish, however; she always looked like an ad from some magazine. She saw my collection of antique smoking pipes and commented on a pornographic carved ivory one. She asked if I ever smoked any of them.

"No. I only smoke my water pipe." I replied with a smile.

"What do you smoke in it?" She asked.

"Hashish,"

"Do you have any?"

She had smoked marijuana before but had never had hashish. I hadn't smoked for quite a while, and I didn't know if the dried, rock like cube I had was still potent. We tried a little before dinner, just a sampling to see if it was any good. Well, it was strong; we had two brief hits and were soaring. We laughed at ourselves and then realized, in our condition, we would have to stay in for the evening. I asked her, "What are we going to do with all of this time?"

"I think we'll find something to do." She was grinning from ear to ear as she approached me.

She was so sexy I had been fantasizing about her for days. It happened, and we were like magic together. It was so intense and perfect for both of us we didn't eat dinner until eleven that night. She spent the night, and we were together the next day. I skipped school and we made the rounds of all the sights she hadn't seen. She was leaving on Friday for a tour that would take her away for several weeks, but then she would return to Paris. We had an on and off arrangement during the next couple of months. The time we were together, which was probably only ten days total, was very special. We never talked about the future, and she never spoke of the past. She wanted to learn and experience everything in the present.

I found she had quiet moods where she stopped and lingered as if in a trance. These were moments where we shared a silent understanding of ourselves. I fell in love with her though I knew it would be transient. We never had a disagreement or a time that wasn't harmonious. During the years, I watched as her fame grew, and she showed the world what a great performer and person she was. She came from nothing and gained a stature of global importance. I saw her only once after that. Our paths just never crossed again and I never even knew if she got a letter that I sent her some months later.

Julietta

Julietta was the ex-wife of a movie producer in Los Angeles. We had met in the American Express office in Madrid where I was waiting for money to arrive from Paris. Frank Salazar, my artist friend, was holding money for me to send it to me if needed while I was traveling. At the time, I had a three-week engagement at the Cosmos Café on the Ramblas in Barcelona. I'd stayed a week after that waiting to appear at the concert hall in Palma, Mallorca. It was only a two-night affair, but I was so enthralled with the magic island I rented a house on the beach and remained there until I started to run out of money.

I had been every day to the American Express office to get mail, but no money had arrived. In the meantime, I was eating cheap but still couldn't pay for my hotel. Julietta was in line with me and I mentioned to her how desperate I had become. When there was again no mail, she smiled and said. "Let me help you out until your money comes."

We had coffee together and that led to lunch that was her treat. She was a rather plump woman of 35, not particularly attractive with brassy red hair and prominent freckles. But a wow of a personality. She loved traveling and was at times so boisterous that it embarrassed me. She was fun and a little crazy. When I told her I couldn't pay my hotel bill, she said. "Well let's get it paid and you can move in with me. I'm going to Paris in a few days and you can help me make the drive."

I was so relieved. "You can stay in my apartment in Paris and I'll pay you back when we get there."

That night I felt awkward when we went to her room in a small but elegant hotel. We had given my luggage to the bellhop and he put it in the room. When I saw, there was only one bed I didn't know what to say. We hadn't been romantic or even talked about sleeping together. She saw the look on my face; put her arms around me and said.

"Now we'll be lovers."

She told me how horny she was and how long it'd been since she had had any sex. It was a difficult situation for me as I didn't find her appealing. She was quite round and had unusually large breasts. When she said she would hop in the shower and began stripping down, I was amazed at how open and frank she was about everything. She unfastened the multiple snaps of her bra and her tits loomed before me in their full proportions. They were absolutely the largest I had ever encountered. They hung down on a rather large potbelly adorned, lower down, with a massive amount of red hair. It turned me on in a kind of perverse way. I had also been quite a while without sex and that was unusual for me. But without money, I didn't want to get involved with someone I didn't know. It surely would end up being an expense at some point, but it was too late to back away now.

After she had told me her whole life story during a two-hour dinner, I had felt I knew her well. A virgin from a well-to-do Beverly Hills Jewish family she had married a successful Hollywood producer. Their wedding night was a disaster even though he had planned every detail to be successful. After the wedding, they drove to Santa Barbara where he had a particular suite decorated with flowers and all the trimmings. She had been looking forward to her wedding night.

"I was a virgin to an actual penis, but I put nearly everything else up there I could find. I masturbated so much I had to remind myself to stop a few days before the wedding so I would be nearly desperate for my new husband. After the wedding when we arrived at our room in Santa Barbara, I did everything I knew how to do but he was limp as a noodle. He said he was put off by the fact I was so proficient sucking on it. It was definitely something I had practiced. I was 20 when I met him and that was the only way I could stay a virgin and keep a boyfriend. During our twelve-year marriage, he never got it up. He saw doctors, quacks and the like but never could function. He had a whole library of porn movies and he found many ways to satisfy me, but never himself. The strangest part of it was he was always trying with other women. I guess he hoped there would be some magic woman that would help him, or maybe they did. He never talked about it. He always pretended time spent away from me was on business. Yet, he was jealous of me."

And so on, that's how the description of her marriage went. She told me after the wedding she became a wild woman and had affairs right and left for a couple of years and until she got disgusted with men. Then she tried it with a female and that wasn't right either. Finally, she decided to live in Europe and settled in England for a while. She didn't like English men, she said, they were uniformly dull.

After dinner, we went back to her room and I took a shower. When I came out, I dropped the towel and exposed my body.

Christian Title

"Wow," she looked at me from head to toe. "You're beautiful!"

Christian and Frank in Julietta's MG on the Rue Lauriston.

I'd never been called beautiful before. It did make me feel good and I wanted to perform well after the story of the twelve years she had endured in her marriage. She lay down on the bed and asked if I would like to see her. With only a smile to encourage her, she spread her legs wide. It was a very different sight to me and turned me on. The bright red hair surrounding her lovely instrument framed the silky white flesh. It was by far the prettiest part of her. Her labia was plump and pink and her clitoris made a statement of its own, bulging round and high, squeezed between a crack of great distinction.

We made it twice that night and once the following morning. We went to the museum, seeing all the sights in her new MG. We went back to the hotel for a shower and more sex before dinner. It was strange that often before when a woman was unattractive to me, I had no interest in her beyond a quick episode. But Julietta was so aggressive and expressed so much pleasure, and was so appreciative of my prowess it made me want her even more. She became much prettier and desirable as the days wore on. We talked ourselves silly all the way to Paris and after we got there for the next week. When I paid her back the money I owed her, she didn't want to take it. She actually didn't expect it; I guess she didn't believe I had money there waiting for me.

One morning she jumped up and said she was leaving. She had to fly back to Los Angeles to see her mother. She handed me the keys to the car and said I could use it while she was gone. She was very vague about when she'd be back.

"I may have to take care of my mother for a while and I'll let you know what's going on."

Many months later, without a letter or word since she left, she showed up at the apartment Frank was sharing with Birgetta, his

Swedish girlfriend. Julietta was definitely a real kick in the ass, as Frank described her. At the time, I had a relationship going with the sister of the great French singer, Charles Trenet. Lucky, his sister and I had met at a dinner party at the château of my friend Gaston. I'd been seeing her a couple of times each week. And she'd wait for me until all hours after the shows. She was quiet and carefree and when I explained to her a lady friend from the United States would be staying with me she accepted it without a flinch. "Let me know when we can get together again," she said.

Julietta had been so kind to me and she was such a great lover I couldn't disappoint her. We continued where we left off and it was as exciting as ever. She and I both knew it didn't have a future; we were so far apart age wise. But it was an experience to remember. Saturday night was Julietta's last night with me. She was driving to Italy the next day. I had plans for Sunday and I knew it was going to involve some exciting sex. So I told Julietta I wasn't feeling well on Saturday night and Sunday morning because I didn't want to be all fucked out for the château games. Later, Frank told me that he had dropped by my apartment, he and Julietta had an exciting time when I left. Frank was closer to her age. I hadn't said much about her, but he wanted to know why the ugly redhead was so interesting to me. He told me a few days later. "Now, I understand. I could've spent a lot more time with her myself." He did, some months later.

Martine

I had worked on and off at The Mars Club for a couple of years. The club was extraordinary in that many tourists and transients happened in. The location was fruitful for meeting women as there were numerous hotels in the area. I learned the best targets for my sexual escapades were the tourists spending their last night in the city. Most of them are now just a blur, but it was a time when I sowed my wild oats. Women of every description and background became my joy and focus. When I reflect on the sheer numbers of them in those years, I marvel. We must all remember those horny years, and make allowances for our children, and the passion of youth. I recall several women that were special, and a few that were beyond special.

One such woman came into the club on occasion. She was always alone, drank little and didn't smoke. Always dressed in the highest of fashion she had the l'aire of money and prestige. She was very friendly in a reserved manner. I hadn't given her much thought as she was at least ten years my senior, and although attractive, she didn't exude sexuality. One night she arrived with a very distinguished looking gentleman. She wore a large diamond ring and a wedding band. I don't know if I hadn't noticed the rings before or she hadn't worn them. They sat right in front of me and seemed to be evaluating my performance. They invited me to their table when the set was finished, and offered me a drink. This happened often and I always accepted since the owner insisted performers accept customer offers to increase the alcohol count. But I only had nonalcoholic beverages as alcohol was the demon of the profession. If you had alcohol each time, you would soon become what so many have become on the nightclub circuit. And it was not, to me, an appealing sight; having seen so many with talent dissipate it with booze is tragic.

The man with the woman turned out to be her husband. He was there to give his approval on her choice of the partner in some games that they played at their château. Andre and Martine as we will call them invited me to be their guest for a party and to spend the night. They wanted me to perform with a jazz combo they had engaged for the party. They told me it would be quite formal and had

114

been arranged with Big Ben if I wished to accept. The pay would be in French francs and would be several times what I was earning at The Mars Club. [This incidentally was ten dollars a night on weeknights and fifteen on weekends. Four nights a week came to a livable amount of money for the times. One could stay at a reasonably nice hotel for five dollars.]

Two weeks later, on a sunny afternoon, I met their chauffeur driven American Lincoln black limo in front of my apartment. Three black entertainers from the Crazy Horse Saloon were aboard. I had not met them before, and we compared notes and experiences in Paris while on the trip to the château. They had finished at the Crazy Horse and each was going in different directions. Lou Robinson was the only one staying in Paris; he was going to join Sydney Bechet at the Veau Colombier.

We arrived at the château's gate around three o'clock. Stone pillars spaced the wrought iron fence and a stone base stretched for as far as the eye could see in both directions. Behind the fence were neatly planted and groomed trees. The gate itself was massive and on one side was a small house constructed of the same stone as the pillars. The view up the cobblestone drive looked like it was leading to Versailles. The group started making comments and gasping at the view. When I asked if they had been to Versailles, they didn't respond. I then asked if they had been to the Louvre or the Jeu de Palme. They recognized the Louvre name and showed some interest, but they had never been to see it. They had, however, seen the Arc de Triomphe and the Tour Eiffel. This wasn't a great surprise to me. In the clubs, I had found there were few that shared my love of art.

Saxophone player Coleman Hawkins led the musicians. He collected people around him that were well-known on the jazz circuit in Paris. Big Ben had arranged to arrive earlier in the afternoon to set up the amplifier and speakers. I felt fortunate to join this group as I had worked with some of the others before, but not Coleman. We set up behind the house on the terrace which looked out over eight or ten acres of groomed garden area, with fountains and marble sculptures. The staff was laying Persian carpets and helping workmen with the tables, chairs and flower arrangements; extra staff was being briefed by the house manager. I went through the kitchen area where at least a dozen chefs and twenty helpers were busy at work. The kitchen had a commercial oven with a large rotating wheel and hanging spits that had perhaps two dozen, large, pork roasts browning, all at the same time. I have never seen such a large oven before or since and the volume of food was astounding. Kitchen and wait staff fetched wine from the extensive cellars located beneath the terrace.

The weather was most accommodating. A light breeze rustled through the trees and the air was fresh with the fragrance of the flower gardens. The warmth of the day lingered well into the night. When the scene was set, it was something to behold; the biggest budget movies of that time couldn't equal it. The guests started to arrive at 7:45 in a steady stream until about 8:30. Drinks flowed and Coleman and his group played straight through until they started dinner at 10 o'clock. When the Hawkins group took a break, I stepped in without missing a beat with Aaron Bridgers on piano and Billy Perlman on base. We were definitely background music, as the level of conversation was loud and continual. The 200+ guests dressed in their elegant robes made a fascinating sight to someone who had never experienced such an extravagant affair.

I stopped singing between the break for Coleman at one in the morning, he did one last set. I joined him for the *Saints Go Marching*

In as the closing number. Only a few of the guests had left by that time. Coleman and his group retired to the kitchen where they ate to their hearts content. I ate lightly and had my first glass of wine. It wasn't like the Vin Ordinaire I usually consumed. The musicians were all returning to Paris and would wait until the guests left to pack up their gear. My hostess's secretary led me to my quarters in the guesthouse near the long pool. I was tired so I immediately showered and enjoyed the splendor of my guest suite. I fell asleep around two in the morning and was sleeping very soundly when I felt someone rubbing my forehead.

"The pool is heated and it's a beautiful night for a swim."

At first, I didn't know what Martine was saying as I was groggy. She pulled on my hand. As I got out of bed, she slipped a silk robe over my nude body. I had suspicions that she was interested, but when she had showed up at The Mars Club with her husband, I wasn't so sure. I now knew she played a unique game and this was the first match. As we slipped into the pool, I could almost make out her form. It was very dark and there was only a small light coming through the drapes of the guesthouse. I knew what a superb body she had; I couldn't help but notice the tight fitting clothes she wore. She had a straight nose and large eyes. She was just at that point in her 40s where age began to show. I knew she'd be the oldest woman I had ever made love to and I appreciated older women; they knew when to savor the moment as young women seldom did. Martine's body was very much like Carolyn's and in the darkness when I embraced her and explored her form, I couldn't help remembering. This, of course, excited me; Carolyn had been the subject of many of my fantasies since my relationship with her ended. She didn't want to kiss me passionately, just a nibble here and there. Touching and swimming away, each time going a little further with the passion. The pool was enormous, so chasing around must've started to wear on her, after all, the tremendous energy she had expended on the party. When we finally merged our mouths, she touched me for the first time.

"Come with me," she instructed.

She took me to a large cushioned chaise under the soft light of the draped window. She beckoned and I stretched out on it. I was on my back with her kneeling over me. She rubbed her body on mine until I was very hard. She remained above me without kissing, just brazenly exciting herself. Then she moved higher on me, rubbing her wetness on my stomach, then my chest. She lifted her legs over my arms and gently put herself to my face. I grasped her ass with both hands and proceeded to show her my expertise. She played tag with my mouth just as she had done in the pool. When she came, it was without a whimper, arched her back and head to the sky. She put her hand down and held my head away as she quivered slightly for a few minutes.

"I cannot do more, take me to bed." We went inside the guesthouse. "Make love to me softly and slowly for a long time. If I fall asleep, don't stop; just enjoy yourself."

She didn't fall asleep and I did as she asked. Slowly she responded again. When she reached a climax, again I was right with her. It was good, but I hoped we would have a chance when I had her full energy.

In the morning when I awoke, she was gone. I dressed and there was a knock on the door. A young woman, I learned her name was Helene, asked that I join them for breakfast. Helene, Martine,

Bernard and I had a lovely fruit salad, croissants, and coffee. When I left, they asked me to accompany Helene back to the city.

In the car on the way Helene said, "Did you make love to Martine? If you did, I hope it was successful. Was it?"

"I think so." I was wondering just where this was going. "Were you the partner for Bernard for the evening?"

"Yes," she said quietly.

"How old are you Helene?"

"Next week I'm going to be 19 and they're going to have a party for me. You're invited. Martine will call you."

[Only once, many years later with my wife Joyce, did I attend a party that was the equal of Andre and Martine's. It was a Roman extravaganza staged by Joe and Jay Haddad. Their home was the former home of movie star Marion Davies, built for her by William Randolph Hearst. Joe had restored it to level even above that of its previous glory. He had exquisite taste and spared no expense to make the entire estate a work of art. Several weeks before the event, a Roman soldier dressed in full garb knocked at our door. When we opened it, he proceeded to open a parchment scroll and read the invitation to us. After reading, he rolled it back on the hand-painted scrollbars and handed it to us. The requirement was to wear authentic Roman dress. We hustled the next day to Western Costume, a large firm catering to the movie industry. Having guessed the size of the coming event we picked knowing that there might not be the best selection if we waited. When we arrived at seven the evening of the party, two columns of trumpeters with French horns announced our arrival. Then a photographer took pictures of us with

Joe and Jay, and of just the two of us.

A full orchestra filled the air with the themes of some of Hollywood's most memorable scores from the great Roman movies. Topless wine maidens served the wine, tightrope walkers balanced overhead, jugglers and magicians moved among the crowd. The large tent held twenty-four tables, each sitting eight. In the center of each table was a bust of Joe; a plaster cast with a flowered wreath around his head and adorned with his horn-rimmed glasses. It was a fitting tribute to his 50th birthday.

There was a separate tent for the carvers of every kind of meat and foul you can imagine. One with salads and appetizers, in the center, was a sterling silver chalice of monstrous proportions, piled high with giant crab claws. It was the most staggering display of decadence I've ever seen; every conceivable desert one could imagine was there in perfection. Joe was a wonderful friend and had a flair for the spectacular. Evenings such as these are indelible in the memory. The one, so long ago, at the château, with Martine, was in particular because of her unique plans with me as her finale to the evening.]

The following Thursday I appeared at The Mars Club. At eleven that night, Martine came in with a handsome dark-haired Italian man in his 30s. They asked me to join them. At their table, I sat on one side and the Italian, Frederico, on the other. Martine put her hand on my leg and at times moved slowly toward my crotch. I put my hand on top of hers; I couldn't take a chance on getting hard and then having Art announce I was singing the next song. Martine was alternating drinking with her right hand and then left; whichever hand wasn't holding her drink would be under the table. I was sure she was taking turns exciting us as one of her games.

"I'm having a party Sunday afternoon and evening and you're invited. Helene will be there and so will Frederico. We're celebrating Helene's birthday."

I was hesitant but agreed to come. I tried to fathom the picture with Federico. Was he gay? Would they expect me to be with him as well? I waited for the moment I could say something to her without Frederico being a party to it.

"I'm not interested in anything intimate with another man. I want to make that clear to you."

She laughed. "There's nothing to worry about... I know instinctively you're all about women."

When Frederico arrived Sunday morning to pick me up, he was driving a Citroen two-cylinder car that was quite popular in France at that time. It was rickety and had a motorcycle engine, which got forty or fifty miles to the gallon. Fuel was very expensive. When I left home in California gas was about forty cents per gallon, in France it was a dollar fifty and very costly across Europe.

I had seen many of these cars, but I had never been in one of them. It was most uncomfortable, and, fortunately, Helene took the back seat. I had become so used to having a vehicle I realized I must buy one even though I would probably still use the metro most of the time.

When we arrived, the grounds and house seemed deserted. Martine and Bernard's teenage children and most of the servants were not there. For a house that I estimate was around eighty thousand square-feet, it had a strange quiet atmosphere. I found it more beguiling than before with the hustle and bustle of the party.

Our hosts had a lavish table set up and we had drinks on the terrace. Then we sat down to some treats which were new to me. I had never had Beluga caviar with scrambled eggs, but it was something I've thought about many times since. They had Pain de Raisen fresh out of the oven; the best I've ever had.

[As I sit here writing this, I'm eating a Pain de Raisen, which we purchased in Tristam, a neighborhood about thirty minutes out of Auckland. We make this trip to a German bakery that is the best we've found in New Zealand. The food we get here has improved and we now have many of the delicacies which were unknown a few years ago. Over the years I have, every once in a while, bought a large jar of Beluga caviar as a special treat, and it has always brought back memories of that special brunch.]

It seemed like an ordinary group for most of the day, sitting around the pool and talking about the recent party and the comments made by the various prominent figures that attended. We drank many toasts to Helene on her nineteenth birthday. I was thinking to myself that she looked 15; she had big wide eyes and a round face. She was very cute, still with a little baby fat, and bubbly in her manner. That stage before she quite reached the full look of a woman. Bernard suggested they go for a walk, and Federico and Helene went with him.

After about twenty minutes, they hadn't come back Martine said she'd like to show me something. We went into the grand hallway and up the circular central stair. It had a magnificent dome ceiling, with murals of figures and clouds and a representation of the warriors of the heavens. Upstairs the hall seemed a city block long. We went to the end and again there was another lengthy passageway. The great door at the end was carved in the Renaissance style;

elaborate, with burnished gold. Martine opened the door and the suite it opened to was one of incredible splendor. It would compare favorably with Versailles. Martine explained the room had been built for the wife of one of France's great families. There was a long and interesting tale of intrigue and tragedy, and Martine became a little bit of a drama queen while relating the story. We had our afternoon of love and passion in this magnificent setting. I pretended I was Louis XIV; serviced by one of my many concubines. It was a day of fantasies.

As evening approached, the big limousine came with the chauffeur and the children. The daughter wasn't much younger than Helene. She was drop dead beautiful; the younger son was handsome as was his older brother. They were laughing and having fun and we met and said goodbye at the same time. The chauffeur drove Helene and me back to the city. Federico remained at the château.

The chauffeur dropped me at my apartment on the Rue de Beaux Arts, and Helene asked if she could have dinner with me. I had nothing planned, so we spent the evening discussing what had happened on her special day. She said she was repulsed by being with both Federico and Bernard; the Italian had nearly jumped out of his skin when she attempted to touch him. She had never had two men at the same time, but it didn't turn out that way. Bernard seemed much more occupied with Freddie, and she was quite uncomfortable with the action. She said Martine told her I was a beautiful lover, but she didn't want Helene to intrude on the relationship. Helene said she took this as a challenge. Then bluntly told me she'd like to spend some time with me. We arranged to meet the following Sunday.

It was an exciting day and I started to see Helene along with the continuation of my affair with Lucky Trenet. Helene became jealous and that became a problem. She'd turn up at the apartment uninvited and although I asked her many times to not do that, she continued. One day when I was with Lucky, she knocked loudly on the door, I didn't answer because I knew it was her. She must have waited for a couple of hours down the street at a café because when Lucky and I went out for dinner, she confronted us. I told her I had no commitment to her and I didn't want to see her again. It was a little more brutal than what I wanted to say, but she put me on the spot.

Like many young girls, she had a lot of baggage. Her father and uncle had been killed in the war, and she lived with her mother and her aunt. She had a bitter hatred for the Germans and she made a spectacle of herself on one occasion that was very embarrassing. We were sitting in the Select Café in Montparnasse; she heard two German couples speaking loudly. She jumped up and told them in French they were pigs and to go home, they were not welcome in France. I doubt they spoke French, but it was obvious what she was saying. I tried to reason with her, but she kept glaring and yelling at them until the management asked us to leave. I went to the Select often and her behavior was very embarrassing. When we discussed it later, I found out her father and uncle had been in the underground and were caught and executed by the Gestapo. When I told her that those people, the Germans she had screamed at, might not have had anything to do with the war. And that maybe they had suffered themselves significantly, she just looked at me, squinted her eyes and said, "Fuck 'em they can stay out of my country; they're not welcome here."

I related this story to French friends at school and found there were many that shared her hatred. Like Alex, the Poet of Saint Germain-des-Prés, said, "It is best the Germans wait fifteen or twenty years before they come here, or they may just disappear." There were many maimed, crippled people in France and those with severe psychological damage. They carried with them hatred, like a disease that remained in the hearts of the population. Interestingly, the English, who had sacrificed so much, still had rationing and shortages, and meager products even after seven years. While Germany, France and Italy and many other European countries had copious amounts of all the luxuries. As my father said to me when I was quite young, "Don't expect fair."

[The experience with Helene was another reason I concentrated on older women. Over the next two years, I saw Martine several times. We always had a great relationship, but it dwindled away as each of us had other commitments.]

* * *

[While writing these stories I researched many of the musicians I worked with. Nearly all had passed away at a very early age. Most in their fifties and early sixties. Aaron Bridgers, the great jazz pianist, has lived well into his eighties and in 1997 while in Paris I went to see him at the Hilton Hotel. He was about 80 at the time and still playing piano with artistry. Although American, he had spent his entire life in France. The acceptance of black people was the factor that convinced him to remain there. He told me he never drank alcohol while he was working. Art Simmons didn't follow that rule and even in the years of The Mars Club, he was hitting the juice every time someone offered. He became so bad he had to return home. Not steady enough to play, he went to work for his brother. The last time I talked to Art he was 85, doing well and living in West Virginia. Maybe piano players live longer. Blossom Dearie, who was very popular in Paris for many years, was still making the nightclub rounds in the U.S.; fifty years of pounding the keyboard and doing the same thing practically. To hold up on the circuit for that long takes an indomitable spirit. [I heard just recently that she passed away.]

8

STEPHANIE

Pen Pals, Oil on canvas

Over a period of years, I worked at The Mars Club many times, usually for a week or two between other engagements. Big Ben was a cheap guy, he paid me cash in dollars, but it wasn't much money. He knew it was impossible to work legally unless one of the big players signed you to a contract. All of the little clubs paid cash and overlooked the work permits. Ben was paying me ten dollars a night when I worked during the week and fifteen on the weekends. He didn't want me on Mondays or Tuesdays so I usually only worked three nights during the week and Saturday and Sunday, which gave me an income of about fifty or sixty dollars. It was enough, but I was always trying to get something better.

To give you some measure of the times. A meal at one of the student restaurants was about one dollar; a meal at a more elegant restaurant was about two to two and a half dollars for a several course meal. At the time Frank and I shared a room at the Hotel de Seine, we were paying three dollars a night. When we moved into a comfortable two-bedroom apartment, we were paying sixty dollars a month. I had tasted the good life while at the Lido and making five hundred dollars a week. I had put away a nice little cushion and with my savings, if bad times did come I wouldn't have a problem. I had sold my car in Los Angeles before I left and raised money any way I could. I gave it to my father and he was holding nearly three thousand dollars for me which I could call upon. This gave me a sense of wellbeing so I could be independent when negotiating with the club owners.

A traumatic episode happened to me one night while I was singing in a place called the A La Romance, a small bar in Mabillion. The owner, Artiss, was an over the hill but still quite an attractive lesbian. She had two younger women of the same persuasion that worked the room. I played guitar and sang some of my repertoire of old folk songs I had done in my high school years. Alternating with me was a black calypso singer from British Guiana, Ivar Grant, who sang only to the accompaniment of bongo drums. I had worked for a week at a time over a long period for Artiss and I liked her and the girls. We had a good relationship which was fortunate. One night I was sitting up on a mini box stage at the back of the bar. A GI in uniform was just opposite me. I had noticed him when he came in as he was an unusually large black man. I did a couple of sets while this man drank heavily and started to glare at me. He was drunk and asked, "Are you American? What the hell are you doing here in this dump?"

"Making a living while I go to art school," I answered.

I could see he was trouble and he started making loud comments during my songs. Artiss came over and asked him to please not interrupt the singing. He got up and pushed the table over, spilling the drinks. Then he pushed the next table over and people started getting out of his way. He hit Artiss and knocked her down and then came after me. The small stage I sat on was about twenty inches up from the floor level so I had an advantage. I grabbed a large beer bottle and struck him on the side of the head. I couldn't believe how much blood went splattering over the wall and tables. He went down and the bar cleared within a minute.

Artiss told me, "Take your guitar and leave; come and see me next week." She looked hard at me, "You were not here tonight."

I left and I had never been so shaken up by anything in my life to that point. I couldn't sleep that night; I didn't realize I had hit him that hard. I thought I had killed him. I didn't say anything to anyone but Frank. I had waited about ten days before I went to see Artiss.

She told me that night she had called the police; they arrived and had rushed the man to the hospital. The American Military Police came and she told them it was another American in everyday clothes; probably a GI as well. There was an investigation, but no one knew the fate of the man. Artiss thought he must have been okay as nothing more was done after a few weeks. But I never worked at her club again.

* * *

After my first real heartbreak with Noddy, I decided I would play the field and pursue every opportunity. During that year, my technique improved and I was beginning to have much more success. I remained aloof at school and this seemed to make many of the girls more interested. My method was to invite them to the club and direct my love songs to them, and the softening up usually worked. It seemed when I told them I didn't want any relationships and it was just for fun; that was the catalyst for a successful pursuit. The women, especially very attractive ones, would take up the challenge of such a ploy.

Often when I made the rounds sitting with various single ladies who came into the club, I would be able to determine if they were likely prey to my voracious sexual appetite. American women spending their last night in Paris at an intimate club, before returning home and back to work, were prime targets. Usually, they were older as I was only 21. Although I was tall and good looking, I looked younger than my age. When I asked them out for a drink after the last set, they'd often tell me I was too young, or they were robbing the cradle. But the women in their 30s and 40s wouldn't mention age; they were delighted to be with someone that returned them to their younger years.

I liked the older women, they didn't talk about love and they knew exactly what was going to happen. They seemed to enjoy it more and seldom were looking for a continuing relationship unless they were French. Some of the older French women came in repeatedly and I had some fun episodes with them. Sometimes they were married and just out for a fling. We would go to my place; other times they had beautiful apartments and they would invite me there. Some were gorgeous and a few were very famous in fashion or films.

The Mars Club was truly a training ground for me. I honed my skills there until I had great confidence. That along with maturity and polish helped me graduate to more fulfilling sexual conquests. My studies suffered during those years. But my painting became focused and I did some good work. Unfortunately, it wasn't as inspired as it should have been if I had directed more of my energies to the canvas rather than women.

One afternoon I was sitting at the Dome Café in Montparnasse. Don Stewart, an artist at the Académie Julian, joined me. I was happy to see he was in good spirits. The year before, a car in Saint Germain-des-Prés struck and killed his wife and many of us had been very concerned he would take his own life. We tried to have someone with him at all times for weeks after it happened. He was in a state of complete depression for nearly a year. He had been very much in love, studying on the GI Bill. He had a good life and it came to an abrupt end with his wife's death.

Burt Gore, another painter from the Académie, joined us. We had sat for about an hour or so when a young, leggy, sandy-haired blond emerged from the crosswalk with a crowd of people. She walked directly toward us, her lithe figure swaying. Our eyes connected for a long moment. I guess she caught herself and was a little embarrassed she had held my gaze longer than might be considered conservative. Her face was angular, full lips, and long, thin, neck. I was so immediately attracted that when she turned and headed away I almost panicked. Both Don and Burt had noticed her too and commented on her beauty. I quickly threw down some money and said, "I can't let this one just walk away without an effort to meet her."

I didn't want to startle her so I quickly walked to get alongside, then I turned and asked her in French if I could speak to her for a moment. "Would you stop and have a coffee with me?"

She recognized the accent and replied in English. "I don't think so, maybe some other time."

"I know if I can't talk to you now there will not be another time, please speak with me for just ten minutes."

She laughed. "Okay, with the agreement you'll not insist on more, I'm meeting a friend and I'm never late."

"Then you're not French or Italian," I quipped.

"No, but you're right. One cannot be punctual and be French or Italian."

I could see she liked a sense of humor. We sat in that café for nearly two hours, and although I told her almost all my life story, she shared only what she wanted me to know. I knew she must be married, but she wasn't wearing a ring. Her clothes were elegant and Italian, everything about her was class and money. She had been born and raised in England. Her parents were divorced and evidently, her mother was some kind of social climber who put her into the best of Swiss schools, with the help of a friend. We laughed and had a wonderful time. It was the first time, since the heartbreak of Noddy, that I felt something beyond that of another conquest. I invited her to come to The Mars Club where I was singing the next few evenings. I didn't think she'd come; she was a few years older than I was, and obviously in a different league socially and financially. Our two hours together was a complete joy. Afterward, I told myself one day I would be successful and polished enough and would meet a lady of her stature and charm and never need another woman in my life.

That evening about eleven o'clock, she entered the club with another, older, woman, it was obvious they were sisters. Big Ben seated them. I had described her to him and, if she came in, asked him to put her close to the piano where I usually sat with a hand microphone. I nodded to Ben; he had it right for a change. Art Simmons was playing piano for me and picked up what was going on right away. He introduced me as Paris's most popular American singer; the brother of Josephine. That was his big joke as I sang under the name of Chris Baker. [For those of you that don't know, Josephine Baker was the toast of Paris for thirty years, she was black, attractive, talented, and also a friend.]

I sang two songs, directly to her as if there wasn't another living soul in the place. When I finished, I joined them. Bonnie Dana took over and sang some Ella Fitzgerald favorites. Bonnie was a sexy redhead with a voluptuous figure. She lived with Art Simmons, who was probably the best jazz pianist in Paris, with maybe the exception of Aaron Bridgers. Bonnie's mother was Amy Sample McPherson, the famous evangelist.

Stephanie and her sister left with me as soon as Bonnie

finished. We walked to the Champs-Élysées and sat in a sidewalk café for about an hour. Stephanie was impressed and thought I had an exceptional voice and predicted future stardom for me. She was surprised it wasn't my aim or desire to pursue singing and that it was the means to an end to support my first love, painting. "I wouldn't be surprised to find you a very talented painter, too."

I asked her to pose for me. "I always capture something exceptional when I have strong feelings about my subject."

She smiled. Her sister was married to a Frenchman and lived in Paris. She was very sweet, but it was obvious she didn't have the grace and stature of her little sister. Before they left, Stephanie asked me about my schedule, when I was working, going to school, where I lived and other personal questions. When I told her, I would be available for dinners or whenever she was free, she laughed.

"You must like me."

"I find you lovely and wonderful."

"I'll come to be with you tomorrow night, around the same time at the club."

I spent the hours before I went to bed and again all day that Saturday wondering what she meant by coming to be with me for that night. Did she want to be my lover, or just spend some more pleasant hours in some café? I cleaned the apartment. I wanted it presentable in case we came back to my place. I didn't want to go there, but maybe she wouldn't want to be seen at a hotel with me. I would have gladly spent the money for a first class hotel, but I didn't mean to be presumptuous either.

Christian Title

At about eleven o'clock just like the night before, she came through the door. The place was so crowded Ben gave up his seat to her at the end of the bar. I think he was curious about who this beautiful, classy, woman was; I learned later he had been quite pushy and asked her many questions. She was much too sharp and used the opportunity to torment him with just enough information to make him that much more curious. The club was very responsive to me that night and I was fortunate not to have some loud drunk mouthing off, as was often the case.

We didn't get out of the club until one-thirty. Al 'Fats' Edwards invited us to join him and his girlfriend at the Pied de Cochon; an after-hours hotspot known for its onion soup. Many of the entertainers and night people would go there after the shows, until the early morning hours. It was located in the market section in Les Halles and during the week, starting at four in the morning, vendors unloaded all the produce, fish, and meat for the various stalls. It was picturesque with all the activity on the streets. They piled cabbages and melons up on the sidewalks and throughout the streets as the marketplace had expanded far beyond the boundaries of the original market. Some years later, the market moved out of Paris and the area became the nucleus of the Centre Pompidou.

Stephanie wanted to join them so we caught a cab and fought our way through still considerable traffic. The restaurant was also crowded. We waited about ten minutes and then were seated on the second floor. We greeted friends and familiar faces and sat for hours entertained by Al, who was a considerable character. He told stories and jokes and roared with laughter at his own humor. On his six-foot-three frame hung about three hundred pounds and it all shook. But he was solid and young, and quite handsome. His girlfriend was German, blond with light blue eyes and tiny, probably not more than

135

a hundred pounds. She said very little all evening as her English wasn't fluent. Stephanie spoke to her in German and seemed very much at ease in several languages.

It was four in the morning and I was tired though I had slept late trying to catch up on the week as I often did. School usually started at eight or nine depending on what classes I had that day. If I were working, I would only sleep six hours or less. When the weekend came, I would often sleep twelve hours as I had the previous night. We said goodbye to our friends and walked to the corner where there was a cab stand. The metal green ornate pole with the white taxi standard on the top overlooked a desolate scene. The streets were empty. A couple of cars went by; we were in luck that the third car was a taxi. We got in the cab and I didn't know what to tell the driver. We hadn't talked about where we were going. It was an uncomfortable few seconds.

"Hotel Wagram," she said, smiling at me.

"You saved the moment," I said. "Am I dropping you there?"

"Yes," she looked at me, "if you don't want to spend the night with me."

"I want to spend the year with you, or maybe forever if you wish."

"I'm feeling the same way. I want to be in your arms and hold you close." At that instant, she had a sweet vulnerability to her. "If we continue to blend so smoothly I'd like to be with you until Wednesday. Then I must return to Italy." She looked at me again; I assume gauging how I felt about that. "If we're not feeling the same in the morning I'll take my leave."

"No, I want to be with you and if there's something that doesn't please you, you must tell me. We've so little time together, it must be perfect. I'm going to cancel everything and be with you until it's time for you to go. I won't inquire about anything. I'll treat these few days as a brief and beautiful time in my life."

We arrived at the hotel and went to her room. We sat on a small sofa for a short while when she suddenly jumped up laughing.

"Take a shower with me and we'll wash the city away."

She started to remove her clothes and was quickly down to panties and bra. Every inch of her was white, smooth, and beautiful.

"Do you like my body?" This was a question that women seemed to like to ask.

As I removed my shoes and slacks, I glanced up at her. "MMMMMMMMMMM."

She went into the bathroom and I could hear the water come on. When I entered, she was already in the shower. I joined her.

"Do you like my body?" I asked.

"MMMMMMMM," she said.

I pulled her to me and we kissed. With that wonderful first meeting, she opened her mouth ever so slightly. Our tongues just barely touched the others lips. We instinctively knew the kisses would generate an uncontrollable passion, so we held back, just teasing ever so tenderly. We laughed and talked about our first encounter being like an old married couple.

"Well," she said, "there's only been one man in my life and it's been quite a formal and arranged relationship."

"I want it this way too," I said. "If it's abrupt and clumsy, then it isn't honest. This isn't an affair you know; it's a milestone, one of both love and passion. It matters not the length of time it occupies but only the depth and intensity of our feelings."

We got into the large bed and she turned the silk sheets all the way to the foot. She lighted a small lamp on the table across the large room. "It's a lovely place isn't it?"

"Yes," I said. "I thought you were probably staying with your sister."

"I was, but she understood after meeting you I wanted you to be my last fling before I left. What I'm feeling right now is so much more than I had hoped for."

With that, she was beside me in the soft yellow light. When we kissed this time, our lips parted and our mouths entwined. I felt her body; it was smooth, firm and I could feel her desperate need. She was grasping and pressing against me with surprising wiry strength from her lean body. When she felt my hardness, she pulled me on top, convulsing in expectation. It was moving very fast for me, I wanted to savor her body kissing every part and giving her a first climax before anything else. That would have to wait until later or tomorrow I thought, she wants me right now. As I thrust inside her, I could feel her almost go into a spastic climax. I moved ever so slow and it lasted for a very long time. It was everything I could do to hold back; I wanted it to last so much longer. She went limp and I continued to move in her with a slow, methodical motion. Her legs went flat and her arms dropped to the sides. She was unable to respond except with the moans and groans of a quiet pleasure. I kept moving slowly, kissing her face and running my hands through her hair. After a while, she started to pulsate again and pump her hips, rocking them into mine. I couldn't hold back much longer. She felt what was happening.

"Now my darling, now, now, now..." she cried.

We reached into the galaxy together. It was euphoric, and we drifted into a dream trance for what seemed like hours. The sky was lightening outside when she whispered softly. "It was the most incredible love I've ever felt."

We went to sleep tightly intertwined.

* * *

The next morning or I should say afternoon, I laid there contemplating the night before. In the night, she told me we would never meet again after Paris. I knew it was the truth so I wanted every moment possible with her. I was filled with regret at the thought even though it was days away before she would leave me. I had promised not to pursue the future and I meant to keep my bargain. As I held her, I wanted to have her again but I knew from experience that waiting and not overdoing it would be better in the long run.

It was Sunday and I suggested we go to the flea market. We took the metro to Coulaincourt and stopped at a local sidewalk café for a croissant and café au lait. We wandered the streets of the market nearly all of the afternoon. She thought she had made a find at one of the stalls; a pencil drawing with the initials A. D.

Flea Market, 1954, Oil on canvas

"Do you think it could be Andre Derain?" she asked.

"No, it doesn't look quite like his work," I said,

"But it's so inexpensive; don't you think it's worth taking a chance?"

I shook my head. "No, it's an old game here. What you're thinking is what they, these type dealers, depend on to sell a variety of works with vague indications it might be old and of some significant value. They remove worthless art from old frames, dirty up some new drawing by coating the paper with strong tea using a large varnish brush and add a few spots and smudges. Most likely, it was done by a local artist commissioned to do just such a drawing based on others by Derain. I've seen Vincent Van Gogh's early dark paintings like *The Potato Eaters*, repainted over old canvases. And just the van at the edge of the canvas on the right-hand side, made to look as if it had been cut to fit the frame. They use a Van Dyke Brown in a Damar varnish, after several coats to give the face of the canvas the age to match the back and sides of the piece. They even rub it with what we call rotten stone, a powder used in antiquing furniture and picture frames. The con is perfected by the individuals in the stalls; they let the customer, mostly Americans, just find it in some corner as if it had been there collecting dust for decades. Then they act like it's some piece of junk. When asked about the price, it's usually quite low by American standards, but high enough that it's a substantial profit on the dealer's investment. The buyer's act as if they kind of like it but never say what they think it is–they don't want to tip their hand. This works in the favor of the dealer as he has made no representations at all."

She looked at me with a quizzical expression. "How do you know all of this?"

"I have a friend that's quite brilliant at mimicking various styles, and it's what he does for a living."

I could see the suspicion in her eyes and figured that some further explanation should clear it all up before she started jumping to conclusions. "My friend is on the GI Bill going to school here. He has a total of about eighty-seven dollars a month, and it's just not enough to get by. And what he does isn't dishonest; he's providing a service to the sellers. The buyer thinks he has made a great discovery at a cheap price. And even when he finds out it isn't authentic, he hangs it on his wall and has a good story to tell. The setting for the misrepresentation is provided to him, but it's he, the buyer, that makes it to himself. Many of the pieces I've seen look like someone's work with which you might be familiar, but they're unsigned. I would object strenuously if it were an exact copy of the style or a particular work, and included a fake signature as well."

"But don't you think there are people who will then add the signatures to competent works which then will find their way to the marketplace?" she asked.

"Yes, I'm sure there are people counterfeiting everything of value in the world; especially those artists with simplistic styles. Because there is little to give them away. If it's a piece of modern art with some black slashes on white such as Franz Kline, it would be far simpler to make the work convincing than to try to make a significant Degas. Unfortunately, very few people can distinguish even good from terrible, let alone a decent fake. But it's my opinion most people are fakes; they produce little of lasting value." I concluded my explanation with an abrupt, "Are you hungry?" She smiled and I could tell I had been rambling on too long. "What would you consider a special and fun treat?"

"I would like to eat at some small family restaurant, where the food is good, but which is what you would consider a typical local atmosphere." Then she added: "I've always been taken to the fancy spots where I was supposed to be impressed. My benefactor wouldn't eat at such a place as I've just suggested, and it's only with him that I've been to Paris."

"I have just the place," I said. We flagged a cab and a surly little man with a dead cigarette butt hanging from the corner of his lip nodded for us to get in. "Do you know a restaurant named the Auberge Basque in Saint Germain-des-Prés?" I asked.

"No," and he jerked to a sudden forward movement. After a minute, he asked, "Where in Saint Germain-des-Prés?"

"Just take us to the Eglise de Saint Germain-des-Prés."

It was an easy walk from the church and one of my paintings was in a gallery window on the way. When we stopped in front of it, she knew immediately it was my work. She looked carefully at the signature and I said nothing. After a long period of contemplation, she looked fondly at me.

"You're truly a very talented young man, I'm proud to be your friend, even if it's a friendship without a future." She laughed and I could see she wanted to keep it light.

"You'll be in the heart of many of my paintings; it's the way I'll still give you my love when you're gone," I said more seriously. "You know we haven't eaten all day. I usually eat a good lunch. At school, we get a bottle of wine for several of us and share Brie cheese and some of the excellent salads they make, very close to here on the Rue de Seine. Mabillion is my favorite marketplace. I live on the Rue du Beaux Arts now, and I always shop there after school since the Académie de Beaux Arts is just down the street."

Stephanie had a far off look in her eyes.

"I guess all this talk of markets and shopping is boring you," I said feeling embarrassed I had talked about such a mundane subject. But it was hard to be stimulating, which I so desperately wanted to be. I was continually making small talk at the club because my French wasn't fluent enough for profound and serious conversation with many comrades at school.

"No," she said. "Just the contrary, I never have the opportunity to go to a marketplace, to go shopping and the only schools I know have been private girls' schools in Switzerland. My benefactor chose the schools, and his personal assistant has chosen all of my clothes and accessories."

"Well, she certainly has chosen well, everything you've worn is superb, and the way you walk and talk and move is like... well, perfect."

She sighed and I could tell that wasn't what she wanted to hear.

"I've been groomed for a particular life, but it has not allowed me to be with men my own age or even women my own age. I long to do the things you describe as boring." She smiled wistfully at me. "I would like to have a bottle of wine and some Brie cheese and bread and sit by the Seine and picnic with you. And go to your school with you to see the art classes and meet your friends." She stopped and the vulnerable look was on her face again. "Could we do that tomorrow?"

I was so relieved she wasn't criticizing. My heart was so full with her at that moment; it meant more time together. "Of course we will. I'm delighted you want to share these things."

Soon we were at the Auberge Basque. When we entered, the owner greeted me because I was a regular. It was my favorite restaurant, and I frequented it as often as I could. It was a single menu for the evening, where eight people sat together and passed the food and drink around. Fixed menu restaurants were quite ordinary in those years. But most were price oriented rather than quality. Sunday night was probably the only night you could get in without a reservation. It was an extremely popular place. If you wanted to go on a Saturday or Friday night, you would need a reservation a week or two in advance.

We sat off to one side which was the first table to be seated. They wouldn't serve until the table was full, and often it was a twenty or thirty-minute wait if you were early on a Sunday. Regular seatings were at eight and ten, but Sunday's were at five and seven o'clock. It was just past five and we were short only one couple. They served us the house wine, which was quite good by my standards, but I'm sure it was considered Vin Ordinaire at the house of her great benefactor. We sat for a while and talked to a young working couple who were out for a special treat. The restaurant specialized in Basque dishes, and the food was always outstanding. It consisted of an appetizer, a light specialty dish, the main course, fruit with bread and cheese, a dessert and coffee.

The last couple arrived and sat next to us at the end of the table. The man was Tom Rowe and the woman with him was beautiful, as were all that accompanied Tom. He was a regular at the Auberge Basque and had recommended it to me. We had dinner there many times together. Tom immediately poured the charm on Stephanie. He was a classy guy; had lived in L.A. and was involved in the movie business. He was about ten years older than I but had a handsome, boyish, look. I had always felt if Tom wanted the girl I was with; he would have no problem taking over. I think it's exactly what he thought when he saw Stephanie was too old and sophisticated for me. His date just sat there during the meal while he paid equal attention to the two women. I was relieved, as it had been many hours of conversation with Stephanie and I needed a break. But I knew, for once with Tom, not all the appeal in the world would benefit him this time. She just wasn't available. I knew we had a certain magic that couldn't be dispelled by Sir Galahad. I actually enjoyed watching him and Stephanie. What would inevitably happen would take him down a notch.

Tom was highly intelligent, fluent in French and several other languages. Brought up in a diplomas family in Japan, speaking that language like a native, during the war he had been a special officer in intelligence. With his dark curly hair and Robert Taylor good looks, he was an admirable package. Stephanie noticed the confidence and assertiveness Tom displayed. She made a special effort to continually touch me and show signs of affection to let him know whom she had chosen. And that she wasn't making any changes. It made the meal fun and I could relax and just listen. We spoke French as his lady didn't speak any English. Unfortunately, French was always a strain for me in a group situation, especially if I was tired. Stephanie loved the meal and company that was so different from her friends and life. We returned to her hotel, sat in bed, and talked for hours. It was such a joy to be with her. She made everything smooth and comfortable.

"Will you make love to me in the morning?" she asked.

I was tired, too. "Yes."

We held each other and talked until we drifted off to sleep.

* * *

In the morning, she was up and had already showered when I awoke. I was disappointed; I'd hoped to join her, but I was truly at her command. She was setting the timing and the pace. I showered and when I came out, in the hotel robe, she had coffee and croissants and cold cuts and jam on a table by the window. She was wearing a sheer negligee. I wondered where it came from. It was very sexy and displayed her slim body and delicate limbs to perfection. What a delicious scene.

"I don't know what to eat first," I said.

She actually blushed for the first time, and I sensed that was something with which she wasn't too comfortable. But I had found in similar situations that sneaking up on it and letting it happen might make her even more uncomfortable.

"I want to please you the first time by kissing your mouth, your breasts, and your sex. I want you to lay back and just feel. Don't talk or look. Just feel. Of course moan, groan, and make sufficient noises so I know what feels best for you."

She laughed, still a little embarrassed. "You're the doctor and I suspect you know well how to perform this operation." When we started kissing, she said, "I've never had anyone want to please me. It's always been that I was expected to please."

With that, I became ever so much more excited. I slipped my robe off and the next half hour was devoted to her pleasure. She was so heightened I couldn't touch her for a long while. I put my head on her belly and lay quietly for a while.

"Look at me," she said.

I pulled myself up to her and she stared into my eyes.

"That was wonderful, I can't describe quite how I feel about it, but we must talk about it later in some quiet moment."

We hugged, kissed and made love for hours after that. She repeatedly climaxed, as did I and we fell into a soft slumber. We awoke and took the metro to my apartment. The climb to the 3rd etage seemed long and tiring that particular afternoon. I remember feeling a little embarrassed the building didn't have an elevator.

When we entered, she gasped. "It's just what I pictured, where did you get all these beautiful things?"

I loved all the little antique shops and the flea markets of Paris. I was always collecting antiques, paintings, dolls, toys, and anything that had a good shape and color. Especially if it amused me. So the place was filled with my paintings and every conceivable goodie I had found. I had painted all the kitchen cabinets with flowers and the walls with cartoon-like faces. The living room walls were solid with my paintings.

Stephanie sat in an old-style rocker the woman downstairs had made soft cushions for; it was something I had never seen before. It rocked back and forth on a level plane, as it had springs underneath on both ends. It allowed you to slide back on little rails like a railroad track. It was very solid. She seemed to take great pleasure in the motion. [I have often wished I had shipped it home, as I've never in my years on this planet seen another one even remotely like it.]

She enjoyed the crazy array of funny things I surrounded myself with; she was fascinated by my collection of pornographic pipes. It surprised her anyone would create such beautiful works of art from such subjects. I had seen one in Sidney Bechet's apartment. Since then, I had found if you asked the antique dealers, they often had something of the like hidden away. They were often made of ivory or exotic woods and were like magnificent miniature carvings on a pipe you could smoke. My living room was filled with such items and Stephanie kept herself well occupied while I changed clothes.

When I emerged, I said, "Well what do you think?"

She smiled with an incredible look that made my whole being love her. "It's the kind of place I would like to have for myself as a hideaway. Somewhere I could have everything that just pleased me; a place in this world just for me. If I have a place someday like that, maybe, well maybe if we could... oh, it's just a dream!"

"Dreams come true if you want them enough," I said.

"I'm surprised the apartment is so perfect," she said. "When you dashed off to change and didn't seem to want me to accompany you, I wrongly presumed you were ashamed of it."

"Well," I said. "It's far from elegant, but it's me, I guess."

After we had left my apartment, we walked the block to the Beaux Arts Académie. We toured the studios and I introduced her to some friends, and to my favorite professor, Pierre Jerome. [I visited with Pierre thirty-five years later. He was in his 90s and still painting in his studio next to the Académie de la Grande Chaumière.]

Stephanie loved the Académie atmosphere and spoke of maybe becoming an art student at some school in the future. When we left, we walked down the Rue des Beaux Arts and made a left turn to the Rue de Seine. A short walk and we were in the marketplace in Mabillion. We bought Brie cheese, a bottle of red wine and a baguette ancienne. She loved this bustling market section. I took her to my favorite charcuterie, where the selection of readymade salads was displayed like works of art. We purchased my favorite, Salade Espagnole. [I returned to Paris over a period of forty years and the shop, still there, always had this delicious dish. On my last trip in 1996 I learned that they no longer made this specialty.]

We walked back down the Rue de Seine to the river and took the steps to the quay. We settled on a bench, ate our lunch and watched the barges navigate the river. The time I spent with Stephanie was a benchmark in my relationships. She had a level of class and sophistication and education and incredible people skills beyond anyone I had ever dated. Everyone, I introduced her to never forgot her; months later friends would still ask about her.

We spent the next two days in perfect harmony and when we said our goodbyes, it was a very emotional time. I wondered if I would ever meet another that would captivate me so completely. I got a note from her the following week, thanking me for our time together saying she'd never forget, and wishing me success and happiness.

* * *

[In 1956 while sailing in the Mediterranean, we were anchored in the outer bay of Portofino. We went ashore in the tender and tied up to the jetty. As we walked along, toward the cafes and restaurants on the main wharf, I saw there was an elegant looking launch sitting at the end of one of the pontoons. I saw a group of very fashionable people coming toward me. I recognized Stephanie immediately; she was dressed in a white silky looking creation right out of Vogue. She was gay and laughing; they all seemed to be having fun. As we approached, I could see she was looking at me. I didn't know if it was recognition at first, but then our eyes met and we held our gaze on each other for a moment. As we passed, she smiled at me and did not look back.

When I inquired on the dock, I was told the enormous yacht in the bay was that of a Tuscan count of a famous family. I assumed it was the distinguished looking man in his late 50s. That final glimpse of Stephanie and her position as the Grand Dame of Tuscan royalty was a fitting closure. We ended with a similar moment to our introduction, just an intense glance; a brief point in the span of our life. But those often lead to significant events and meeting people, we remember for all time. We live and find happiness in the friendships and loves of our past; it gives us stability and pleasure throughout our lives. So I say to young people, build the stepping stones that will form your path.]

* * *

[In the San Fernando Valley where I grew up, there were four groups of people as I saw it. From a kids point of view, of course, perhaps an over simplification but I believe it remains true. There were the people with money who lived based on recognition from their peers. They belonged to the social clubs and groups that were the elite, in their estimation. They indulged in creative things that were fashionable but didn't have individuality. They used the top decorators and many of my friends' homes looked amazingly similar to me as a boy. The unfortunate part is that the level of their enjoyment and understanding is very limited. I find this also applies to music and good literature.

The group I admire most has success, but when it's enough to live and spend their time in interesting and comfortable ways, they retire early. They are often much more sensitive not only to the arts but also to old people and children. The group to which I had the most exposure as a child and to which my greatest reference was at that time was the still working successful people who at the same time had an appreciation of the arts.

The fourth class was the class my family was a part of. They worked hard, smoked and drank excessively. They didn't put much time into learning or caring about the arts. It was a subject I spent some time explaining to Stephanie, about my frustrations of not having anyone in my family that cared about any of the passions I was pursuing. I wanted to be successful, but I was very much aware it wouldn't be worthwhile unless it were on my own terms. To be successful and not be fulfilled would be a frustrating experience. I had already learned with very talented friends in junior high school and high school that early success in show business distorted one's perspective of life and one's future.

A good example of this was the group of exceptionally talented kids I had the pleasure of being with as part of the Keenan Wynn Camp troupe. Barbara Ruick, the daughter of actress, Laurene Tuttle, was a friend and one of the most talented girls. We used to rehearse in their playroom over the years and I watched this lovely girl grow into a stunning talent. She was romantically involved with another great talent at North Hollywood high school, John Williams. He had an orchestra in our high school and was even then an incredible musical talent. Some years later John, who we called Curly, (before he lost his hair); married Barbara and they had three children. Barbara died young of a cerebral hemorrhage, which broke the heart of not only John but everyone who knew her. Her only significant success had been when she co-starred with Shirley Jones in the musical, 'Carousel.' I visited her and Shirley in New York at that time and I had never seen her happier. John, of course, went on to win more Oscars than you can count and to take the Boston Pops Symphony Orchestra to new heights.

As I mentioned previously, another of the troupe was Debbie Reynolds. She and I did some fun numbers together, and I was very much in love with her. She went through so many bad experiences with men; she was so trusting and loving. And with her early success never had the basics of what men were all about. I can't recall ever knowing a more giving and kind person, but when it came to happiness, she was cheated by her fame.]

* * *

Africa

I made two trips outside France to North Africa; to Tangier and later to Algiers. On those trips, I found I wasn't comfortable with the people. They were always selling or trying to get something and didn't appear to me to be sincere.

My third adventure was to the Niger River country in Central Africa. This safari, with French biologist Andre Metereau, wasn't a good experience. I was 23 years old; I had completed my master's degree and was open to any adventure which presented itself. Pierre Jerome contacted me to see if I would be interested in doing the illustrations for a project sponsored by the University of Paris. I had made a successful series of watercolors of the city, which were reproduced and sold to tourists. He had seen the work and was interested in the technique.

We flew in a DC-3, a twin-engine propeller plane, making several stops to refuel until we got to the staging area in Dakar. We were eight people at first and took on two more French Africans for the flight to an airstrip where we would join a small river boat outside of Timbuktu. We made slow progress on the river for two days before our first stop. The plane ride was bumpy and cramped and the cabin on the boat was five feet wide and nine feet long. So far, it wasn't my idea of a pleasant trip. The photographer was a foul-tempered, chubby little snot-nosed fellow, and his wife had a mouth that never stopped. Conflicts began soon after we left Dakar. The French are very particular about food and the food on the boat was about as bad as it gets.

As we progressed the trip became even more unpleasant. I kept to myself and tried to enjoy the native people that surrounded us. In the far reaches of the Niger River country, we made our land-based camp. The people were extremely primitive. I think I must have been the first very light complexioned, blond, person they had ever seen. They not only stared at me, but the children thought I was some kind of freak, and laughed at my every move.

Our guide and translator made it difficult, as he spoke French with a very different inflection. Since it wasn't my native language, it was very hard to understand him. What I gathered was that the people thought if they touched me, it would bring them luck. I was like an albino monkey! But if that was the case why did they constantly pick at the hair on my arms and head? I think they were just curious about the texture, and it was driving me crazy. Imagine dozens of people around you all of the time, touching you and pulling your hair with less than clean hands. This presented problems when trying to execute exacting drawings and watercolors. A council and a head governed their society; we might call the leader their chief. The council was made up of previous leaders and elders. Finally, the guide talked to the leader about my problem, and he made an edict to his people they were forbidden to touch me. So instead, they'd put their heads six inches away to study my skin and hair.

One evening I was playing my guitar and serenading Jacqueline, the wife of our leader. I had collected quite a crowd of people and Andre asked if I could move to the bank of the river as they were crowding so close to the tents they couldn't prepare our dinner. I sat on the edge of the steep bank and played some early American folk songs. That drew an even more sizeable audience. I did this on several evenings and it changed the atmosphere and relationship I had with the people. I was no longer a curiosity, but someone that made them happy. Soon they were always greeting me and helping me with everything I did.

We spent ten days venturing from our campsite to interesting places to examine the terrain and plant life. I was just trying to survive and get back to Paris. I didn't like the people I was with; there was a constant conflict between them and the air was thick with dissension. I spent as much time as I could drawing cartoons and characters for the children and enjoying the association I had developed with them.

The night before we were to leave, the chief made me the gift of his daughter to bed with. The guide explained he wanted her to have a blond child just like me. I refused. She wasn't exactly my type; not attractive and unquestionably not very clean. I thanked him though and he got quite angry. Then several in the group were consulted and they determined it would be a terrible insult if I rejected her. I was stuck.

Her mother and some of the women prepared her for the occasion. She was groomed and some awful perfumes were applied.

Fortunately, for me, they don't make love, they just fuck. She was satisfied in about three minutes and then just wanted to look at my body. After an hour or so, I got dressed and left the shack. I spent the next few days while on the trip back to Paris, examining myself to see if there was any indication of disease. It was an unpleasant journey and I never wanted to see any of them again. I finished the illustrations and that ended an unpleasant but still learning experience and an interesting adventure.

[I have visited Africa several more times, and Joyce and I covered some of South Africa. One incident in Botswana while on a safari is memorable. We were in a tent in the compound; the base of the tent was wood flooring with wood siding up to about three and a half feet. It had a wood frame, but the sides and roof were canvas tent material. It was about seven in the morning and Joyce and I were startled into alertness by the tent stretching down toward us with great force; accompanied by the screeching of the monkeys. They were jumping from a tree branch well above the tent, leaping onto the slanted sides where they could catapult to the ground. As they hit the side of the tent just above our bed, it looked as if it would stretch down to where we were lying. It scared the hell out of us and we quickly moved to another area of the tent to get dressed. The native population and our fellow companions all thought it was hilarious. When we went outside and watched it, it was indeed comical.]

African Safari, Christian and his buddies.

9

THE PHILLIPE MARCHAND PAINTINGS

The Académie accepted that I wished to work in the Impressionist style after the French masters. After this understanding, my life as a painter improved and was much more exciting. The Sorbonne University was offering a doctorate program which was a continuation of studies after a master's degree, with only a one-year extension. The primary requirement was the sponsorship of two professors, and the authorship of a thesis on an aspect of art history not fully examined. It was my desire to do this on some of the Impressionist painters, but it wasn't accepted. My advisors and I finally narrowed it down to Georges Rouault and Chaim Soutine; artists that hadn't been thoroughly investigated for their unique styles. During this investigation, I became enamored with these artists, but also with the realm of other Expressionist painters such as Modigliani, Van Gogh, and Paul Gauguin and the German Expressionists. These studies led to a lot of experimentation into Expressionist philosophies and opened the door to understanding many other neglected areas which soon started to enter my thoughts and work.

When I finished my degree at the Beaux Arts, I continued with individual classes at the studios of living masters, Andre L'hote, and Fernand Leger. I had over a period of years taken special classes with these exceptional men and the teachers they had hired to continue their philosophies. This led me to study the Fauve group of artists, referred to in English as the Wild Beasts, because of their arbitrary techniques with pure color. Cubism, abstract expressionism and an array of nonobjective methods were discussed and practiced.

* * *

During a break from school, a friend of mine asked if I would like to join him, in the beautiful city of Nancy, as he was returning home for a few days. His family was charming and his father was a professional working artist. His primary gallery was a small art shop and store on a side street in the city. He also exhibited at several, mostly tourist-type, galleries on the French Riviera. His paintings were colorful and commercial, but rigid by my standards. His son was one of the better students at the Académie Julian; better than his father in his artistic talent but hadn't arrived at an individual style.

Since I had time to work freely, I took some of my experimental work with me to finish. I had seen the work of Claude Venard at a Left Bank gallery. I was fascinated with the idea of putting a painted surface on the canvas and then sketching into the surface with a sharpened pencil or the sharpened end of a wood brush. As I sketched, the paint would have to be wiped off the sketching tool with each stroke. The one thing I didn't like about the Venard work was it had many disturbing blobs of paint from not cleaning the instrument used for the sketch-in, which distracted in the finished work. The several works I took were dry, but the lines were not very discernable. I put a coat of black paint over the sketch and then wiped out the canvas, leaving a gray tone on most of it, but the deep lines of the drawing were left entirely black. I got this idea from the work of Bernard Buffet, whose work was the rage, at the time, in Paris; he was so prolific with his black outline and quick style. I then worked in the bold decorative strokes which left some of the background showing through. By the weekend, I had finished all three paintings.

The local gallery dealer came to the house to see Jacques' fathers work, but when he saw what I had done, he was very interested. We discussed leaving the work with him for sale, but there was a catch. He said he couldn't sell the work of an American to his clientele. "The French want only the French; they think they're the best painters on Earth." So that evening we thought up the pen name of Phillipe Marchand. The next day I signed them with a bold black mimic of the way Buffet signed his work. The Marchand work was immediately popular.

It was only a couple of weeks later when the gallery contacted me and said they wanted an additional ten paintings. The owner came to see me at the Veau Colombier where I was working the weekends. When he asked for more, I told him I was paid cash at the nightclubs, and I couldn't afford the time with my schedule to produce the number he wanted. He paid me a nice sum for the three works I had left with him. And said he would pick up additional works if I could do them, and pay me cash provided it was of the same quality. The decision that night, to produce more of the Marchand work, was essentially the end of my singing career, although I was working more and had achieved some real popularity on the nightclub circuit. I had been singing for a couple of years, in mostly the same places:

- The 'Metro Jazz' in St. Michael,
- The 'A la Romance' in Mabillion,
- The 'Veau Columbier' in Saint Germain-des-Prés,
- The 'Calavados,' across the street from the 'George V Hotel,'

- The 'Mars Club' near the Champs-Élysées; and my first job in Paris at,
- The 'Lido de Paris.'

But I was tired of the nightclub scene. I enjoyed the singing, but the long periods talking to drunken idiots and people I had nothing in common with was wearing on me. I often slept only a couple of hours a night and then caught up on the weekends, and mornings when I didn't have an early class. The schedule was hard on my body and taking a toll. The time spent working the clubs could have been used for painting, and that was a problem. I never made enough money to live well and I was spending more than I was earning, only getting ahead when I received an important club contract. The drinking and atmosphere weren't conducive to the future I had planned for myself.

"The English Tourists," Oil on canvas

But the problem was that I couldn't paint any volume of work from my apartment. Then I found a solution. Many of the American students went to the American Students Center on the Boulevard Raspail in Montparnasse. Upstairs there was a large and beautiful studio with skylights. Very few students ever used it and it was empty most of the time. A wealthy American woman had bought the property and built a center for the American students that would live there so they would have a place to congregate. It is very sad, but some years later, it was torn down and replaced with commercial buildings. I never found out how and why this happened. It was a landmark and a unique place, and should have easily found sponsors to continue the tradition.

I decided to work from the upstairs studio at the Center. The next day, which was a Saturday, I stopped by the Rousseau art shop on the Rue du Dragon. I picked up ten canvases of various sizes, a broad palette knife, and the material to start the work. By the afternoon when I took a lunch break, I had covered all of the canvases with a film of titanium white and sketched in the subjects from a sketchbook I had been working on. Some large cupboards in the studio were dusty but empty. I cleaned them out and placed the wet works, in them, leaning each individually on the sides. I used a cobalt dryer in the paint and I expected they would be ready within four or five days.

The following weekend I had no commitments and I worked twelve to fifteen hours that Saturday and a full day on Sunday. Frank came by that Sunday. He was curious about this new found venture. When he saw the work, he was very impressed. He said it wasn't as good as my other work but, it had a great appeal. After watching for an hour or so, he said it was growing on him, and he could see why it was so popular. I personally didn't think much of it. I was quite happy to work on them under another name.

I decided I would keep the Marchand work a secret as the galleries would be quite upset if they knew the artist was an American using a pen name. The paintings at that point were in several galleries including the prestigious Rene Druet Gallery. Concerned about it leaking out, we got around it by stating Phillipe Marchand had his beginning in Nancy. [Later on once I was back in the United States, when the book of the Marchand works was published, the background was directly related to my actual experience, but just by bits and pieces.] For the remainder of my time in Paris, the Marchand paintings and my own Impressionist works continued to pay the bills. It was demanding, but I lived very well. I sang only when I had a worthwhile club date, and made myself available only on the weekends.

* * *

The next school year was harder, but when Frank came to tell me of the possibility of a nightclub of our own that was the beginning of The Calypso Club on the Rue de Rennes. At the time my friends and I also had another side business, I had promoted and organized a team that conducted guided tours of the Paris nightlife. I would sell, make the contacts, and direct the guys for the advance purchase of tickets to the Casino de Paris, the Folies Bergère, and the Moulin Rouge. It employed Frank and two other friends, Trent, and Ken. Each of them had a car and would do the pickup and tour for a group of four or five. On very busy nights, we would schedule the clubs so each driver could take two groups. The early group taking in the big shows and the second group starting late and taking in three jazz clubs on the Left Bank. We had it down to a science, and at one point, we often had as many tours as the big operators. We called it the

'ASO' an acronym for American Students Organization. It was confused purposely with the USO, which all knew was an entertainment organization for U.S. soldiers.

* * *

Paris continued to be a passion and inspiration for me. The architecture, the cafes, and street-life were so different from life in Los Angeles. An ambiance and mood prevailed in the Latin Quarter; one of comfort and excitement at the same time. The familiarity with the area around the Académie fostered my love for the city.

The restaurants I frequented were mostly mama and papa eateries, but the food was always excellent. I think it was so consistently good because a Frenchman wouldn't accept anything less than good. In the U.S. people generally will not send food back or complain, they just won't go back a second time. In a way, this is unfair, as the restaurateur cannot sustain the business and doesn't know why. In France, everything was sent back if it isn't good. They learned and had to present tasty food or they would soon be out of business. I had special places where they knew I was a student. Often the mama would ask if I had enough, or she'd just walk up with a pan in her hand and say, "Try this." That personal relationship made each meal special, and I found myself eating at the same places. One such place was the Chez Martin; a little hole in the wall run by a woman and her son and his wife. She made a Veal Marsala dish with Morelle mushrooms in a pastry cup that would blow your socks off! I would always look at other items on the menu, but I couldn't resist this dish.

My studies at the Beaux Arts Académie progressed and I formed an alliance with one of my professors, Pierre Jerome. Pierre was impressed by my talent and he, like Mr. Wright in high school, took me under his wing. He gave me a considerable amount of his time and shared his passions. I had started painting the live models in the grand atelier, and my work so impressed the teachers that Pierre saw to it I could work in the restoration department of the Louvre. A Russian painter by the name of Renowskov taught me the glazing techniques of the masters, and I worked several times a week there along with my other studies at the Académie.

After the first year, big Jack had gone to Copenhagen to study. He still had family in Denmark and didn't return for a year and a half. Walt stayed during this entire period in his flat on the fifth etage near the Julian Académie. Frank had a Swedish girlfriend that shared the apartment with him, and he remained on the Rue Lauriston for an extended period. He had to avoid Shar as she was always asking about me. He told her I wasn't coming back because of family problems at home. I remained concerned Shar would one day come into my life again. I had all but given up the singing except for occasional gigs, one or two nights a week, just for fun. But I was spending some time organizing and operating the tour business along with the late shows at The Calypso.

III

SAILING

10

SAILING ADVENTURES

Black Tarquin

In 1953, I finished my contract with the Lido Cabaret in Paris, and the Beaux Arts Académie had recessed for the summer break. A friend who was taking sketch classes at the Académie Julian with me said he must return home immediately because his father had passed away. He was quickly putting things in order for his departure.

He told me of the boat he had purchased in England and left in Copenhagen and the adventures he had while sailing along the coast of France, Belgium, Holland and Denmark. He gave me the keys and explained he had left it in the care of a fisherman and that if I didn't want it, he would have to abandon it. It sounded romantic and I had visions of taking the summer and just cruising around the Baltic Countries. I accepted the boat.

Black Tarquin was a converted Clinker built lifeboat; the edges of hull planks overlap instead of joining evenly, it had a mast, keel and sails and a small cabin built forward. When I found the boat, it was in poor condition cosmetically, but sound in construction and condition. I met the two sons of the fisherman who had inherited the job of caring for the vessel. A friendship ensued and I paid them to help me refinish the topsides and get it in sailing order. A few weeks later, I was on my way. The older son was an experienced sailor and when the boat was ready, he sailed with me for several days. I was a quick learner and I was overconfident with my newfound skills.

After a few weeks in and around Copenhagen, a splendid city, I proceeded first across to Sweden and then around the whole of Denmark, sailing only during the daylight hours. The trip around Denmark, stopping at little village harbors, was a complete delight. The people took me into their homes, fed me and treated me like a visiting prince. A few weeks later, I was on the west coast, preparing for a North Sea crossing unaware it had a reputation as one of the worst bodies of water on Earth. Early one Sunday morning as the first church bells were ringing, a group of well-wishers saw me off. The mothers of my new friends packed food and supplies and nearly everyone brought me a useful gift. As I motored out of the breakwater with my two horsepower Seagull outboard, the sea was calm and the sun was warm and inviting. That first day was perfect, I had a fair wind on a broad reach and I was averaging over four knots. My spirits were soaring; I was feeling an independence of the soul that was new to a 21-year-old.

[I had experienced a similar feeling when I was 17 and hiking the High Sierra Trail. I started with two friends well-equipped with food and camping gear. Two days into the trip, with the pitch dark nights and animal sounds, my two friends decided to go back. I continued alone for three weeks to Yosemite National Park. While hiking the trail, I encountered many hikers and families. I joined their camps at night and the women were always most concerned about me being alone, and if I was eating right. After the first week or ten days, I found myself leaving the trail and avoiding others, as I was enjoying more the solitude of my adventure. It was during this first journey in my life that I fell under the spell of being one with nature. I feel this has profoundly affected my career as an artist, and even my decision to remain a painter against all odds. The experience in the mountains had somewhat prepared me mentally for the solitude which one has when isolated in a small boat sailing on the vast expanse of the sea.]

**

The second day out, the clouds became dark on the horizon and I could see the dense front coming in from the northwest. It grew calm late in the afternoon, but the murky, ominous cover continued to move toward me. I didn't have any kind of communications equipment and I wasn't sure exactly what the weather signs meant. The forecast, according to the fishermen, was perfect for a crossing. However, it did look scary!

The wind started to pick up about six in the evening and steadily got stronger until it was beginning to get dark, around eight-thirty. I didn't have a lifeline or harness to hold me aboard, so I decided to tie in a reef while it was still not too risky. The boys in Copenhagen had taught me what to do, but I hadn't done it since we practiced nearly two months before. It was a primitive system of canvas strips hanging in a row in two lines going up the sail. When you tie all the lines in a row to the boom, it constitutes a reef and reduces the sail area. It was slow and difficult to do while the boat was bouncing about over four and five-foot waves. When I finished, the boat was moving quite well on a close reach toward my compass course to the Thames estuary, the entrance of the river that leads to London. The winds continued to get stronger and I was becoming exhausted. I had squandered much of my sleeping hours star watching the night before, which had been the most beautiful night of my young life.

During the day when becalmed, I dozed when I should have

taken the opportunity to get some much-needed full sleep. As the evening wore on, the winds got stronger. I took another reef in the main sail and left the jib loose so it wasn't drawing too much. The wind continued to strengthen and the seas were getting larger. The only thing I could see was the white crests of the waves breaking on the starboard bow. I had my running lights on but the night before I hadn't turned them on because I was awake most of the night and the moon was three-quarters full. Fortunately, I didn't see any ships nearby.

As the seas started to get nasty, I realized I would be in deep trouble if I had to go forward without anything to hold me aboard. I took a spare jib sheet line and ran it forward around the forestay and back to the cockpit on the other side. I tied it down to the aft cleats and then proceeded to take some strong line and make loops as arm holds. I had no sooner completed this task when the winds increased again. They were putting a great strain on the mainsail rigging and I had let out as much as I could without it flogging and ripping itself to shreds. It was time to take the main down. Using my safety system and pulling myself forward on the line with my arms through the loops, I had a certain security. From a sitting position, I pulled the sail down. It seemed to take forever as the slides wouldn't move because of the pressure of the wind. I took the main halyard, looped it over one slide at a time, and pulled down with every bit of strength I had left. I was so tired that reason and judgment were now failing me. I experienced long periods of confusion before I could fathom the next step to ensure my survival. I sat in the cockpit, tied down at the waist, trying to muster enough energy to get the jib down and drag it into the cockpit and then into the cabin. The foredeck was plunging underwater with every wave. The seas had grown to ten or twelve feet and the faces were almost vertical with the crests tumbling into white water. I tied off the helm again after bringing the boat into the wind. Then crawled forward to the mast and unleashed the jib halyard. Every time I had done this before, the sail came down immediately. Now the wind was holding it as the boat would fall off and catch the wind soon after I pointed it up. It wasn't coming down at all!

I worked my way forward. With each wave, I was under water holding on for dear life. Between waves, I reached up and tried to pull it down, but it was impossible. I went back to the cockpit like a drowned rat. But my adrenaline was pumping and I knew if I didn't get it down and the wind got stronger I would be in even a worse predicament. I turned the tiller and put the boat downwind and the motion became quieter. I released the sheet line and raced forward with one arm through the safety device and crawled on all fours to the bow. It was bouncing all over the place. The jib wasn't pulling and instead was flapping violently as the boat turned beam on to the seas. The jib flew out to the side and part of the sail was in the water with every roll. The minute the tension was off the sheet line the sail started to work its way down. Taking the hanks off the sail and bundling it up while hanging onto my makeshift apparatus was a dangerous and frightening experience.

Finally, after pushing it into the cabin, I sat cold, hungry and confused. I started to try to figure how I could turn the boat stern or bow to the seas and avoid this terrible rolling. The bow was out of the question, as I couldn't chance going forward again. I had been lucky and might not have the same outcome. The stern was the only option. After a long time, I figured I didn't need the lifeline anymore. The line was strong and the bucket was very sturdy. If I could tie it to the galvanized bucket and put it over the stern, it might be enough drag to keep the boat stern to the seas. It worked. The stern was pulled around and suddenly the motion of the boat changed. I figured by my rough calculations I was heading toward the German coast, but at the present speed it would take a day or two before this would be a problem. I took a small heavy metal tool box, emptied the tools out except for some rusty bolts and nuts, clamped it shut and added ties around it. I took several dock lines, tied them together, and let the box go over the stern about sixty feet back. This improved the motion even more. I wasn't turning to a beam position in the trough as much. The winds continued to build and the seas started to tower over the stern, breaking toward me. I estimated they were approaching twenty feet high. The wind had turned more to the north and cross waves were presenting another problem. Every five minutes or so two wave trains would meet creating a wall of water that would break over the stern and make the boat surf down the wave at high speed.

I prayed the line and bucket would hold; the strain on it seemed more than it could take. Finally, a big wave broke completely over the boat and the cockpit filled with water. The cockpit was the entire vessel; there was no bulkhead to keep the water from the cabin. The boat was nearly half-full of water and I knew another wave like that would sink it. The boat didn't have a pump; just a one-liter paint can with a string for bailing. I bailed furiously, and each time I would get the water down to the floorboards, another wave would fill it again. The gods were playing tricks on me, their timing seemed uncanny. For the next few hours, I bailed as fast as I could. Just before dawn, while so busy with my chore, I looked up to see the wall of a great freighter not more than a hundred feet away. I was so tired that the threat and significance of the incident escaped me, it was only later I realized how lucky I was.

As it started to get light the third day, the winds had come all around and were now blowing me toward my destination. The waves were so confused I could hardly tell the principal direction of the seas. The winds were high but had subsided considerably. I started to realize how cold I was, and how completely exhausted. I began to hallucinate. One minute I would be there with my full faculties and the next I would be off in some strange fantasy of color and shapes not even mindful of any plan or strategy needed to continue to survive. I fell asleep, awoke in the afternoon and started to mend my broken brain. Fortunately, I had been moving in the right direction. The winds continued to diminish and I put the jib back up and brought in the drag lines. Two and a half days later, I followed the coast into Ramsgate on the English mainland.

It was the experience of a lifetime. I learned a bigger boat would be better and that I didn't have the necessary knowledge to attempt such a crossing. I did, however, feel a great sense of accomplishment and cherished the feeling I had while it was going well. When ashore I learned the winds that night blew over forty knots and everyone described it as a nasty low. My little boat, *Black Tarquin* had served me well and I spent several weeks in Ramsgate and around the coast looking for a place to cross to Le Havre on the French side.

[The next year I toured England with an orchestra and spent many nights in English and Scottish ports, but I never quite had the real feeling of the coastal people like I had when living on the boat in the port. They were a hardy lot, friendly and still recovering from the pains of war.]

When I arrived in Ramsgate, I was required to go through customs and immigration. But I was so tired I just went forward and slept until I heard people screaming at me from the dock. I had in my tired state just put the bow line and stern line to the dock in a space quite far out on the main wall. I had put more slack on the stern line as the steel ring I had attached my line to was much further away. When I poked my head out, there was a pair of men who looked like fishermen looking down at me. I immediately realized the problem. The tide there was twenty-six feet and it had dropped another fifteen feet as I slept and the bow was practically out of the water. There was so much tension on it I couldn't untie it and let out more line. The fishermen threw me another line to attach to the bow, and then I cut the bow line, then we did the same to the stem. The men reversed the lines so the bow went a long way aft down the dock and the stern line went well forward. The crisscross of the lines was called scissor mooring. This way the boat would stay against the dock but still be able to move up and down without strain. When I recovered my cut lines, I had no way of getting up to the dock. One of the men left and returned with a ladder he hung from the dock. It had blocks on one side to hold it from the wall so there was room to put your feet while climbing. All of this was new to me. When I apologized, the men just laughed and said it had happened many times before. Some people didn't return soon enough and found their boat hanging in midair.

I made friends with these men and that evening I took them with their wives to a local restaurant. I bought new lines and they helped me to replace the loaned lines they had given me. I liked Ramsgate and the people there. A few days later, it was clear and the sun was shining. It was only about seventy degrees and to me it was a little chilly. When I went into the village that Saturday the beach, just small stones, and gravel, was crowded with people carrying blankets, umbrellas, and towels, just as if it was hot weather. Being from California, this was an unusual sight, how desperate people were for a little sun on their bodies. I played darts every night with a group I had befriended. It was something that I would do many times while in England, and being good at it I had an entry into joining fun groups.

I spent some exciting times along the coast and made a daylight crossing of the channel. I had good winds and it was a pleasant sail. I cleared customs and immigration in Le Havre and headed to a spot where I would be in a good position to ride the tide up the Seine River. The following day, fortified with two extra containers of fuel for the outboard, I caught the tide at five in the morning and motored as far as I could go until it changed. It would run up to four knots on the river and my outboard would only push me at about three knots maximum. The trick was the minute you realized you were no longer making headway to pull to the side and put the anchor down. This was complicated as you had to find a place where it was wide enough you could anchor fairly far out toward the middle. If not the boat would lie over to the side and being an open vessel, it might flood before it floated if you dried out on the bottom. The best place, of course, would be on the quay of a village.

After two days, I finally got to the first lock. The Keepers of the Locks had homes right beside the lock and had food from their gardens and homemade items for sale. They were always friendly and helped with the lines when they saw I was alone. The progress after that was slow. I averaged about two miles per hour, so if I traveled twelve hours, I would only make twenty-four miles. The third day I tied up to a commercial barge operated by a husband and wife team that transported goods on the river. They invited me to dinner aboard and it was the best meal I had had since in Denmark. They towed me with a bridle from their stern from there to Paris. In Paris, I moored at the Touring Club de France under the Alexander III Bridge. The club had toilets, bar, and a lounge. I had stayed on the boat only a couple of nights before I joined Frank, who was alternating living in the two apartments on the Rue Lauriston and the Rue des Beaux Arts.

The Director

Black Tarquin had been my first experience with sailing and I loved that boat because she had always come through for me. I liked the idea of living on the river at the Touring Club de France and had met many of the cruisers and canal people while keeping *Tarquin* there. They were interesting people, from many lands and backgrounds. A few months later, I sold *Black Tarquin* to a Frenchman, who planned to put a much larger outboard on her and take her through to the Mediterranean. My next boat wouldn't come until over a year later, but I had the sailing bug and couldn't wait for the next adventure.

My friend Ken Mackie, from the tour operation venture, was a Scotsman, who grew up in the Northumberland border country between England and Scotland. I went with him to visit his mother. Alnmouth was a very provincial place that seemed from another century. The little stone houses and shops that lined the main street were built mostly in the 1900s. He never spoke of his father; even when asked about him he would avoid the question. There was some deep rift between them. It must have been something he was deeply ashamed of, as he would get quite upset if you pursued any line of questioning about him. I assumed from different stories I had heard that his father was a fisherman. He often related tales of his boyhood of being out on the double-ender type North Sea fishing boats. Ken never talked very much about anything else in his childhood except for the war years when he would sneak onto the Duke of Northumberland's estate and poach rabbits for food. He was quite resentful of the people of Alnmouth because he felt they had treated his mother unkindly. I think it had something to do with his father, who apparently was a scoundrel. Even though I pumped him about his father, he never would open up and talk about him.

I felt it was a good time to get away from school and the nightclub and my commitments for paintings. After we had left Alnmouth, we visited several ports on the coast looking for the double-ended fishing boats Ken was so proud of. In Berwick on Tweed, we found a thirty-six-foot trawler in excellent shape. Berwick was an old and interesting port; I had appeared there the year before while on tour. The place was right out of the storybooks. I loved the old seaports and this one was a classic. The trawler was named *The Director*. I bought it and we made the journey south to Newcastle on Tine, which was a large ship building and wrecking area. We filled the hold with wood and several brass ports and bunks and all that Ken thought would be necessary to convert the boat to a yacht. He represented himself as being capable of all of this work, and I was gullible enough to believe him. I put up most of the money and he was to do the work. We had been gone longer than I had expected and I had to get back to school and other demands. Ken found a place to put the boat and he would work on it while I financed the project.

I returned in June to find he hadn't done very much to make the boat livable. He had put a cabin top on it and installed the bunks crudely in the main hold. He had purchased the material to finish it off when we got to the Touring Club de France in Paris. The boat had a big two-cylinder petrol/paraffin (gasoline/kerosene) engine which gave us a hull speed of five plus knots. It was a hand crank start that usually took several turns to get running and often would kick back and almost tear your arm off. It was designed to push the boat at hull speed even when towing the fishing nets.

One day off the coast, at the Crouch River, we spotted four

men waving to us from a thirty-foot fishing smack. They were rolling wildly, and one seemed to be working on the engine which was covered by an engine box in an open position. One man was holding the box up while another had his head buried beneath it. The others were trying desperately to get our attention. We pulled alongside and threw a line to them. When we proceeded to tow them into Burnham, our boat didn't slow at all.

We went up the Crouch River and anchored in the bight. Two of the guys were young like Ken and I. They were brothers and the other two were their father and uncle. We left the boat at anchor and used the heavy oars to push our way to their dock which was close by. They called the father Spence, as their last name was Spencer. We had dinner with them that night and stayed in a little shed with two bunks. The next morning we all had breakfast together. It was raining steadily and they decided not to try to fix the boat in that weather; the day before it had been overcast and misty as well. Ken and I were quite happy to be away from the damp interior of the trawler. They asked us to stay another day until the weather was more forgiving. Their cottage was quite small, but it had a charm and tradition that made it different from any place I had ever stayed. They burned a fire nonstop, in a giant potbelly coal burning stove that heated the house and served for cooking as well. There were little carvings, old memorabilia, and art everywhere. Their mother made Afghans and embroidered blankets and she had put her unique touch on everything around. Ken was attracted to the father; he seemed to want to bond with him more than the sons. I figured it might just be the father figure he desperately needed. The older brother and I were the same age, 22. We were both fascinated by our upbringing in different lands. His name was Ken, but his mother called him Kenny; we called him that, too, to make less confusion with two Kens around.

When we left the next day, Kenny and I had probably talked some ten hours. We covered more about ourselves than I had ever experienced with any relationship in my life. His sister Jacqueline sat in much of the time, as she was also interested in the life of a young American from Hollywood. Our lives and experiences were so different; they had done without so much during the war. While we at home in the U.S. had hardly any inconvenience at all. We had gasoline rationing, food stamps, and you couldn't buy a new car. But as a young boy, the only thing tragic I remember was my friend Jimmy Benmat's father didn't come home from the war. In England, even on tour in 1954, less than a year previously, the food was rationed. We had eggs only on occasion, meat was scarce, and restaurants were abominable. The first bed and breakfast the orchestra stayed at in Manchester, served kippered herrings and beans on toast for breakfast. I remembered I was horrified that anyone would serve such awful food. Mrs. Spencer, however, seemed to make appetizing dishes out of very little. Her talent came from innovation and necessity; she had few products available to work with. Jacqueline was smitten with me and I promised to stay in touch with Kenny and the family.

When Ken and I left early the next morning, the father expressed how grateful he was we had turned back and rescued them. I told him that it was a very special time for me to spend it with his gracious family. The morning was overcast with the sun peeking through only now and then. I was happy just to have a warmer day without the rain. Spence had recommended a wharf area run by a man named Emil Chartoff, who was a diesel mechanic with a slipway and a couple of docks. When we arrived there, in the suburbs of London, he thought we wanted to have mechanical work done. We told him our story and he said he would be most happy to let us use the dock until he needed it. If the other empty slip were filled, then we would have to leave in the event someone needed emergency service.

I had to get away from Ken for a while; his deep moods at times were difficult to endure. I called Kimberly Martin, a talented young singer, and pianist I had met at The Mars Club. We had had a brief affair that left us both wanting more. She was working at the Regency Bar in London, where she had been for some four or five months. That was like becoming a permanent fixture in the business. I asked if I could stay with her for a day or two, and she welcomed the request. I told Ken I was going to be gone for a while and it didn't seem to mean much to him one way or the other. He was a strange guy. I knew I was his best friend and at times, he would be open and involved with what was going on. But after the days with the Spencer's, where he seemed so happy, he became quiet and moody. After we had left there, he was in a complete withdrawal. Later I decided it must have reminded him of the family life he didn't have. I realized that no matter how close someone would be with him, he was a loner and selfish. But, he could play a useful role if he wanted something and had a long-term objective in mind. [I learned in life that it isn't bad to use someone to further your own desires. Provided you give something to them to fulfill their desires, too. There is always something you can give; love being the most precious, and the most needed. It took far too long for me to learn this. As a young man, the direction of my organ guided me more than anything else. Where it pointed, I would go!]

At the Regency, Kimberly finished at midnight. I had hung around all evening drinking a beer or two and sang a couple of songs so the management didn't mind me being there and talking to her. We went to eat at an all-night fish and chips place. Back at her place, we talked for hours. We were both exhausted and after I had taken a quick, hot, shower, I crawled into bed and was out like a light before she finished her shower. It was one of the few times, at that age, I can remember being more tired than horny.

It was noon before we even stirred. I felt like I had been drugged. Usually, I awoke alert and bouncy, but somehow the trip and the tension of being with Ken during his moods took more out of me than I had thought. We got up like two zombies and made our way to the local café; a chain called Lion House. Kimberly drank tea, which I learned to have while in England, as the coffee was unbearable, particularly after my French coffees and croissants in Paris. It was a lovely day and we took a long walk through the park and around town for several hours. Kimberly didn't cook; I remembered that from Paris, so I offered to make dinner for us. She had some other errands to do and gave me her keys.

I went back to the flat to investigate what pans and pots were available to plan my dinner. It wasn't much, but enough to get by, especially after cooking on the boat's single burner stove. I bought candles and a funny looking stuffed dog I put on her pillow. We ate dinner at six because she had to be at the bar by eight. We had a romantic evening and she loved the dog. The apartment was only one room with a kitchen and a bathroom, but she had it looking quite chic. She had so many pillows on the bed that it didn't look like a bed at all. The wall held dozens of framed drawings and prints. She said she copied that from something she had seen in a Cary Grant movie. She was a lovely person and we just fit together as neatly as we had in Paris. I was with her for three days. We talked, laughed and made love like the most natural thing in the world.

I was reluctant to leave. The days with her were fun and I was happy. I knew I would have trouble finding someone so compatible and comfortable to be with back in Paris. I had more feelings for her than I had in a long time and physically she was much like Noddy. She was slim, small busted with black hair and blue eyes. Carolyn had set the standard for my attractions, and every woman I had been serious about had measured up to those same qualities. Kimberly didn't have the sexual energy of Carolyn or Noddy, but she was more laid back and easy to please in every way. She was very grounded and sure of herself; seldom got very serious and never put any pressure on me to see her, call her or fill any void she might have in her life. It was very attractive to me that she expressed how much she enjoyed our relationship without requesting any commitment. I wasn't ready for any deep relationship, and the light and simple things we shared were what made it a perfect time.

* * *

Ken and I headed out the day after I left, Kimberly. We put a few stores aboard and moved out onto the Thames River through all the London suburbs and industrial areas that had been bombed so heavily in the war. Much of the city was still rebuilding. There were bombed out lots filled with rubble between buildings throughout the city.

We went directly out to the estuary, where we became fogbound. Although we couldn't see them, we could hear the foghorns and churning propellers of the big ships as they slipped past us. We heard a buoy bell to the starboard and headed that way until we almost rammed it head on. I was on the bow listening and giving hand signals to Ken. The fog was so dense he could barely see my directions only thirty feet away. We pulled out of the shipping lanes and rested in twenty-five feet of water, and put down the hook. We didn't know what stage of the tide it was but estimated it was about half tide, and with twenty-three feet of change, it didn't leave a big margin for error. All night the ships sounded like they were going to ram us. Some were so close I could feel the wall side of the vessel, even though I couldn't see it. During the night, we must have dropped from a large swell and the hull hit the sand. We were up like a shot and Ken heaved the anchor while we moved back toward the buoy.

After listening to that bell buoy clink all night, we were ready to be on our way. The fog had lifted slightly and we knew it would be light soon. When we were leaving the Goodwin Sands, as this estuary was called, the fog cleared enough that we became more comfortable with our full five-knot speed. Ramsgate was a resort city where thousands came to lie on the gray rocky beach. But it was like a homecoming for me as it was my landfall on my first sailing adventure from Denmark. We moored next to a fishing boat lying against some pilings. The boat looked so dirty and abused I wondered what kept it floating. A young lad of about fourteen years popped his head out from the forward hatch. His dirty little face and grubby clothes matched the boat. With a closer look, I could see he was quite a handsome boy, with blond hair and intense blue eyes. He jumped aboard to help us tidy up after securing our lines to his bow and stern.

"Looks just like our boat," he proclaimed.

It was indeed a North Sea double-ended trawler like ours, but larger at about fifty-five feet in length. The similarity ended there. Their decks were strewn with piles of nets, ropes, traps and all the rusting gear for the trade. We invited the boy named Bill to join us for tea. Down in our forward cabin, we put water on the one burner alcohol stove. The stove had to be pumped up to pressure, and it smelled awful. The forward cabin was used by the fisherman as a home while they were at sea. It had berths on each side with a Baby Blake toilet in between on the forward bulkhead. Ken had made a low, narrow, doorway through from the hold to what had become the main cabin. You had to squeeze through, but it was better than going on deck to go forward. The small boxlike pilot house would only seat two of us out of the weather. There was a long seat, a wooden spoke wheel, and a compass. Charts had to be stuffed and folded on the small dashboard in front of the wheel. When a map was partially opened on it, you couldn't see the engine instruments. The aft engine room had a separate hatch from aft of the pilothouse. Entering the main cabin had to be from forward, so one was always on deck to get to any compartment.

We bought an old canvas tarp from a yard in Newcastle and Bill helped us string a rope from the forestay to the aft stay and make a large V shape tent to cover the boat. It worked out well and made the boat more livable. We had our tea and sat below, warming our hands on the hot mugs, and talking. Bill's father called out to him and we invited him to join us. When he entered, it was almost frightening to see the massive hulk of his body coming down the ladder. He had a mop of hair like none I had ever seen, wiry hair that stuck out like a bush all around. It gave the impression of being twice the normal size. He had a large nose and thick big lips; it seemed to all go together. His face was weathered with a several day growth of beard. I was thinking to myself if I ever had any trouble I would want this guy on my side. When he sat on the bunk next to Ken, his body rounded off right up to the deck, with his knees high in the air.

We learned they lived on the boat and Little Bill went to the local school. He would leave long before school started when Big Bill

184

and his two helpers would go out early in the morning. He went to a local fisherman's café called The Dolphin near the docks, where he would hang out until it was time to go to school. After school, he would go to the same restaurant and do some of his studies and the toothless fat lady and her billiard ball-headed husband would look after him. It served as a daycare center. It must have been tough on Little Bill. I'm sure the local kids looked down on him for his crude clothes and his meager lifestyle. I'm also sure they didn't give him any flak, as he was big and tough like his father and left no quarter for insults. If they ever looked at his six-foot-seven-inch father, with close to three hundred pounds of muscular bulk they'd have second thoughts about making any snide remarks.

One evening when we were on our way to The Dolphin, a couple was trying to maneuver their Morris Minor Car out of a very tight space. Big Bill just picked up the front of the car like a toy and sat it out on the street. The people inside were so wide eyed they couldn't pull themselves together to thank Bill until we were well away. Then the man yelled out behind us and Bill without turning waved his hand at them over his head.

When Big Bill came in each day, we would move the boat over so he could moor inside us to unload his catch. He would take a certain amount of fish each day to The Dolphin café, as he and his son ate nearly all their meals there. It had a cleanup room for the fisherman where they'd wash up, or shower and change their clothes from a locker that had their names crudely printed on the doors. It was like a second home to many of them and there were many kids about. They had an admirable camaraderie between them.

We stayed in Ramsgate for a week and enjoyed some lovely weather. The crowds would grow on the weekend and I was fascinated with the sun-seekers. It was hard to believe people would go out in the clear but chilly weather and lie on the rocks in a bathing suit. If the sun were out, they would erect an umbrella.

I used to think to myself, this is a place right out of a Jack London story. Everyone ate fish and chips night and day, augmented by the occasional bowl of fish stew that seemed to be always brewing on the big stove. I ate a lot of that stew. Next to the pot were stacks of white balloon bread, the only bread I think the English ate at that time. It became an everyday endeavor to walk the town, sit and watch the tourists and visit with our neighbors, the Bills.

The night before we left to cross the channel to Le Havre, we sat aboard their boat, in a similar forward cabin. It was much larger and had dual bunks on each side. The head was forward, and an excellent double burner stove and the oven was against the aft bulkhead. We drank a lot of beer and smoked many cigarettes. I fell asleep and the conversation seemed like it was from another world; in my stupor, I was just vaguely aware of it. They let me sleep there until morning when they were leaving at five AM. It gave Ken and me an early start to France.

The trip to Paris from Le Havre took only three days, including the time for customs and immigration. It was very different from my first trip to Paris on *Black Tarquin* with its limited power. With *The Director,* we pushed at full speed and got far enough that the tide wasn't so strong. After the first lock, the river flow was only about one to two knots in the center so we hugged the side where it was half a knot or less.

When we arrived in Paris, we moored at the Touring Club de France. They had full facilities and a lounge for the guests at the dock.

186

They put a phone aboard and it was quite civilized with our tent neatly covering the boat. I moved back to the Rue de Beaux Arts apartment and got back into the swing of getting paintings done. I helped Ken, Frank and Trent get more going on with the tours. Things had been slow during the winter and spring months and Ross Trent was handling most of the tours. Ken didn't run any day tours but worked on the boat to get the main cabin more livable.

Once things had picked up, I was no longer very active in running the tours for the GIs. Frank and I had started The Calypso, a small nightclub off the Boulevard Raspail on the Left Bank. Our partner that owned the club was having an affair with Frank. When he met her, she was running the club as just a local bar. She didn't use the large room which adjoined the small bar area. There was a stage, with an amplifier system, that was set up to hold forty or fifty people. The piano was out of tune and I suspected it hadn't been used for several years. We got the club in shape and started running the tours into the club as a last stop of the evening. It became quite popular with the military guys from SHAPE headquarters in Neuilly. I did a lot of the entertaining myself, harking back to the guitar and folk music of my youth.

Ken continued to live on the river. During the summer, we had cruise tours up and down the river with the GIs that came to Paris from the various camps. We always invited girls for a free ride to keep the military boys happy. Some of the girls were Americans and some were hookers we had at The Calypso Club. Some of the guys just wanted to talk to an American gal. They were homesick and this made it a lovely day for them. We had evening cruises too, and it was the night tours when we mostly had the working girls. If they made a score, we would usually get an envelope with two thousand francs so they would be invited again. I didn't think of myself as a pimp, but I guess it boiled down to that. On occasion, I would get a quick blowjob from one of the girls before the GIs would show up. I rarely fucked them as I was always afraid of VD. At that time, however, they had penicillin which had created a new freedom for the young soldiers, students and the entertainers of the era.

* * *

When I had been back in Paris for a period, toward the end of the summer, Frank and I lost The Calypso Club. The woman that owned it got greedy and wanted a much bigger cut of the pie. She saw it was doing well and I guess thought she could hire entertainers and keep the American crowd that met there every evening. She overlooked the fact most of the clientele was from our crowd of Americans that lived in Paris and a small group of military men based in other areas of Europe that came back on visits.

Frank was quite bitter as he had helped her so much. She was making many times the money she had been when we took over. We always let her stay behind the bar and watch the cash, and Frank thought she was probably dipping into the till also. Three months later she was back to just the bar; the regulars had found a new home. She called Frank and wanted to put things back as they were, but we weren't interested.

Big Ben had called me from The Mars Club and I went back for a few weeks, but the Marchand paintings demand was such I needed to spend my time doing what I loved most. I talked Ben into raising the salary to get Kimberly. He was always such a cheapskate, but finally he said he would do it. Things had changed in Paris and the talented piano singers were getting more expensive. I told him what Blossom Dearie was getting, and she wasn't even close to

Kimberly when it came to talent. I wanted Kimberly to come to Paris for selfish reasons also. I was tired of just shacking up with my list of available women. I wanted to be with someone as easy as she was. It came as quite a shock when she told me she was getting married. She had good sense, as he was a successful man with a large business and an exceptional family. She had known him for many years and they had drifted apart after school. But he had never forgotten her and when he came back into her life, he wanted it to be permanent. After that, I lost track of her but I chalk it up as a heavy weighted plus in my life. She, like Carolyn and Stephanie, was a positive force tucked away somewhere deep in my heart.

The following year we sold *The Director*. [I had many good times on her. As I reflect on all of the boats I've owned, the North Sea experiences traveling down the east coast of England and taking the boat up the Thames River to London were very memorable.]

* * *

During my visits to the Touring Club de France on *The Director*, I met a man that would become a friend and a sailing companion. The boating facility was next to the Place de la Concorde. It had a lounge and a bar that was open on occasions. Nigel was a very distinguished gentleman with a gray beard, a long straight nose and a head of wavy gray hair. He was short and a little stout, not over five-foot-eight. He had been a major in the Army and had seen a lot of action, but he mentioned it only in passing. He was on his motor launch; a beautiful fifty-foot boat he had built for him. Aboard were his son Darryl and his friend from the university, Don. Whenever I was near the dock, I would always come by to say hello, and Nigel would ask me aboard. His son was a bit older than I was, but he was quite immature and still sounded like a college locker boy. He was good looking and a few inches taller than his father was. I visited with him sometimes during the summer. Nigel was often not there, as he had a business to run in the U.K.

It was the following year after Nigel had taken his boat back to England that I got a message from him. He didn't have my address so he had left a message with another boater I knew, Kevin, at the Touring Club de France. By that time I had sold *The Director*, so I rarely frequented the club, but Kevin lived on a great old river barge and had been there for many years. Although American he was married to a French woman he had met in the closing years of the war. He loved to walk from the Concorde to the Arc de Triomphe and sit in the cafes on the Champs-Élysées. One day on his walk I happened to be at a sidewalk café when came by and stopped to join me. He immediately said he had tried to get in touch with me at the address which the club had. I had long since moved into my apartment on the Rue de Beaux Arts, and after Birgetta had gone back to Sweden, Frank had left the Rue Lauriston apartment and moved in with me. It was supposed to be temporary, but he stayed for a long time.

I went to Kevin's boat the next day and got the message from Nigel. I contacted him and gave him my new phone number but alerted him to the fact I was seldom home, so it was best to call me early in the morning. A week later, I received a call and Nigel asked if I could join him on his new sailing yacht for a cruise in the Baltic. I couldn't leave school for a month so we made temporary arrangements to meet in Gothenburg the following month. We made final arrangements a few weeks later and I joined him there. I stayed a few days with my family there; Bjorn and Lek were second cousins on my mother's side, and I had visited them a couple of years before. Bjorn and I were about the same age and we had always hit it off together.

***

[I didn't see Bjorn again after that meeting until many years later. We had written a few letters and then everything got lost in time. Thirty-four years later, Joyce and I were sailing our Peterson forty-six, *Tarquin of Malibu* into the harbor of Mitalini on the island of Lesbos in the Greek islands. A man jumped off his boat and aided us with our lines ashore. It was a hot day, we invited him aboard for beer and the three of us sat around and told stories. He was from Sweden and I told him I had family there. Nothing more was said; we exchanged stories of the places we had been and asked questions about interesting places to go. He had sailed single-handed around the world with help here and there from his son when he could get away. We went to dinner together that evening, as he knew of a good restaurant. While eating, I told him of my visits to my cousins. I said he might know Lek as he was a well-known writer in Sweden. He started to laugh and shake his head. He reached for his wallet, pulled out his boating card, and handed it to me. It had a picture of the boat and said, Bjorn Anderberg, Captain. It was my cousin! His physical changes were considerable, but once I knew it was he, I could see clearly the friend I had forgotten so long before.]

***

I joined Nigel and his crew of a captain and his wife, and Nigel's girlfriend aboard his magnificent schooner, a seventy-six-foot masterpiece built by Abeking and Rasmussen in Germany. The boat had been purchased by an Argentine businessman before the war and had been preserved during the years that so many fine yachts were lost, recruited in the service of their country. I spent six weeks cruising the coast of Sweden and Norway. Nigel as always was great company. The captain and his wife were hard-working and pleasant to be with, but Nigel's girlfriend acted as if she was Queen of the Nile. She would never go anywhere without full makeup and pressed and pristine clothes. Betty, the captain's wife, spent most of her time cleaning and pressing the clothes for the queen.

The most memorable part of the cruise was sailing into the fjords. It was my first experience with natural beauty of such proportions. I vowed at the time I would visit many such places when I could be alone or with someone I loved, and just enjoy the beauty and atmosphere. It isn't a feeling you can describe or relate to others, it's truly something that must be experienced.

I returned to Paris wanting to find another boat and plan more adventures at sea.

[Over the years as I've traveled the world in my many boats, this revelation has been unveiled in so many magnificent locations and in so many ways. I can only say to the reader, if you want one of most satisfying adventures possible in this world, buy a boat, sail it with someone you love, and see our incredible planet.]

* * *

Patience

Ken and another friend of mine, Tucker, a very experienced sailor, had found a boat named *Patience* they thought was perfect for an extended sailing trip and that would bring a good price back in the U.S. We began making plans for the adventure.

School would be finished in a few weeks, and I would graduate and finish some paintings to fill commitments until I got back to Paris. The demand for the Marchand paintings had grown steadily, and I was frantically working to keep everyone happy. The last year my studies and the completion of the thesis for my doctorate, along with the increasing popularity of the paintings, had occupied my life. I hadn't had a nightclub engagement or even a healthy relationship with anyone since the boom started. But the money was coming in, it was much more than when I was singing in the average nightclub. It was steady and growing by the day.

Trent handing supplies to Tucker on Patience.

Many American galleries were buying from my Paris gallery, and the reclusive Phillipe Marchand was becoming ever harder to excuse from the scene. I needed a break, but the idea that the work would stop when I was gone might give people a reason to suspect. So I accumulated about twenty canvases my home gallery could continue to bring out periodically. They were not happy with my decision to go for so long, as they were making more than I was. They didn't think I knew what the work was selling for but, friends had gone to price things at the galleries in New York and Chicago. I had no master plan at that time. I just knew I could work as the agent for Phillipe Marchand in the U.S. and reap a much larger slice of the pie.

Ken had gone back to Burnham-on-Crouch to conclude the boat purchase with Colonel Fuller, the owner of *Patience*. Tucker had remained there to do a complete survey of the vessel before closing the deal. I had given Ken the final balance and they started on the boat while I finished my last works and tidied up the other affairs.

When I arrived in Burnham-on-Crouch, I brought my friend Ross Trent with me. He was an ex-GI studying on the GI Bill at the Académie de la Grande Chaumière and was an excellent painter, selling fairly well in Paris. He also had helped me with the tour operations venture. He had enough money and felt he could pay his way and hitch a ride back to the U.S. Trent was from East Patterson, New Jersey. He was outgoing, fun and honest and we all liked him. [Many years later, he came to California and I took him into the portrait business with me. He was truly a great talent, and I regret to this day, what I saw as a lost potential. Unfortunately, he carried a lot of emotional baggage and was plagued with tremendous insecurities and self-doubts and things didn't work out. Trent's real name was Rosario Columbus Trentacosti. He changed it, I believe, to seem less the son of poor immigrants from Sicily. I think his issues also had a lot to do with his early life in an Italian neighborhood and how he was treated. Some years later when I was in New York, I called to see if we could get together. His mother answered the phone and she didn't speak enough English to take a message for him. After over fifty years in America, she hadn't learned a word.]

I was very disappointed when I saw the boat. It looked derelict; torn apart, with all the gear lying on the wharf, and the hull leaning against the pilings. I thought we would never go to sea in that old tub. Colonel Fuller had left the boat on a mooring in the river for many years and it was terribly neglected and weathered. When the tide raised the boat to float again, it looked a little better. Ken and Tucker had completely cleaned the bottom, repaired many of the seams and put on pieces of new copper sheathing. But the bottom was the only part of the boat that looked presentable.

For two months, the four of us worked ten hours or more a day. We stripped and varnished the masts, the rail, and topsides, and painted the hull. Tucker re-rigged the boat, ordered the sails and pulled everything together. The roughest job of the re-fit was the repairing of the teak decks. The wood had hardened like steel and it was two inches of solid teak, so it was a major job to plane, sand and caulk. When we finished, the decks looked new, the varnish sparkled and the white hull glistened with the fresh coats of paint. Finally, the rigging was complete, the sails bent on, and we were ready to set sail.

It wouldn't be a whole story without mentioning the help and fun brought to us by the female companions that joined us after work, or after school. Often on the weekends, the girls would pitch in and work hard. They did it just to be with us and to do some local sailing when we did the trials. Jacqueline was an 18-year-old local girl going to business school that I had met while staying with her family when I was sailing *The Director*. She was pretty and had a sensational figure. We had been attracted to each other at that time and seeing her again rekindled it. A serious affair between us started and she fixed my companions up with her girlfriends.

It was at that time seeds of dissent were starting to grow between Ken and Tucker. Tucker was the ultimate sailor, with much experience and profound knowledge. It was natural he would be the captain. Ken was an Englishman in his own country, so it was best that he handle the negotiating and dealing with the locals. They, of course, thought he was the captain and Ken began to think he was as well.

Ken had been a successful middleweight boxer in Scotland, but he had a match which left him with a headache that lasted for two weeks and he decided not to fight again. He wasn't very bright and had a gruff exterior to cover up his insecurities. He was quite handsome and stood about five-foot-nine, with a great mop of wavy blond hair. Women found him very attractive. He made love like an ape; a wham bam type of guy, as he was described many times over several years by women in his life. As a result, he too didn't have lasting relationships. He was very English in his manner with women, not open, and didn't share a great deal even with good friends. His guarded personality and intellectual shortcomings would be an important factor in the compatibility of the group. He resented Tucker's knowledge and ability as captain of the boat, and never fully recognized they didn't share that position.

Tucker didn't push it and realized early on Ken wanted to be the head honcho but just wasn't equipped for the job. Tucker was about five-foot-nine and had a sturdy build. He was an Army GI, who had visited Paris and took one of our tours. When I heard his name, I recognized it immediately. Known as the Iron Man of North Hollywood High School, he was a star in many sports and the Herald

Express Newspaper Athlete of the Year in Los Angeles. I went to high school with him, but he was one year ahead of me. We didn't have a friendship then, but he knew my brother, I don't think he knew me at all except for my tennis accomplishments. Tucker wasn't artistic and we never had anything in common as far as literature, music and art were concerned. But we had both grown up in San Fernando Valley and went to the same schools and that gave us some common ground. He was a very attractive guy and the women all seemed to like him. He didn't communicate with them very well and was a directional and determined type of person, so they found him distant and self-centered.

Trent thought he was a ladies man, but in the thirty-odd years I knew him he never had any lasting relationships with anyone. Jacqueline's friend said he was a clumsy lover. He was quite dark and about five-foot-seven inches tall with a nice-looking face and medium-build. Many women were attracted to him, but I think his short height was also a factor in his multiple complexes. He was very artistic and loved to laugh and have fun, which made him a good companion for the trip though he was never a good crew member, as I think he was afraid of the sea.

I used to take my guitar to the Star Pub and play American folk songs. They had a tea shop also where we would hang out. The singing was an advantage; many of the people in Burnham-on-Crouch recalled I had singing engagements with Ted Heath's band and he was well-known. So that gave me a certain prestige with the local girls. But Jacqueline was the pick of the litter. She was deathly afraid of getting pregnant, so we would only make love when it was her safer period and then I wore a condom as well.

I shared the aft cabin, which had the best berths on the boat, with Tucker. My bunk was the largest and most comfortable because I was the biggest investor. Tucker and the guys were good about vacating for an evening to the movies or to the pub to play darts, and we all did this when one of us had something lined up.

The others were not seeing much action so there was a standard joke about my escapades. Trent would twist his face up in this gooney love pose and thought he was mimicking the way Jacqueline looked at me. Then they'd all laugh. "Just wait until her belly starts to bulge, the Bobbies will be out in force looking for you. But, Chris will certainly marry her, the fine gentleman he is!" They had great fun arranging and discussing my marriage to the local queen of Burnham-on-Crouch. Then the invitation list would start with a description of the action of all the local characters who would attend. They decided Driftwood would be best man. Driftwood was a scruffy local character that collected debris along the shore. He put it in a big sack on his back, and would sell it to the locals. He would come by at low tide, survey the situation then exclaim, "Tides comin' in here." He was a likable old codger, always smiling and seemed to have a great time picking up the wood along the shore and greeting the local folk.

The weather was cold, and misting rain a good portion of the time, but was improving, and soon we would be on our way. The village was a friendly place and the older local men liked us. But the very young men our age thought of us as a threat. We tried to make friends many times with them, but they treated us with great suspicion. We were competition for the girls and the fact many of them came to the boat and spent a lot of time with us was a factor. This wasn't approved of by the young guys and many of the girls' families. Some fathers even forbade their daughters to be aboard the boat. There were a few times when some of the locals became aggressive toward one of us when we were alone in town and Trent seemed to be their favorite patsy. They didn't pick on Tucker, Ken, or me. Ken, who was a tough cookie, straightened them out. He had Trent point out the ones that were bugging him, and would go up to them and let them know clearly that anyone that started anything with any of us would have to deal with him. Before I got there, a big six-foot-four village bully had picked on Tucker. He didn't back down and Ken was afraid if Tucker got hurt they wouldn't get the work done on the boat. Ken stepped in and flattened the guy in about ten seconds, so the story goes. After that, no one wanted to deal with Ken.

When the food and gear were aboard, and everything was in place; it all seemed perfect. The last week we were there, we lived out on the anchor near the mouth of the river where it was deep. We went out and sailed every day, worked the bugs out in the rigging and were quite happy with the result.

The Duke of Northumberland, who commissioned the boat in 1896, named her *Patience*. She was a sixty-seven-foot gaff-rigged ketch with a topsail rig, and a sixteen-foot bowsprit, with three headsails; thick solid spruce mast and spars. The forward headsail had a Waco Martin furling Genoa, and two triangle-shaped jibs aft to the mast. Admiral Muir of the British Navy rebuilt and re-commissioned the boat and helped in the final redesign and rigging in 1932, the year I was born. He was retired from the Navy and sailed *Patience* around the world. He then wrote a book entitled, *Around the World with Patience*. In the day this was done, between the great wars, it was a great accomplishment as I understand it. The boat had become well-known and was sold to Colonel Fuller of the British Commandos, who wrote a book as well called, *Messing About with Boats* and *Patience* played a prominent role in his writings.

We were commencing our journey in 1956. It was a time that life was good in England, the people had finally recovered from the hardships of the war, and the rationing was gone. People could go out and buy a rasher of bacon, eggs, steak and other luxuries for the first time since the late 1930s. Many items were available in tins, (tin cans) including butter. We had a cooler which would preserve vegetables for near to a week, but after that, it was dried food and tins. But, nearly everything was available in tins in those days. I did most of the planning and purchasing of the food. Trent helped as we were the only two that had any cooking and food experience. Trent being Italian, and myself a great Italian food fan, loaded up with pasta and all the products we could keep long-term for good meals. We had a few dinner parties before we left, just to entertain the girls, as a thank you for their excellent help on all levels. They went out sailing with us on the final weekend, and it was perhaps the nicest weather we had had for two months. It was a great day, emotional with their crying at our departure but the beginning of an adventure.

We left on a Monday morning and sailed through the Goodwin Sands, which guarded the mouth of the Thames. We put into Ramsgate where I had been with *The Director* cruising the east coast and with *Black Tarquin* after my crossing from Denmark. We had a few things to fix, but we were anxious to get on our way. I went to see some friends I hadn't seen for a couple of years, but they were not home. I asked about them in The Dolphin pub that was the hangout for the fishermen and their families to find they had moved to better harbor facilities and better fishing up near Newcastle.

We set off again and made a couple of easy hops until we arrived on the Isle of Wight, near South Hampton. We anchored out in the bay where there were no mooring fees. Our first night ashore we were in a fish and chips shop and met three girls. After eating our meal together, they asked if they could see the boat. After two trips in the longboat, we were all aboard. Ken made up a concoction of Hot Buttered Rum. I serenaded with the guitar and some funny songs and we all joined in a rather rowdy performance. Ken excused himself with one of the girls and went up forward to his cabin. Tucker went aft with a sleazy one that looked like a cheap hooker and I was surprised he was horny enough to settle for her. The other girl stayed with Trent and me and we talked for a long time. I wasn't interested so I went up on deck and wrapped myself in a blanket, as it was quite chilly.

I was in the Dog House, which was partially protected from the elements when I heard a loud knock on the hull. I was groggy and confused as I heard the strong language of a police officer and another man called to me.

"Do you have some girls aboard?" he asked.

"Yes," I said. "I'll get them."

My head clearing, I ran below and they were all back, fortunately, in the main cabin.

"Is the captain aboard?" yelled out the policeman.

Tucker went up on the deck with the cheap-looking blonde. The man with the officer was her father. She obviously was one to worry about and I guess he knew it. As it turned out, she was only 16 years old. It was hard to believe, as I would have guessed her to be at least 22 or 23. The girl cried out several times to her father.

"Nothing happened... we were just playing music."

The officer instructed the girls to get in the boat and asked Tucker to accompany him to the police station. Ken and I took our dinghy in as well and waited in the outer office while they questioned Tucker. About two hours later they let Tucker go. The officer said it would be best if we were on our way in the morning.

We were ready and fully stocked so we left first thing in the morning. Since we were in a hurry to get out of there, we didn't try to get any local weather reports. We heard on AM radio that the winds were ten to fifteen knots and it sounded like another good day. We were with the tide and could get a good start before the tidal current would hold us back. The tide in the English Channel runs up to four knots, and if with the winds, even more. In fifteen knots of wind, we could sail at six or seven knots. *Patience* was a slow boat in light winds; she was nine-feet-six-inches depth and weighed thirty-two tons, before all the gear and provisions. We didn't head for Finisterre on the French coast as it was choppy and not a comfortable course, so we went straight out and down the middle of the English Channel toward the Atlantic.

We were on a close reach and making about ten knots with the tide. The wind was blowing about fifteen knots and clocking around to the north. We were making good time with the wind and tide with us. After a few hours, the winds went light but we continued to make headway with the flow of the tide. When it started changing, we were more in the open entrance to the channel and the current wasn't nearly so strong. The winds died and we started the engine, with about a two-knot tide against us, we were only making about four knots.

We motored through the night and by early morning we had cleared the corner of France at Finisterre. The winds were starting again with a light breeze off the French shore. We picked up some speed and motor sailed well out to get some clearance from the land. About noon, we could barely see land in the distance and made a directional change to make a course to Corunia, Spain. The wind went light and then died again, the seas were calm and we were making about six knots under power. A couple of hours later the wind came up again and since we couldn't make any headway with the wind directly on the bow, we had to set a course west heading out into mid-Atlantic. There wasn't much point in running the engine, so we headed slowly on a southwesterly course. We considered running into the French coast and waiting for more favorable winds, but Tucker thought it best to get some sea room and not take a chance of being on a lee shore. Ken wanted to get into an anchorage somewhere. I agreed with Tucker as I had more confidence in his judgment.

In the next few hours, the winds continued to increase out of the same direction. Tucker's decision was correct because in the four hours it would have taken us to close the coast the wind had built to over forty knots and the seas were twelve to fifteen feet. We reefed down to half of the main and mizzen, rolled the Genoa up completely and left both staysails flying and changed course to the Irish coast. The winds kept building and Tucker said he thought we might be in for something bad. We had better take the necessary steps to ensure our safety. When we had refinished and caulked the decks, Tucker installed some deck fittings to be able to tie the booms and gaffs down and other things I didn't know what they were for, at the time. Ken had objected to spending the money on that expensive deck hardware.

As it turned out everything Tucker did was what gave us the edge in our fight for survival. The winds reached fifty knots plus and

Tucker and Ken started tying ropes together. They made a harness around the mizzen mast and out around the galvanized shrouds. They took a large extra anchor line and put the old Genoa sail on it. We tied old sail bags to the other lines and made them ready to put over the stern. I kept thinking about the old bucket I used to keep my stern to the wind in *Black Tarquin*. I had done that just out of instinct.

The winds continued to build. Trent was trying to steer, but the helm was getting hard. Tucker changed our course to directly downwind and put two of the drogues overboard. The winds reached hurricane force and the waves were now twenty-five and thirty feet high with white foam everywhere. The tops of the waves were starting to roll down the face. We had everything out now, and Tucker told Trent he could leave the wheel. Frozen in place, his eyes were wide and his body rigid. It took all three of us to get Trent down below. We put him in Tucker's berth as it was the best riding area of the boat. The berth was a single and we tied him down with ropes. He laid there staring at the cabin top completely paralyzed. I asked Tucker what he thought was wrong. He replied that he knew of cases of fright where this had happened; had read about it but didn't know anything more about the duration, or long-term conditions.

It was a good thing we got Trent below when we did. The conditions worsened, and by nightfall, we were pulled back through breaking waves by the warps. The boat was reacting well, according to Tucker, but we could do nothing more but wait below and hope for the best. When the light was fading, I looked again by opening the main hatch. The seas loomed like towers and the waves were breaking and rolling down over the decks with a crushing sound. I watched until I had to slam the hatch shut because the sea began running toward me.

I had never felt winds of such strength, or seen the sea as mountains of white foam. Scared and certain it was the end I couldn't see how the boat could possibly survive the endless pounding. The creaking and groaning of the hull, the smashing sound of water on the deck, was unnerving. We were running off into the Irish Sea between Ireland and England and had no bearing on where we were. Tucker had made some dead reckoning estimates and felt we were safe, but we didn't know. We knew we were edging toward the English coastline and just hoped we had enough sea room to see us through the night.

As it happened, the wind was backing and slowly it was turning us away from the coast. By morning, the wind was from the southeast and had calmed to forty knots. The noise had lessened. We were exhausted, but thankful to be alive and making ready to sail again. The Waco Martin furling gear was flying out to windward, it had parted from the bowsprit, but it looked like it could be repaired. The stanchions were bent and the mizzen boom had broken away from the mast but was still lying there. The preparations and adjustments Tucker had made saved the day. It was evident, even to Ken, that Tucker was the man!

We jury rigged the boat and headed for Corunia. Ken thought we should put back into an English port for repairs, but we decided Spain would be cheaper and better for us. The high winds pushed us with good speed to our destination and we were in Corunia on the fourth day. We moored against a wall in a busy part of the city. Trent was several days in his comatose state, but once the boat was still and after we had fed him soup and some protein, he responded. At sea, Ken had managed to get some water down him with a spoon, but that was all he had had for five days. It was a couple of weeks before he seemed normal again, and we made him rest while we pulled the boat back together. It took about ten days and then we were off to Portugal.

We anchored in Cascais about fifteen miles north of Lisbon and went into Estoril to clear customs. As we made the rounds of this magnificent resort area, one of the most memorable taste treats of my life was from a small ice cream shop that made their own ice cream. That day they made a raspberry treat churned with fresh cream from a local farm. It was so special I've thought about it so many times when I eat the ice cream people tout as the best. The local yacht club invited us to dinner at the club. In those days, visiting yachtsmen were rare. The locals were curious as to where we were going and what the plans were for these young adventurers. We told our harrowing story of the hurricane and we learned of the many losses of fishing boats and ships during the storm. The seas were reported to be eighty and ninety feet and winds of near a hundred miles per hour with gusts far beyond. We, my shipmates and I, felt a certain pride in surviving, and still sailing on in our journey. I didn't mention to my friends that, at the height of the fury around us, I promised myself if I survived the storm I would never set foot on a boat again. The mind has a wonderful way of forgetting the worst of life and remembering the good times.

We moved the boat to Lisbon and found a safe anchorage close to the city. In a café near the naval installations, we met a handsome young sailor who spoke good English. He was training as a naval officer in the Portuguese Navy. The Portuguese have great pride in their maritime heritage and they had several great, old square-rigged, classic boats as training ships. Mateo was about our age and we ended up having dinner together and making the rounds of the local brothels.

In Spain and Portugal, it was a custom to visit the local houses and make evaluations of the talent. No one participated in the fun and games, but there was one house where Mateo knew all the girls. It was a Saturday night and the place was busy. One of the girls looked like Elizabeth Taylor; she was exceptionally beautiful and I was surprised she worked as a hooker. The girls were friendly and they liked us, as we were a handsome group and quite unlike the other men in the place. There was a guitar there and I picked it up and sang some funny American folk songs. The girls loved it. A sexy redhead couldn't keep away from Ken. He asked her to come to the boat the next day and she accepted. One thing led to another and soon we had Mateo bringing several of the girls with him for a sail and lunch on the boat. They were supposed to be there at eleven in the morning, but eleven came and there was no sign of Mateo and his crew. At noon, we had all but given up when Tucker cried out.

"There he is. In that longboat... with the whole brothel!"

Mateo had with him seven of the girls and a local man was rowing them out toward us. They brought lunch baskets, wine, and pastries. They looked very different from the girls the night before; prettier, fresher and happier. I guess it was a day out and they seldom had the chance to sail on a large yacht. When he came aboard Mateo said it would be best that we get out of the marina area.

We sailed down the coast to a deserted bay that was quite beautiful. We cruised into a protected finger of the bay and anchored. The girls loved the sailing and nearly all of them spoke a little English. We set up the table on deck and Trent took over the arranging of seating and the food. He had prepared spaghetti sauce the previous day, which he did in volume so it would last for several days. It was a warm day and the girls all went below and changed into their bathing suits. I thought it was funny that women that exposed their bodies to men for a living would be so shy when changing. Back topside they laughed, swam, and cavorted like school girls.

Mateo was enamored with the dark beauty and made it quite clear she was his private property. He was showing off his physique and prowess as a swimmer and diver to impress the group. We didn't care we were just having fun. He climbed up the mast and made a big deal out of posing on the spreaders before making a swan dive into the sea from twenty-five feet up. It was a good one. He hit the water cleanly and was gone for a few seconds then popped up about twenty feet out from the boat. The girls clapped and screamed at their hero. When he came aboard, they felt his muscles, stroked his body and made a considerable fuss.

Tucker wouldn't be outdone. He was a diving champion and truly one of the greatest athletes I've ever known. He went up the ropes of the mast, holding a V shape with his legs, hand over hand displaying his incredible strength. When he got to the spreaders, he stood, back to the sea, and performed a perfect two and a half somersault dive, striking the water straight as an arrow. He disappeared below for a long time. Mateo started to look around the perimeter of the boat for him, but he wasn't there. The girls began to look worried. After a very long, time Tucker burst out of the water some sixty or seventy feet out from the beam of the boat. I knew immediately where he had been. The transom looked as if it went directly into the water, but there was about a foot where the angle changed which created a breathing space under the stern. He had rested there and then pushed off from the keel and swam under water for an incredible distance. When he came aboard the girls went crazy, Mateo was quiet and kept looking at him. I think he just couldn't believe what he had seen. Although I knew what Tucker had done it was still an incredible feat. After that display, the chubby little blond that giggled relentlessly made her move. She wanted to try out Superman, and she and Tucker went below for an hour or more.

Trent tried to take a couple of them below, but no one took him up on the offer. Ken had gone below with his admirer before Tucker did his act. A shy little nymph-like girl who hardly said a word all day cozied up to me. I hadn't seen her the night before and I assumed that she had had a trick and was busy. But, she soon told me she was the younger sister of the dark-haired beauty that had gone below with Mateo. We had the dinghy over the side and the spare girls were sitting there and making the swim to the rocks near the bow. I took the little nymph to the aft cabin where Tucker was pumping away with the blond. We stretched out on the berth next to them and she was fascinated with their romping not far from us. Soon she got excited and we got into it, but she wouldn't take her clothes off. I played with her breasts and her pussy. I could tell she came, but she wasn't going beyond the limits. She stayed hot and we played for a long time, but I was getting frustrated and didn't want to continue. We just laid there and I cooled off. Tucker left and she took out my tool and finished me off with her mouth and then her hand. I discovered afterward she wasn't a hooker at all. She and her sister lived together and she liked the girls her sister worked with.

After our perfect day with the hookers, we sailed on down the coast of Portugal into Gibraltar. The mooring fees were very high so we anchored out in the bay. We bought much-needed stores and boat material for the repairs we had not made in Corunia. We worked on the boat and then made the crossing to Tangier in Morocco.

I had been there once before while working for a crazy friend, Eric Sweeney, running cigarettes from the Canary Islands into Spain.

The port for Eric's boat was in Tangier and I had been there several days before and had the chance to investigate the area. That's a long story so here's the short version: I was arrested in Malaga while transferring contraband onto a local fishing boat. The American cigarettes we carried were manufactured in the Canaries with tobacco purchased in the United States and then packaged under all the popular American labels. The duty on American cigarettes, coming from the United States, was so high it was a profitable business. For a long time, it was easy to make the drops. Eric's boat did thirty-eight knots, which was about five knots faster than the Spanish and French patrol boats. Unfortunately, I did this first run at Eric's request and it coincided with when the patrols had new boats that would do over forty knots. Because Eric was my friend, I was bought out of the local prison two days later before any legal procedures could take place. The others in the crew were left behind; as it was the chance they took.

While in Tangier this time, we met two English men who asked if they could charter *Patience* to take them to Palma Mallorca. They agreed to give us a token fee and to supply all the food for the trip. We went to the market and loaded up with all kinds of great things from the international market. We left the next day with Sam and Lenny aboard. We anchored off the coast of Spain for the night and the next day went into Valencia. A very attractive gypsy girl came to the boat soliciting her wares. Sam invited her aboard and when I came back, she was in the saloon with the whole bunch watching her display her body. I sat down and realized she was pregnant; her belly was just showing a round protrusion. When she spread her legs, Sam jumped down and started eating her pussy. It almost made me sick, his ugly little twisted up face in the cunt of a ragged gypsy. Who knew when she last washed and what diseases she carried. Sam got her excited, jumped on top, and lasted about three minutes.

Lenny took her by the hand into the aft cabin. Tucker and I had given it up for the charter and we were sleeping in the saloon. When Lenny came out about ten minutes later, Ken decided he would give it a go. Tucker, Trent and I looked at each other and shrugged our shoulders in wonderment. At one point, Tucker voiced his disgust. Ken was gone about a half hour and came back in sheepishly, saying he was horny, and she was quite good. Lenny slipped her a couple of English pounds as she left.

I asked if anyone wanted to go ashore and get something to eat. They all stayed on the boat and Tucker and I went into the town. We sat in a bodega and had fried fish and octopus in its own ink, French fries and a couple of glasses of wine. Thinking back on what had just happened aboard our boat we looked at each other. Sam and Lenny were uncouth pigs; we would be happy to be rid of them. We dropped them in Palma and no real discussion ever took place about the incident.

I had been there a couple of years before after a gig in Barcelona; I had a two-night engagement at the auditorium in Palma. I had taken the overnight ferry and found a nice little hotel near the harbor. I met two Army guys from Los Angeles and they were on a four-day holiday in the islands. They had been to Ibiza the day before. When they realized, it was a gay dominated place they came back to Palma. We rented a car together and set off to make a grand tour. It was truly a beautiful island. We stayed one night in a little hotel on the north coast and the next day circumnavigated the island and returned to Palma, where I appeared that night. I went to the theater early to check on the microphone situation. It was a standard stage platform microphone with a giant head. I didn't like these mics as they blocked the audience from seeing your face and expressions. But it had good sound and I practiced for a few minutes to check it out.

At the theater, I met two German girls. They were twins, pretty, and contortionists with an act like I had never seen before. They were identical and I couldn't tell them apart. Off stage, I thought it strange that they'd still dress and make themselves up the same. They were twenty-five years old and I thought at that age they'd be tired of the twin thing and would want to express themselves as individuals. When I watched their act the first night, I was turned on. They had incredible bodies and a level of flexibility not to be believed. They could sit on top of their own head. I thought to myself what exciting and unusual positions one could find with such a partner. I got their names and tried in vain to find some marking or telltale mannerism that would help me distinguish between them.

The next day I decided I would stay in Palma for a while. I rented a furnished house on the beach in Terrano, an area just along the coast from the harbor. The second night was the last night for everyone, as the performance was a once a month program arranged by the city council. I invited Heidi and Florene to stay with me for as long as they wished, and they joined me for the next five or six days. The first night we went out and did some shopping and the girls made dinner. We drank a lot of wine and got high.

"Which one of you would like to sleep with me?" I asked. I didn't expect them to, but in my inebriated condition, it seemed like the right question. Heidi volunteered, and I said they could share me if they liked.

Florene said she was tired. "You two have fun."

After she had gone to bed, Heidi and I got into a passionate session of the sofa. I told her I would like to kiss her pussy. She said she could do that herself. It was my tool she was after. We laughed, undressed, and proceeded with a routine affair. We made it long and hard and she took a very long time to reach her summit. We went upstairs to bed and made it again. She explained she had not had sex for a very long time. They had been doing shows all over Europe for months, but she hadn't found an attractive partner. Her ability to get into positions was exciting, but we didn't do anything extraordinary. In this close contact, I started to recognize some subtle differences, and I thought I could tell them apart.

The next night, we started flirting while having dinner at an Italian restaurant. Florene made a few comments about how late we got up that morning. She had taken a long walk, found a small bakery, and bought some special breakfast delights. That day they had dressed differently and as we spent the evening, I was convinced that it was Heidi I was giving all my consideration. The two of them were fun and devilish in their attention to me. We drank a lot. I heard many stories about their family and how they, at a very early age, became contortionists. Their mother was like them, and they tried to mimic her contortions from the time they were quite young. They were recognized from a very early age while still living in Munich. Their career was fascinating, and royalty had wined and dined them throughout Europe. Heidi and I slept together again that night.

The next morning the two of them were giggling while I was making breakfast. When I inquired, they looked at each other and said, "We both think you're an excellent lover."

I said, "It's interesting you both function and react very much the same, and physically there are no telltale marks."

They laughed. "There're some ways and marks you could discover, but we won't tell you… you must discover them."

I asked if their mother and father had any problem with their identification.

"Not at all."

I thought as an artist I was particularly observant and as a singer, I had a superb ear for voice. As a lover, I thought I had mastered the nuances of a woman's reactions. But they had completely fooled me, and my confidence in my prowess suffered. Over the next days, the three of us had wonderful times and I did find some subtle differences. I realized that the first few days they kept changing names, so just when I thought I could identify something, I was thrown off. They were playing their little game with me.

Finally, they admitted they had often switched partners and played their game of intrigue many times. I made love to both of them for the rest of their visit. Morning to night we had great encounters, but never did they join me together. I tried to convince them, but they had a code, which in retrospect was probably a good thing. They were so close that going beyond a particular point might be destructive in their relationship. What I found truly amazing about them was the real harmony between them; I never witnessed any disagreements or conflict. They said, when I remarked about it, they had had many fights when they were younger but had very few after they started working the circuit.

When they left me, it was very sad. We all cried and planned that they would come to Paris to see me. Unfortunately, sometime in the following year I heard that a motorcycle in Italy hit Heidi. I never found out exactly what happened. Or the extent of her injuries but I did get a note from her in answer to a letter I had sent some months before to their family address. She said they wouldn't be coming to Paris that year, but she was doing well.

Errol Flynn

We had to move from our initial spot in Palma because *Patience* was in the space of a yacht that was returning. We re-moored alongside a big gaff-rigged schooner named the *Zaca*. The afternoon we arrived, a boy of about 14 years old sat on the cabin top well above us. He asked that if we went ashore, across their foredeck, to remove our shoes if it was early in the morning, as his father often slept late.

Later that morning Errol Flynn came on deck. I was varnishing *Patience's* rail, and he stood and watched me for a few minutes. He nodded with a smile and I recognized him immediately. I said hello, but he just went about his arranging of a deck chair below a sun awning and started to read. Several days went by and we were careful to cross his deck very quietly. In the evening when we went ashore, we boarded our tender and rowed around to a ladder at the dock. Tucker and I were on deck, sprawled out recovering from our adventures of the night before and watching Errol as he proceeded down the steps near the bow to a small platform on the water.

Patience was less than half the length of the *Zaca* and we were in a good watching position from our low stern to see him assemble his diving gear and ready himself for a dive. We had guessed he was going to check the hull or do some underwater chore. We were curious why he would do such work himself, but he seemed to do quite a few things around the boat himself. He slipped his arms through the straps of the tank, tightened his weight belt, put the mouthpiece in, and was over the side in seconds.

I hadn't been watching very carefully, but Tucker stood up immediately and said, "He didn't even check his tank!"

Tucker was over the side in a flash. As I watched from the deck, I saw some bubbles coming up, so I knew the tank must be working. In less than a minute, they surfaced and Tucker helped him on the platform. Tucker jumped up, took the gear from his back, and helped him remove the weights. Errol was gasping for breath and didn't seem coherent. I jumped aboard *Zaca* and went down the steps and helped bring the gear back aboard while Tucker helped Errol back to the ship. Patrice Wymore, his wife, was ashore with Sean, his son. We sat Errol in his deck chair and slowly he seemed to adjust to what was going on.

He said. "I couldn't get any air."

"No," Tucker said. "Your tank valve was closed. I saw you hadn't checked it, so I dived down and opened the valve. I thought it best you come up and take a break and maybe do whatever it was you were going to do, later."

Errol thanked us and after a few minutes had said, he was going below to rest.

Trent and Ken hadn't returned by the afternoon and Tucker and I were on deck watching for them. Tucker had described what he'd found when he went in the water. "I didn't have a face mask on so I couldn't see well, but there he was on the bottom drowning." I was very impressed he had noticed and acted so quickly, but that was Tucker; he wasn't only a superb athlete but also a very experienced diver.

Errol came on deck and asked us to join him for a drink. We went below, had drinks and Sean joined us. Patrice came to meet us and seemed to be attending to personal tasks scurrying about in and out of the saloon. He told his son.

"They saved my life. You be sure that anything they want... you get it for them."

He didn't seem to know which of us had made the dive to help, but we explained it to him. We compared notes and he became very interested when we discussed Hollywood and the people we knew. He had met Debbie Reynolds and thought she was a great talent. We talked about her, Keenan Wynn, and others we knew. Tucker wasn't a great communicator but Errol and I seemed to hit it off from the beginning. The next day he asked me if I wanted to do a little sailing around the bay. He had a daysailer; a nifty little twenty-foot racer. We raced around the bay for an hour or so and had some good fun. When we returned, Patrice fixed us some lunch and we continued to talk. Errol was a flamboyant storyteller and he seemed to dwell mostly on the sailing and his early life. He didn't talk about his acting life or all the years in Hollywood.

For the next month, we sailed, drank and became friends. He seemed to want to escape from the boat so we frequented a little club where he would hang out. I would go there with him and sing a few songs with their awful piano player. When we left Palma, I gave Errol my mother and my father's phone numbers, and he said he would call me when he was back in Hollywood.

***

[After the cruise in the Mediterranean, when I was back in the United

States, my mother called to tell me: "Errol Flynn called and left his phone number. Is he that actor?" When I said it was, she asked me not to hang around with unsavory people like him. It was interesting that even someone like my mother, who wasn't the least in touch with what went on in show business, had already formed an opinion of him.

I called him back at the Garden of Allah, a motel/hotel of some note in early Hollywood years and went to meet him for dinner. I was shocked at his apartment's accommodation. I always thought it was a classy place, but it was run down. We went to a nearby restaurant and had something to eat. Errol was drinking heavily and in just over a year since I had seen him last he had deteriorated significantly. He wasn't coherent and his senses seemed to be dulled. He spoke of his disappointments and how much he hated people in Hollywood.

It was hard for me to take, as I had returned home to find my mother who was an alcoholic had also deteriorated. She was difficult to be with and I would always have to visit her in the early evening before she drank too much and got muddled. I felt sad and when I excused myself that night, I knew I wouldn't see him again. To this day, I cannot be with people who have an alcoholic personality. Errol said I was one of his best friends and that made me realize there were not many left he related to. It was only about two years later I learned of his death.]

Barcelona

Before the gig in Palma, I had appeared at a club and bar by the name of Cosmos on the Ramblas. I arrived in Barcelona by train and, being famished, I purchased a sausage sandwich at the station. When I arrived at my hotel, I was feeling nauseous and weak, I went to the room and lay down and went to sleep. A short time later, I became violently ill and felt I might pass out. I called the desk and the clerk said he would be right up to my room. When he saw me, he physically picked me up and carried me down to the street. He sat me down on a bench near the door, got a cab and accompanied me to the hospital. He translated as they took me inside the hospital on a stretcher. I passed out. When I came to I was in bed. My throat was sore and my stomach felt like it had been used as a punching bag. I had food poisoning. I spent the night and woke the next morning feeling much better. A burly and rugged looking man came to my bedside. The doctor who had taken care of me had summoned him. His name was Raymond Hansen, a language teacher, and he was going to take me to a place where they could care for me for a couple of days.

We went to the hotel and the same man was at the desk. It was a tiny place and he was alone. I got my suitcase which was heavy with my stage clothes. Raymond grabbed it and threw it up over his shoulder as if it was nothing; in the other hand, he had my guitar case. I found out later he had previously been a boxer in Denmark and, as I understood later, a contender for the heavyweight championship.

I wanted to pay the hotel bill, but the desk clerk said he had rented the room anyway and had just put my suitcase in the office when he got back; so there was no charge. I signed a fifty-dollar traveler's check and gave it to him. He didn't want to take it, but Raymond and he had a short conversation in Spanish, which I only partly understood. He took the check and we left.

Raymond said. "I'm taking you to the Pension Maria on the Rambla Capuchinos; that's where I live. It costs one dollar a night and for that you also get breakfast and dinner." He looked at me. "So fifty dollars was a great deal of money to the good man that helped you."

I nodded. "He left the hotel unattended, which could have caused him some severe problems, and without him I might not have made it!"

I rested that day, but the following evening I was starting at the Cosmos bar. Raymond came to see me there and hung out for most of the evening. He talked to the bar owner and convinced him it would be best if I didn't work too long.

During the next week, Raymond and I became friends. He was serious about his work. He had many people that came to him to learn English as well as Spanish, French and German, and, of course, his native Danish. One evening, one of his students stayed for dinner at the pension. His name was Angel Montero, but everyone called him Monty. Monty was a clerk at the Avenida Palace Hotel, which was the finest hotel in Barcelona at that time. He had started as a bellboy and worked his way up to a night clerk.

Monty and I hit it off right away. He wanted to practice his English, so I helped him and he helped me with Spanish. We both were working nights, so during the day he showed me the city. One day he wanted me to meet his mother and took me to his home in the hills above the city. It was just a shack with dirt floors and poor beyond anyone I had ever associated with. His mother was sweet and seemed so pleased he had an American friend.

When I finished at the Cosmos, I still had nearly a week before I needed to be in Palma, Mallorca. Monty said he had a week off and wanted to show me the coast. The next day I left my gear with

Raymond and we took off for our adventure. We went on Monty's light weight motorcycle and for five days, we romped through the small coastal towns. We stayed in pensions mostly but spent one night in a gypsy camp where Monty had a good friend. The evening with a group of gypsies, singing and eating was very different and fun.

When I left Barcelona, Monty and Raymond saw me off on the overnight ferry to Palma. Monty was a humble and pleasant man. I promised I would write and that we would meet again at some future time.

* * *

[After a while, I lost track of Raymond, but Monty was good about writing and letting me know where he was. He became the manager of the hotel. His flair for languages and his good looks and suave manner made him appealing to the owners. A few years went by and I didn't hear from him. Then one day I received an announcement he had become the manager of the Prado Hotel in Madrid. I remembered the hotel was a colossal and fancy place and I was so pleased he had come so far. A note with the announcement explained he was getting married and he said he would like me to meet his soon to be wife if I ever came to Madrid. Some years later, I stayed in the hotel and we had a brief lunch together, but the timing wasn't good, he was very apologetic we didn't have more time together. He had become an important man and I could see the pressure that was part of his world.

Monty and I eventually lost touch completely and some forty years later, I sold my yacht in Palma and Joyce and I went to Barcelona and stayed at the Avenida Palace. I asked the manager if he knew Monty and interestingly, he had been there the day before we arrived. The manager told me he was living in the Dominican Republic and had a hotel there. He gave me the address. Knowing I was taking delivery of my new yacht which was being built in Rhode Island, I planned to travel throughout the Caribbean on our way to the Pacific and stop to see him.

Two years later we anchored in Samana Bay in the Dominican Republic. We hired a car and in an hour and a half were at a most magnificent hotel and casino. It was old and classic, obviously Five Star, and one of the grandest in the city. Joyce and I went to the desk and I said I would like to see Mr. Angel Montero. The man quizzed me about my reasons and I explained we had been friends many years before and I was sure he would want to see me. He said, "I'll call him and see if he is available." In a few minutes, he came back and told me, Monty was at his home and it would take him a half hour to come and meet me. He asked us to be the guest of the hotel and to wait in the dining room where Mr. Montero would join us.

About thirty minutes later the manager approached us and I knew it was Monty with him. He was still handsome, with a full head of gray hair, still slim, but looking quite frail. Monty was several years older than I, which would have made him about 67 or 68 at that time. He hugged me very hard and started to cry, I had tears in my eyes as well as we just stood there and looked at each other. My heart felt the same friendship we had known forty-three years before. We had lunch and I could see Monty wasn't well. Joyce, who was a nurse, also noticed his frailty.

Monty told us of his marriage of forty years and that his two daughters were both physicians living and practicing in Spain. He said he had so many times thought of our motorcycle adventure down the coast, and the night with the gypsies. It was one of the most fun experiences of his life. We talked and I told him of my life and my success and I promised to send him a book of my work and a serigraph for his home.

Monty didn't complain or say anything about his health. It was a wonderful time even though it was just a few hours. The manager came over and said the car was waiting for him and they had arranged a limousine to take us back to Bahia Samana. We said our goodbyes and waved to Monty as his car drove off. Next, a limousine with two motorcycle escorts pulled up to us. It had flags on the two aerial-like posts on each fender. We learned it was the car of the president of the Dominican Republic. They took us back and dropped us at the sleazy yacht club at the head of the bay as the other cruisers looked on with great curiosity. I had never been in a president's car before or since. I faxed my secretary from the boat and asked her to expedite the book and serigraph to Monty at the hotel. Joyce and I knew Monty was dying. She thought it must be cancer and that he had dressed impeccably and worked very hard not to show his condition. I never had contact with Monty again, but he was very special in my life.]

Marseille

Our next stop was Marseille and the port was crowded with fishing and work boats. We found a place on some pilings and had to use our plank boards with the fenders to keep the rough slimy posts from damaging the hull. We went into the port and I asked the local fisherman where there was a good place to eat.

I had to do all the talking in Spain and France. Even though Trent and Ken had been there for quite a while, they spoke only a few words. Ken had no aptitude for languages and no ear for music either. For the many months we cruised, I often played the guitar and the guys sang. Tucker couldn't carry a tune very well either, and he seldom chimed in. Trent had a good voice and he liked to sing, so did Ken, but he was always off key.

The fisherman sent us to a local port bistro, which was a very interesting place. They had a giant caldron of fish soup with a ladle, large bowls, and near it, a stack of baguettes piled four feet high and six feet wide. The pot probably held some thirty gallons and had a large flat burner under it. A huge gas bottle sat next to it, unadorned by any camouflage. Every day they had something different in the caldron. And it was delicious the two evenings we ate there. A big bowl with a half a baguette was about fifty cents; a large beer was twenty cents. It was a happy place and people dressed as bums ate next to people who looked like they just walked out of Vogue magazine. I had seen this kind of simple food provision before but never on the scale of that fisherman's bistro.

Onward

When we left Marseille, we stopped at each of the elegant ports along the coast of France. We always anchored out, which was allowed in those days. Years later on my second *Tarquin*, you had to try to get a space in a berth which was outrageously expensive. We had more money at that time so it wasn't a problem, but I continually thought back on this first experience.

We covered the coast of France, then Italy, the Peloponnese and made our way to Athens. Even though we anchored out most of the time, occasionally we moored right in the city. It was exciting but noisy and uncomfortable; all sorts of odd people in boats hustling their wares often approached us. Yachts were rare in those years and everyone thought we were millionaires waiting to give them money. We investigated many of the Greek islands and found the people generally friendly, but lazy. The young men, our age, were arrogant and ignorant, so we had little in common with them.

Mikonos

In Mikonos, I had a very exciting experience. We were moored against the wall in the small, picturesque, city and there was a hard-chinned French boat just in front of us. As I passed it on several occasions, I stopped and talked to a stunning, young, blonde girl. Each day that I walked by we would smile at each other and say hello. I learned she had arrived three weeks previously.

One day I saw her down the quay at a local café. She was sitting with another young woman and motioned to me to come and sit with her. As I did, the other woman got up and said, "I'm sorry I can't help you," and left.

I noticed the girl didn't have anything to drink. "Will you join me for a coffee or something?"

She said, "I would love to have a coffee. I haven't been to a café for some time."

I wondered why she'd make such a statement. She was sitting in one and there were others all along the quay. "Why?" I asked.

"Because I don't have any money."

"I don't understand. You're with your husband or boyfriend. I've seen him many times with friends in the cafes."

She didn't reply and was quiet as we sat enjoying our coffee and watching the scene. Mikonos was a mecca for gay men and there was several cavorting in the café quite near us. I commented on them. "I'm surprised at the number of gay men on the island."

She shook her head and with a sad smile said. "My name is Brigette Henson, I'm from Sweden. Can I tell you my story without chasing you away?"

"Of course!"

"I'm in an awful situation. Like those men," she waved a hand at them, "the man I'm with is also gay. We became lovers when I was in Athens. I'm a medical student at the university in Stockholm and was on a tour with friends when I met him. He was handsome and dashing... he had a boat and took me sailing. We became lovers and have spent five months sailing through the islands since the weather has become warm. But we haven't had a good relationship since we arrived here and fight continually. He has a male lover, too, and he wants to keep us both. I want to leave and go back to Sweden, but I've spent all of my money and he will not give me any because he knows I'll leave. I can't believe he has become so mean." She gestured at the chair next to where I was sitting. "The woman that was here is from England. I asked her to help me, as I've asked others, but no one wishes to get involved. I've missed my chance to be in school this year. It will be very embarrassing for me to call my family and ask for money, as they're very upset with me. But I must get enough from someone to make a call."

"How much do you need?

"About ten dollars." She looked down then back up to me. "I'm afraid of him and want to take my clothes and leave, but I don't know where I could stay."

Her eyes filled with tears and I thought, how incredibly beautiful she was. How could it be that no one would help her? We talked for two hours and I took her to dinner at a place well away from the port. The more I heard of the story, the more I realized the man she was with was unstable and perhaps even dangerous. We made a plan and that evening when he was out with his boyfriend, Brigette packed her bags and came aboard *Patience*. I explained to the guys it wasn't a love affair and that I wasn't seeking anything from her, but only wanted to help her in a difficult situation. They agreed to take her with us to where she could call her parents. We were a three-day sail from Istanbul, where she could get a plane and fly directly home. Tucker generously said he would sleep in the saloon so she could take his berth.

When she was aboard, we left port and headed to another anchorage on the island. That night we all had dinner and she insisted on cleaning up. Trent made some Spaghetti Putanesca, and we had fresh bread from one of the bakeries in port. That night we all had a lot of fun. She fit in well and even seemed to add some harmony to the group. Ken and Tucker had never quite got along; a competitive issue with them that appeared to be getting worse as the trip wore on. She lightened the mood between them.

Brigette's personality and good humor made everyone realize we had become bored with our daily life aboard. That first night, she and I talked half the night away. When we finally went to bed, I felt I knew her better than I knew some people I had known for years. She was completely open and direct. She realized her recent escapade was foolish and, that thankfully, we had saved her.

The second day we spent in Samos, an old port with ancient walls. No yachts, just fishing boats and a rough waterfront. She tried to make a call from there but couldn't get through. It cost nearly all the ten dollars I had given her. She fretted and was disturbed by the difficulty of making a call. I had experienced that myself. I tried to call my mother many times while we were in the Greek islands, but could never get a line and make a connection. Their phone system and reluctance to deal with foreigners made it a frustrating effort. That evening on deck I put my arms around her. I told her I was going to buy her a plane ticket to get back home and some extra money so she could get from the airport to where she needed to go. We became lovers that night and seemed to make the transition with great passion and comfort.

In Istanbul, we made flight arrangements and stayed together for another few days before she left. She promised to send the money back to me in Paris and, if possible, maybe she could come to see me the following year. I told her I didn't know where I would be and that the money was a gift. But we would stay in touch and one day could see each other again. On the day she left, I took her to the airport and we both cried.

Onward Again and Back to France

We continued up the Bosporus to the Black Sea and things aboard were getting very tense. Both Trent and I tried to talk to Ken, who was becoming even more of a hard case to deal with. He got it in his head we were all ganging up on him, and he became more impossible by the day. I felt Ken owed me a lot; I'd employed him and carried the financial burden of our sailing. But he was just a bull-headed jerk that had no appreciation for anything I had done for him. We finally headed back to the French Riviera; a fast and not too pleasant journey.

When we got back in Cannes, we listed *Patience* for sale. After a couple of weeks getting her in shape, Tucker and I returned to Paris. Ken was to sell the boat and send us our shares. He didn't have any money left and he was too proud to ask. He got some jobs working on other boats, but it was meager so Trent stayed on for about a month and supported him. After Trent had left him, Ken sold the boat and kept the money for himself. He apparently had forged Tucker and my signatures as we were all equal partners.

[I was never able to track down the boat, but seven years later people in Cannes told me he had used the boat for smuggling and it had been confiscated. Years after that I read about its restoration in a sailing magazine; another Englishman owned it.

Brigette and I stayed in contact and when I returned to Los Angeles, there was a letter thanking me for my help, and telling me she was returning to school. I wrote back and gave her the address of my Hollywood Boulevard studio. I told her how wonderful she was, and that I would never forget her. We wrote a few letters back and forth, and soon the time passed and I was on my second marriage to Marie. It was at the time Marie and I were about to split (as told in a later chapter); more than twelve years had passed, and a letter arrived at the studio. Brigette explained she was going to a medical convention in New York, and asked if it was possible that I meet her there. I went to New York often and planned to be there and stay at the Hilton where she also would be staying. She called my room as I had arrived a day earlier than she had. Her message asked if we could have dinner that evening and she'd meet me at the bar at eight o'clock.

When she walked into the bar that evening, every man in the room turned and watched her. She was exquisite and I hardly recognized her. When we embraced, she kissed me full on the lips and it was a very emotional moment. When we went to dinner, I found she had married another physician. He was a heart surgeon, and she had become a pediatrician. She had given birth to two boys and proudly showed me their pictures. We had an enjoyable evening, and she went on about what an incredible influence I had been. That my encouragement to return to school, and my generosity and love had taught her a life lesson. I knew I had loved her and guided her somewhat, but I didn't realize how much it had meant to her.

We danced until midnight and when we reentered the hotel, she said. "I would like to make love to you if that's okay."

I replied. "I must be dreaming. Through the years, I've relived our time on the boat many times in my head."

We spent the nights in her room in case her husband called. I knew Marie wouldn't call me. For three days, we loved and spoiled each other. She didn't attend any more of the seminars; she said she had accomplished the objective of her trip. When we said goodbye, we both knew it was a final farewell. But we promised should we both be free at some future time we would make contact.

Thirty-five years later, I sent her a note to the hospital where she worked, which I located on the internet. I told her I had contacted her to just see how she was since I thought of her often. We corresponded several times and I found she had a son that was an excellent doctor, and the other was in the advertising business. She had divorced and told me the mail she had sent me had been returned. She saw my work, online at my website, and was very excited I had reached such a level of success. I explained my ongoing love for her and that I appreciated with fond memories our very special times spent together. I told her of my marriage to Joyce and that we were so very happy together.]

IV

COMING HOME
HOLLYWOOD & THE
STUDIO

11

BACK TO THE UNITED STATES

I had completed school and had had many adventures on land and sea, but it was time to go home. When I left Paris and said goodbye to all my friends, it was a sad day. I knew I would come back, but I also knew it would be a long road at home to establish myself and make my mark as an artist.

I returned from France on the *Ile de France*, an old French passenger ship which had a reputation as a party ship after World War Two. I had accumulated a substantial amount of money and I spent it cautiously, traveling by the least expensive class. I shared a cabin on one of the lower decks with three strangers. That first afternoon I went to the cabin to rest. What I found there was an indication of what the voyage was going to be. One of the men was very fat and had the berth above me. His excessive weight caused the bunk to bow down, and it looked as if it might give way at any moment. I could visualize myself being crushed during the night. The two other men were father and son; the father took the lower berth and the son of 20 years or so, was on the upper berth. The son looked to be quite a handsome fellow of about five-foot-eight inches tall. But it was hard to distinguish his looks. He had a scruffy beard; the kind that grew down his neck to his chest but was motley on the checks where he didn't have full growth. He and his father were dressed very poorly. Their shoes were particularly filthy; I'm sure they had never seen any cleaning or polish in their long history.

The stateroom had a sink, a chair, and a hanging locker. There was little space for luggage except for under the lower bunks. And the one porthole had a sign that said, Keep Closed at All Times. The cabin was cold from the air conditioning central vent which hung down from the ceiling. But, it was better than smelling the dirty feet and unwashed clothing of my companions.

The first evening I dressed up a bit knowing I would be seeking someone who might save me from the fat American and the two dirty Frenchmen. The food at dinner was quite good, and the large gallery for dining was packed with a happy lot of travelers on their first night at sea. I sat at a large round table, covered in white damask—its subtle pattern of waves seemed to move under the swaying lights above—with seven other passengers. Across from me was a buxom, dyed-blond with black roots, woman showing off her cleavage, while her companion, a skinny, dried up, stone-faced, self-conscious twit maintained a blank stare. I took an immediate dislike to both of them. But the big blond did grow on me during the dinner as she was quite entertaining; she seemed fun loving and outgoing. Her twit friend just sat there looking under-nourished. They had been traveling in Europe for three weeks and were returning to Ohio. Where I'm sure they went back to the factory assembly line.

Then there was Margaret; someone I will always remember. She was in her sixties, gray hair, beautiful skin, and a regal posture that told of pride and intelligence. I was fortunate to sit next to her. She had charm and an enduring quality that made her an engaging dinner partner. She was on my left, and immediately on my right was an Italian man who was very pleasant. He was short, bald, and overweight, but impeccably dressed, very polite and a gentleman. His English wasn't very good and he apologized for not communicating adequately. During the voyage he and Margaret would spend a lot of

234

time together; they seemed quite happy getting to know each other. The other woman at the table, I don't remember her name, was a school teacher from New York; a middle-aged, well-groomed, person who smiled a lot. She seldom added anything to the dinner conversation. The two young American men were in their early twenties. They had been backpacking through Europe for the summer and were returning to go back to school. I was only a couple of years older, but I felt they were still children. I exchanged pleasantries with them but knew instinctively we had nothing in common.

After dinner that first night, I followed a plan I had come up with earlier while investigating the ship. I made my way to an on deck stairway that led to the upper first and second class areas. I wandered around smiling and greeting people. I particularly greeted the officers and staff of the ship, as I wanted to establish that I belonged in this milieu.

On B deck, there was a very classy bar, and a black piano player, Ken Marble, was just beginning his set. I talked to him at length and discovered we had many mutual friends in Paris. He was from New Orleans and was a close friend of Art Simmons that I had worked with so often at The Mars Club. He had been there and seen me once performing my repertoire of songs. He invited me to sing a few songs. There were only a few people in the bar and it was a good warm up, as I hadn't been singing for some time. I loved these old-timers from the early jazz days. They could play anything, accompany a singer, and subtly smooth out the clumsy mistakes I would make.

Ken was another one of those great talents from out of the south that came and went unnoticed. His fat round face, large gray mustache, and sparkling big eyes gave him warmth felt by all of the patrons of the bar. It was the favorite spot onboard. I sat at the bar drinking beer and became friendly with the French barman. He was pleased I chose to speak French with him and was quite a fun character. The bar soon filled and many were standing behind the seats at the bar. I sat on the piano and sang for about forty-five minutes without a break. The audience was very receptive and amazingly quiet.

I had spotted an attractive woman who had entered earlier. She was very tall and slim. She wore a clinging silk dress that outlined her body, exaggerated her flat chest; a look I had come to learn was the sign of real class. It gave just a hint she might even have breasts. She was in her early 30s with the lines just beginning to show on her face; the kind that make an attractive woman striking... and intriguing. Her face was angular, with a broad smile of gleaming white teeth. She seemed very much like some of the women I had known in Paris. As it turned out, she was from Boston, with the accent just traceable. She wasn't a beauty, but someone I would describe as a handsome creature.

Some people asked me to join them for drinks I smiled and said I would join them later when they wouldn't remember anyway. I approached my lady. Her name was Kate Wellington. She was very receptive and straight forward and invited me to join her. We hit it off from the first minute.

I got up and sang again after many of the patrons requested songs. Since I had been there since opening that evening, everyone thought I worked for the company. I didn't mind as I wanted to establish myself as belonging on the upper decks.

After the next set, Kate and I talked until they were closing the bar at one o'clock. It was a lovely evening and there were still many people in deck chairs and walking the decks. We put a couple of deck chairs together and continued to talk until after two in the morning. I finally admitted to Kate I was dreading going back to my steerage compartment.

"I don't care for my cabin mates... and don't want to go back there. I know Ken, the piano player, a little from Paris. He's invited me to stay with him." I didn't say it and left the 'but...' hanging in the air.

"Wouldn't you rather stay with me?" She smiled.

She never mentioned our age difference and it didn't seem to matter. I went to her cabin without ever returning to the lower decks. She had a spare toothbrush and everything I needed. The suite was large and obviously very expensive, perhaps the best on the ship. By the time, I had showered and we had talked further it was three in the morning. I had taken the train from Paris which left at 7:00 am. It had been a long day though I had taken a two-hour nap, with Mr. Fats above me and the two French men reading or napping. I was fortunate I was one of those people who could go endlessly and I always had reserve energy. It was a good thing, too. We had kissed for a long time in our robes before we got involved. The lovemaking was beautiful and we fit together without a hitch. When we finished, we both went out like a light. We didn't stir until eight in the morning; then hugged and dozed together for a couple of more hours as if an old married couple. She had breakfast brought to the suite.

For eight days, we loved each other; made mad passionate excursions into each other's private being. We became so close in one week that it was hard to understand, but never once did we discuss the future. We drank, sang, danced, and made the best of every moment. When the ship pulled into port, we parted.

"Will I ever see you again?" I asked her.

"I took a break from my life and spent three months searching for a new way, and I didn't find it. When we met in the bar, I was disillusioned and down. Now I know what direction I must follow. I'll not go back to my husband. In ten years, we never had what you and I shared in one week. I know now it's a relationship I need; all my ambitions and false values have come full circle. You and I are not meant to be, but I'd like not to give you up. Maybe we'll meet again after I use what I've learned. That would be special."

She gave me an address that would always reach her and said she'd send me an update when she had settled into her new life. A wealthy father and a social-climbing mother had spoiled Kate. Her mother had pushed her into a marriage to an equally spoiled young man. For ten years, they played the role of the high society fashionable couple. They never had children as Kate wasn't capable. Why, I never learned.

In New York, I sold three un-stretched canvases to Victor Hammer, which gave me confidence success wasn't far away.

I took a Greyhound bus to California. On the trip, I sat next to a girl that had been backpacking in Europe for the summer. She and I talked about our lives, ambitions, and futures. When she got off the bus in Chicago, she invited me to spend a few days with her and her family. She had a very charming mother and I found I related much more to her than the daughter. Their home on the lake was very lovely and it was a pleasant few days to pull myself together for my return to LA.

[Five years later, I was exhibiting paintings at the Durant Galleries in Boston. Paul Durant knew Kate's family and I sent her a note I would be there for a few days. She had married again and had a little boy, so much for the doctors who said she couldn't have children. She came to the opening night with a girlfriend. She still had the glow. Our eyes met and an instant flashback hit me taking me back to that deep connection and time we had spent together. I can only speak for myself, but I think she felt the same. I never saw her again.]

Los Angeles and San Francisco

When I arrived in Los Angeles, I bought a used Pontiac convertible and, after a few weeks, decided not to settle there. I put all my belongings in the trunk and I drove to San Francisco believing I would be able to create better opportunities there. I also had the objective of finding Carolyn, as I knew she had moved nearby.

I stayed with a girlfriend from Paris. Jan Marks was an artist and a superb one. She was with me at the Académie Julian and we had been friends for several years. In Paris, she had lived with Bob Hill, who had given me *Black Tarquin* when I was at the Lido. After Bob had left, she lived with Bud Harborne a drummer that worked around Paris for a time. Jan and I had corresponded a few times after she left. I called her and asked if she knew of a studio where I could live and work. Jan offered for me to stay with her for a couple of weeks until I found a place.

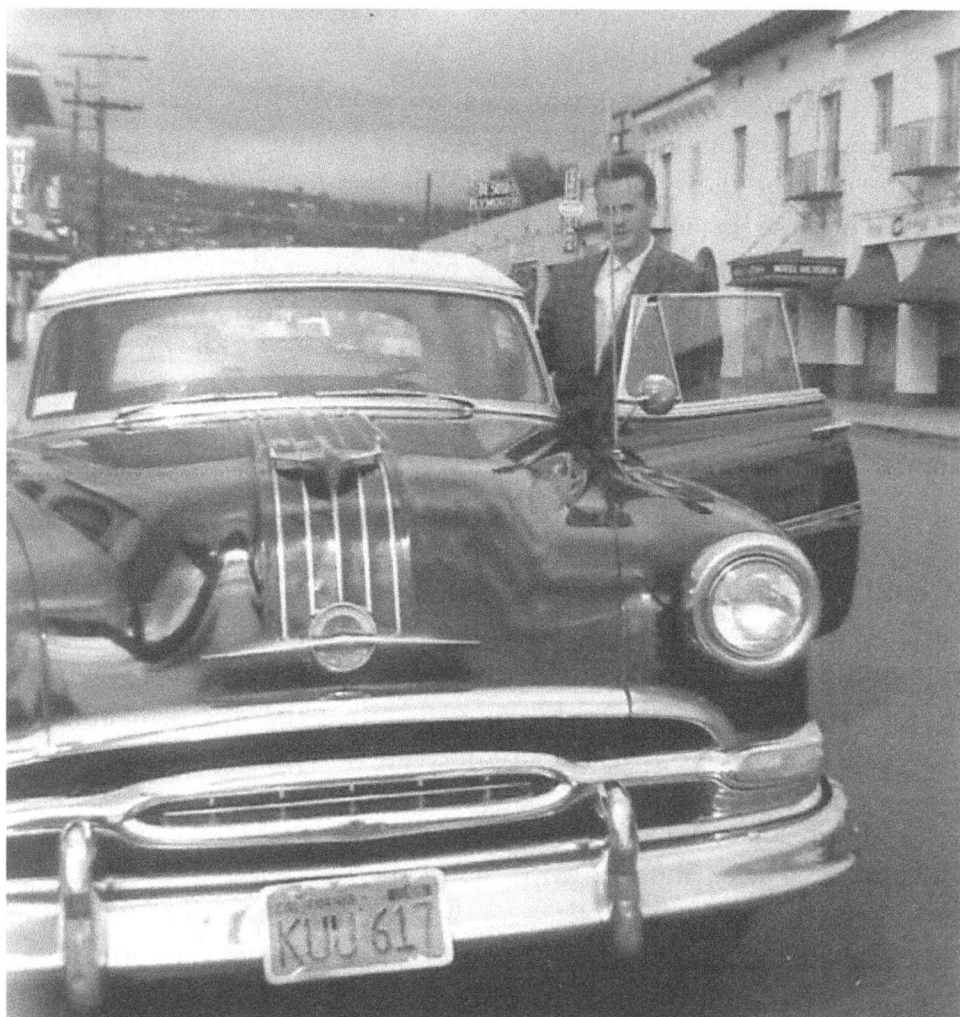

Christian with his Pontiac convertible.

When I got to her studio, she was doing some very wild and impressive landscapes, the color was Fauve in intensity and the patterns unique. I was with Jan for three weeks and during that time, we were intimate together. We got along fine at first, but her strong personality started to grate on me. It was difficult working in the same studio together, but also instructive, as she was a real creative talent. But she was toting a lot of baggage from her family and background and was subject to fits of depression. She had a grand piano in the studio, and would get up in the middle of the night and play classical concertos until dawn. Then she'd want to sleep and not be disturbed. I was paying half the expenses but was treated as an intruder. Needing the exercise, I tried to play tennis in San Francisco, but the weather was so bad all of the time I gave up on the entire situation. I packed up my car and headed back to Los Angeles. There I found a studio where I could live and work on Hollywood Boulevard.

A Hollywood Studio

The building at 5444 Hollywood Boulevard turned out to be a most impressive jumble of artists, derelicts, con men, and would be actors. The two-story brick building was just east of the corner of Western Avenue. The building faced north and had large windows on the second floor, which made the light perfect for an artist. The reflected light from the red brick building across the street was warm and quite even for a good part of the day. Artists who were very accomplished in their particular styles occupied the north side.

I rented the center unit, which was a space eighteen feet wide by thirty-five feet long. The eighteen feet facing the street had three four-foot-wide windows, their eight-foot height was nearly to the eleven-foot ceilings. I also rented a small room over the stairwell that wasn't connected to the studio and measured eighteen by fifteen feet. It had three large windows. The corridor next to the stair was broad enough I was able to keep my trash boxes there without cluttering the studio space. I used the small room as sleeping quarters. My dad gave me an old sofa-bed; it was a single-size with a pull out on the bottom. When the mattress was moved over, it became a regular sized bed. If two slept on it, the crack in the middle was quite uncomfortable, and one side was decidedly comfier than the other was.

It was 1957 and twenty-five dollars a month for the studio was about the least expensive space one could find. I paid an additional fifteen dollars a month for the second space which also was very cheap. The whole place was filthy as the cleaning service came only once each month. At each end of the wide hall that ran down the middle of the building were the bathrooms. It had a shower which was just a pipe with no fitting on the end. The artists used the sinks for cleaning their brushes, so they were disgusting. I repainted the one close to my quarters, cleaned it up and put a proper shower head and curtains on it. I got the two other artists to clean their brushes in the other bathroom and to use that bathroom only if they needed to change clothes or shower. They were pleased as when guests came it wasn't as embarrassing.

I painted my studio walls in sand beige; I did the small room which I called the office, the same. I would never admit to the other artists that it was also my home. I played the role that I was working so many hours I often spent the night there. I put some old readymade curtains on the office windows, added a two burner electric stove top on a cabinet table, and bought a used refrigerator and a table which sat four. I found an old but very interesting looking armoire that had drawers on the bottom and hanging space on the top. I salvaged a working black and white television from my dad's garage.

Around the corner on Western Avenue, there were a couple of antique stores. They were more like thrift shops, as there wasn't much in the way of quality. The area was so poor, with so many transients, that used furniture was in demand. Between the two shops was a small restaurant run by an older Jewish couple. Max and his wife Regina, who they called Reg, were hard-working, kind souls that always had something left over if one of the older, retired, residents ran short for the month. I went there every morning for breakfast when they opened at 7:00 am. Reg would fix me a big pile of hash browns, an egg and a couple of pieces of toast.

After my years in Europe, I couldn't stand the American boiled coffee which was brewed in a large urn by the gallon. I got used to drinking just water with breakfast or a glass of orange juice. I always had my café au lait when I first got up in the morning at the office. After some months there, I started buying croissants at a bakery on Vermont Avenue that I had discovered. I put a stock of them in the freezer, and after a few minutes in my little electric oven toaster, they tasted almost like the Café Royal in Saint Germain-de-Prés.

The cast of characters at my building and the surrounding area was different, to say the least. One of the main characters was the artist Paul Gerchik, a gray-haired, almost distinguished looking man in his 50s. He had a slight frame and stood about five-foot-seven inches tall. He was very high strung and his nervous condition was apparent. But Paul was also a gentle and very kind man. He was easy to get along with, but he guarded his time carefully and didn't want anyone to get too close. He worked only as an artist and his success I think was mostly because his brother-in-law was Edward Lewis, the producer of many films, including, *Spartacus*. He and another artist, Milton Gershgoren, were friends and one thing they had in common was the fact they were not very open. I could never in my life become real friends with anyone so guarded and reserved. I was open and shared what was happening in my life with those whom I loved.

* * *

Finally, I was working again and feeling I was an artist. I had been thinking for some time about how I would proceed to paint and distribute the Marchands and make a living. I knew instinctively that to try to sell my own Impressionist paintings and get ahead would be difficult as I knew nothing of the galleries and distribution channels. I made up several sixteen by twenty stretched canvas portraits from photographs of the movie stars. To attract attention, I wanted personalities that everyone knew. I contacted the buyer for Bullock's department stores. He was impressed and agreed to put them into the Wilshire Boulevard and the Westwood stores; if I would agree to paint four hours each week at each store. But he thought fifty dollars per painting was too much, so we settled on thirty-five, of which I got half. He agreed if they ordered the frame, which was an additional fifteen dollars; the store would only take one-third.

I worked long hours in the studio and made the long drive to Westwood to paint every Wednesday. The Wilshire store set up a display area, but the store manager never arranged a working area for me. As it turned out, I had my hands full with just the contacts and sales from the Westwood store. I collected good crowds while I painted. I don't think many people had ever seen a working artist who could work as fast as I could. I had done so many classical works in school that I could complete a painting in eight to ten hours. I would work the first five or six hours in the studio, and leave a few hours to finish the work in the store. Soon I was doing only the portraits and the Marchands and didn't have time for anything else.

Milton Gershgoren was a five-foot tall Russian immigrant in my building who was a very talented painter. He did explosive emotional figurative concepts, which didn't sell well at all. Only occasionally did he make a sale at one of the local Jewish centers or from his studio. He made his living doing commercial art, creating logos, newspaper ads or the like. Milt was a fun guy; he enjoyed his studio and his life there. I know he also worked at home and had a son and a daughter. I never knew much about his background or his personal life. He was a private man and a little paranoid about any invasion of his privacy from others. I think his Jewish and Russian background had a lot to do with his fears. He admired my ability to do the portraits, as I had asked him if the business got too much for me if he could do some of them. He said he couldn't equal my work and he didn't think there were many around that could. He thought the portraits were underpriced and I should raise them to a minimum of seventy-five dollars. That was a big jump from thirty-five and I doubted the store would go for it.

But I realized, after I figured my travel and time, I was working for a couple of dollars per hour and I couldn't continue at that rate. I was averaging ten dollars or more per hour doing the Marchands. The fact I was putting out considerable time and money for frames and the store had still not paid me anything after about six weeks was frustrating. The Westwood store manager was a nice guy and he expedited the money and agreed to raise the portraits to fifty dollars. The change in price made no difference at all, and the orders continued to come in. I would sell five or six paintings a week and got the occasional order from the Wilshire store.

During this period, I talked to many people during the painting demonstrations. We discussed my Paris years and often even got on to the subject of tennis, as sometimes a viewer would be in tennis clothes. One day Walter Pigeon, who was one of my favorite actors, stood behind me and watched for quite a while. He said he would like to see some of my other work. We discussed my

Impressionist pieces and his passion for the style. He asked me to bring a few paintings to the house and to also look at his collection. That was the wake-up call. At that moment I knew I could open all the doors I desired if I pursued the most affluent clients that passed through that store.

The actor gave me his phone number and I called him the next day. We arranged to bring some of my Impressionist paintings to the house. He and his wife were very complimentary of my work and bought a landscape for three hundred dollars. They didn't want the frame, as it was pretty much just a utility type, to contain the painting. A good French-type frame for an Impressionist painting would cost two or three hundred dollars. I didn't want that kind of investment at first, but I soon learned quality framing sold paintings, and people would pay the additional cost because it looked so much better. When I arrived at his house, he was coming off the tennis court. I told him of my tennis background and he and his friends invited me to play with them at another man's home that following Saturday morning. I remember the man lived off Sunset Boulevard and was the son-in-law of Jack Warner of Warner Bros. Pictures. I played that Saturday and they all realized I was a good player. My years of competitive tennis as a junior had developed a level well above the social tennis crowd. I knew not to show off, and I tried to make everything close so it was an exciting match for everyone. I hit it off with the group and over the next few months, I played a lot of tennis with many in this crowd. I sold quite a few paintings and started putting beautiful frames on them.

I started to frame the Marchand paintings with first class frames as well, and I raised the prices accordingly. These were going to galleries in the United States. This increased my income and I fixed up my studio as a working gallery. I had my works neatly displayed on the walls. I raised the price of the portraits I was selling to seventy-five dollars and put better frames on them. At this price jump, I lost some of the housewife type clientele, but the better presentation helped me to get into the higher social level people. As my contacts grew, I concentrated a lot more on my Impressionist works and the Marchand works for the U.S.

I was working so hard I didn't have much time for women. I had just one girlfriend who came to the studio a day or two each week. She was the secretary to my insurance agent and had a child she was supporting, as well as her mother who took care of him during the day. The father had, according to her, left without a trace. We became a convenience for each other and had some memorable lovemaking sessions.

I was starting to make real money. I bought sharp clothing and continued to pursue the tennis crowd. My game had been getting much better with playing a couple of times a week.

One day I joined Walter Pigeon at the Beverly Wilshire Hotel, which was one of the fancy hotels in Los Angeles. Nearly all the big wigs stayed there, or at the Beverly Hills Hotel. We played doubles with Frank Feltrop, the pro at the hotel and Mickey Rooney, the actor. Rooney was small but a very competitive guy. He and Feltrop beat us, but it was a close and fun match. Rooney was better than Walter was, and I wasn't in Feltrop's class, so it was clearly in their favor. As we finished Howard Duff, the actor, had stopped by and watched the last few games. He loved to bet and said to Frank, "Give this kid two points in each game and I bet he'll whip your ass."

"You're on," said Frank "But he only has time for one set."

No one asked me if I wanted to do that. It was all agreed and Walter left, but Mickey and Howard stood by. I don't know how much money they had riding on it, but it was a lot. I was winning my serve quite easily with the extra points, but losing on his serve until finally I broke it and won the set. Everyone loved seeing Frank lose his money, and a good crowd had gathered, all of whom were rooting for me. Frank took me to lunch that day and it was the beginning of a long friendship. I began to play at the Beverly Wilshire regularly and there are many stories I could tell of our matches with celebrities and scoundrels.

I continued to raise my prices and put even better frames on all of my works. Even at a hundred and fifty dollars, I was still selling a portrait each week. I dropped the Wilshire store to create more of the Impressionist works which were starting to sell. During this period, the Phillipe Marchand paintings were gaining momentum and I was supplying several more galleries. I always worked on these on the weekends when the other artists were not around, or I just didn't open the door. When they were drying, I would face them toward the wall. The Marchand paintings had long been my support and mainstay, but I was determined to arrive at the same point with the work under my own name.

Within a year of my return, I was finished with the department store work. I had gained many good clients and the referrals were mounting. I had raised my price to three hundred dollars and I had the clients come to my studio where I would do the photography, then have them return for one sitting for the final work.

* * *

I had heard a woman in Paris say she had purchased a Marchand in

Chicago, so I researched and found the gallery. The Oldman Gallery in Chicago had all the aspects of an established gallery and, from all appearances, was a successful operation. I called them, representing myself as the agent in the U.S. for the artist, and we arranged an exhibit. The Marchand work had improved considerably, and I framed the show with the best quality. I shipped thirty-two paintings by truck freight, packed in crates I had built in my studio. I remember when the shipment was picked up from my studio both Paul Gerchik and Milton Gershgoren were talking in the hallway. I had carefully concealed my work on the Marchand paintings so I said I was having a show in Chicago. They asked where but I avoided answering the question.

About two weeks later, I flew to Chicago for the show. It was a tremendous success opening night; it was almost sold out and the enthusiasm of the patrons was incredible. Mr. Oldman was eager to get more pieces from me. But I had made a commitment to the Lars Laine Gallery in Palm Springs for a show six weeks later, and everything I could produce would be for that show. I returned to Los Angeles and got to work for the next exhibit.

During the next few weeks, I talked to Mr. Oldman several times and promised him a minimum of six paintings within ninety days. A month later, I still hadn't received a check from the show. I called him to ask for payment on what had sold at the event. He said he was having some collection problems and several clients had not paid him yet, but he would do a final accounting in about a week or ten days. Two weeks later, I called again and he made another series of excuses. He owed me about fifteen thousand dollars and I was beginning to get worried. That was an enormous sum of money in those years.

After about two months, he wouldn't take my calls. The woman who answered told me she had nothing to do with it only that Mr. Oldman said he wouldn't pay me until he received the six paintings I had promised. I wouldn't fall for that as I had determined he was going to stiff me.

After another two months, I had still not received a penny. Because this guy was paying cash to the Paris gallery for the work, I had figured he was solid. I contacted an attorney recommended by a friend. A week later, I learned the gallery had been abandoned; Oldman owed everyone and no one knew where he was. I never heard of him again and never received any money. It was a complete loss. I then made up a rule for myself: a gallery must be in business at least five years and I must have a full credit check done.

The Lars Laine gallery show was also a sellout and Lars paid on time. After the show, he continued to be one of my largest buyers of the Marchand paintings. I still sent part of my production to Paris, but customs and red tape was hindering this part of the operation. It often took two months for the gallery to actually put the paintings in inventory. Those sent to England were not as difficult but still had significant problems.

I had also promoted the Marchand paintings to a local firm by the name of Framecraft. Joe Chabot, the owner, was very successful in selling the work to his clientele. Although I continued to sell the works acting as the American agent for the artist; the selling of my work under my own name was progressing and I had developed a few galleries that wanted the work. Most of the personal contacts I had were reluctant to frequent the Hollywood studio, and I often took pieces to people's homes, which was time-consuming and demeaning, it made me feel like a peddler.

The Gallery

I had established my studio on Hollywood Boulevard producing portraits and creating Marchand paintings to supply the international demand. I decided since I was there nearly every day, I could open a gallery and show my creative work. It would also provide a showplace for dealers who wished to see and choose particular Marchand works. I had developed a mailing list of the various buyers, dealers, and clientele for paintings and the portraits. It was 1957; I had some good publicity when a painting of mine was presented to Nikita Khrushchev when he visited the United States.

Since my living quarters were in my Hollywood studio, I had little expenses and the income from the portrait business and the demand for the Marchand paintings were increasing by the day. I hadn't sent any of the Marchands to France for about six months, as the gallery there owed me money and I hadn't received a check for works I knew had been sold. They claimed the sales had been limited, but if I based the sales on past performance, I was sure they owed me a considerable amount. The only advantage I had was to starve them from a market I knew was thriving. That worked. They realized I didn't trust them at this point and they would lose considerable profit if I didn't send any works to them. When I got the letter and a check from them and the same day received a check from Bullock's for the last month's sales, I saw my account jump over the fifty-thousand-dollar mark. I was flying high thinking about the future.

When I turned 25 that year, I was working an average of more than fifty hours per week and playing tennis at various people's homes. I had a gaggle of women satisfying my needs, and I was expanding the list. Life was great and I had never had everything quite in control at the level I now had. Weeks before I had won the first prize for painting at the west side Jewish Community Center; the second prize was won by Ken Bengor. At the presentation awards, Ken and I sat together with his wife, Barbara. We had a good evening and Ken invited me to his studio in Culver City. I thought he was a very good artist and got his phone number. The following week I called and we had lunch at the greasy spoon near his studio. He was quite industrious and was working on a multitude of canvases, but everything he did was quite different. He had enough technical talent but was trying to do everything, and not concentrating on an objective. Whatever was popular or in vogue became his objective. I asked him why he didn't pursue a single style and purpose. That was the only way his works would become recognizable, which was the key to sales. He rejected this advice and proceeded to tell me what a major talent he was; he considered himself the premier artist of Los Angeles. His basis for this was that Rico Lebrun, regarded as a giant in the art circles of LA, had told him he was of this opinion. He was friends with Rico, and it was through Ken I also developed a friendship with the man.

Some weeks later, I received a phone call from his wife, Barbara. She was having guests over on a Saturday evening and I was invited. The evening was interesting in that most of Ken and Barbara's friends were artists. I didn't move in circles of artists as I had learned in Paris that many developed petty fits of jealousy and would never become clients. I did enjoy the comparative evaluations, which I think every artist needs, but I liked these encounters to be brief, instructional and unemotional, which was very difficult with most painters.

As the evening wore on, I started to understand the man and his frustrations. He was quite small but well built, and he took great pride in bragging about his physical strength. I realized he had a considerable load of complexes which limited his ability to communicate. Although he had a wonderful natural talent, it couldn't be harnessed because of his mental limitations. Barbara, on the other hand, was very down to Earth and intelligent. She was an executive with Prudential Insurance, and I'm sure she paid most of the bills. It was hard to figure out why she was with Ken. He wasn't a very attractive man, and he was only an inch or two taller than Barbara was. He was entirely self-centered, seldom talking about anything but himself and his work. That night I was in the kitchen helping Barbara. I liked her smile; she had a full mouth with gorgeous teeth. She was quite large and robust with brown skin and dark hair. She was of Italian and Greek descent and later in our relationship told me many stories of her family. They were an impressive lot. It became even more bewildering to me she'd be with an uncouth peasant like Ken who was drunk and grandstanding with the guests. Barbara made trips out to bring the food, but I stayed in the kitchen until she returned.

She asked me. "Why don't you want to mix with the guests?"

"I'm quite content to enjoy your company. I'm a one on one kind of person. After many years of nightclubs and crowds, that's just not what I enjoy."

That night Barbara and I laughed and had a fun time together in the kitchen.

The next week she called me. She had thought continually about our evening in the kitchen and asked if we could have some time together. We met that night at a coffee shop on Wilshire Boulevard near the Prudential building. I was returning from a trip to deliver a portrait to Bullock's Westwood. We sat for an hour and a half talking about life, mostly hers. She had great frustrations with Ken's career and she couldn't figure out how he could get into the mainstream art community and start getting some recognition. I was disappointed she just was there to promote her husband. I told her what I could and what I knew. She was appreciative and before I left, I leveled with her and said I was very attracted to her and I had hoped she felt the same.

It was as though the whole conversation before was a sham. She relaxed and told me she also was attracted and had wanted to approach me but didn't quite know how. She said she made many outside calls and could come to my studio and see my work. We made a date for the following Wednesday.

On that Wednesday, I was sure this was going to be an exciting adventure, so I rested well and abstained from my usual rendezvous. About two-thirty in the afternoon she knocked on the door. She had worked from early in the morning and looked a bit tired. I could see she was a little nervous and asked if she smoked grass.

"Oh, yes, that would be wonderful."

I had some smooth stuff that was very electric for lovemaking. After two hits, she wanted more but I told her my rule. I never took more than just enough to get a relaxed high and used it a maximum of one day a week. I explained the years of using it for my singing appearances made me realize too much could become a problem. The two hits were enough. She became very relaxed and after showing her some of my work, I took her in my arms and kissed her. Her reaction was a transformation that took her from the well-groomed and rigid business woman to a passionate and aggressive lover. We were all over each other and barely made it to my living quarters.

After a couple of hours, she began to open up and tell me of her sexual frustrations. Ken rarely made love to her and it was getting less all the time. She suspected that he and a young man I had met at the party were having a relationship. I remembered a Latin looking young actor I had seen there and had thought at the time he was gay. Barbara loved Ken for some reason I couldn't figure out, but that was her cross to bear. I just wanted to enjoy our time together and share her mind and body. A week before my birthday, I told her I was planning a special day for myself and although I would be with friends that day, I would like to see her, too. Lovemaking and painting were my favorite pastimes, so I decided I would plan something that would register my 25th birthday as a landmark.

That morning, on June 13, 1957, I awoke from a very long and good night's rest. At seven I went to Reg's café on Western Avenue and had a light breakfast then returning to the studio at eight-fifteen. I had left the door unlocked and Barbara was early and already there; nude and in bed. As I came through the door, she spread her legs.

"Happy Birthday! This is your pleasure day; I'm doing all the work." It was one of those fun times. We laughed and spoiled each other. I needed it to be somewhat limited as I had planned a busy schedule for the rest of the day. Barbara left about ten and I took another shower and started working on a painting I was enjoying finishing.

The second encounter for the day was with Margo Mirren. She was the wife of Al Mirren, an amateur artist that had approached me at the Bullock's Westwood store when I was giving a portrait painting demonstration. He had asked if I would give him painting lessons. Al was about 68 years old and quite bent over with serious arthritis. He had been a colonel in the Army and retired after a thirty-year career.

He was old beyond his years and in bad shape, but he still had the personality of a military man. He asked me to comes see his work and considering teaching him how to improve. As it turned out, he lived in the Hollywood hills quite close to my studio and I agreed.

When I arrived at his home, my first thought was he must have a lot of money. The house was enormous and impressive, but the furnishings were old. I found out later he had inherited the house and its contents from his mother, along with a very comfortable estate. When I showed up to see Al's paintings I expected to see something fairly accomplished, as he was very knowledgeable about art. He had read extensively and talked as if he was well on his way to exhibiting at a professional level. In Al's eyes, they were special, but to me they were just like the little old lady paintings I had seen in the classes of some of my artist friends. Many of them taught these classes just to get by and continue with their careers. I didn't quite know what to say but complimented him on the considerable effort he had put forth to do so many canvases. I declined to give him any lessons as I was too busy. I wanted to make a run for it and get out of there.

I'm glad I didn't. When we went upstairs from his basement studio, he introduced me to Margo. She was a very young woman. Small but fit; she had a bright and magical personality and was a total contrast to Al. He had met Margo in the Midwest and they had married when he was in his late 40s and she was in her 20s. I can imagine he was quite good looking and dashing in those days. Margo was 40 when we met and later on she explained to me she had such a bad home life she'd have married the devil at that period of her life to get away from it.

When Al went to get something to show to me, Margo asked if she could come and see my work. I gave her my card and asked her to call me. I could see, by the way, that she changed the conversation when Al returned she was planning to come alone. That made me very happy. Al was a bore and Margo was sexy with a firm body that turned me on.

The next day Margo called me. She asked if she could come that afternoon. I had plans, but we set a time for the following day. When she came into the studio and saw my work, she smiled. "Al said you were a real artist, he even admitted you were better than him. I never wanted to burst his bubble; he lives for his paintings, so I encourage and compliment him. But your work is magnificent; I don't know a lot about it, but I can see you're a true artist."

She was open and told me about their life, and they no longer were able to have sex because of Al's physical condition. I asked her what she did about that.

"I try to find partners that are discreet and fun. I don't want to leave Al because he doesn't have long, his health is that bad. So I try to be there as much as I can."

I told her she was a very appealing woman, and I could see she'd be very successful with men. I came right out and told her I would like to be that partner if she felt the same way. She didn't answer, but came close, pressed her body on mine, and looked into my eyes. When we kissed, it went from soft lips to a passion, to mouth orgasm. She was so hot we barely made it into the other studio. We ripped our clothes off and were nude, locked body to body, in seconds. She pulled me on top of her and climaxed during the first penetration. She was small for me and I couldn't push too hard for fear of hurting her, I could feel myself hitting bottom as I thrust forward. She didn't seem to even notice and just became wilder.

That first day cemented our relationship and we had our rendezvous at least once a week from then on. She talked about everything and described her feelings with every action. I found she and Al had been excellent lovers when they were first married, but Al started to slow down in his early 60s, and by 64 he could no longer satisfy her. He thought oral sex was disgusting. She had just masturbated for years and never had anyone who was interested in her satisfaction. I was the first one who made love to and cared for her. She was one of the best lovers I had ever had.

On my birthday, Margo was scheduled for one o'clock. I went out for a quick lunch and tried to eat a lot of protein for energy. I came back and laid down for a quick rest. After a while, I heard Margo's voice in the hallway and went out. She was talking to Paul Gerchik, the artist from next door. His studio was next to my living quarters and he had recognized her from previous visits. He had mentioned how attractive Margo was and had asked me to hold down the screaming when she visited. Paul made a quick exit when I came out. I took her arm and we went into my studio. I showed Margo the painting I was working on.

"I love it... and I have a surprise for you. Al's visiting his sister. I didn't want to go with him so I have the whole day to spend with you!"

I was caught off guard, as she generally would stay no more than a couple of hours. I quickly made up a story that friends were having a party for me, and I had to leave by four o'clock.

"I should have called you because I knew a couple of days ago." She seemed sad then brightened and handed me a small box. I knew right away by the size and the weight it was a watch. When I saw the beautiful gold Bulova, I was a taken aback. Margo was on a tight rein as far as money was concerned. Al gave her a budget for the month and put money in her account. She had told me she had a difficult time not running out of money by the end of the month. I always wondered why Margo would stay with him, and the more I found out about their relationship, the more I couldn't understand why she stayed. I guess she knew he wouldn't be around for a long time and it was too late for her to look for a new life. Margo was much calmer that day, maybe because she wasn't pressed to get home or account for her time. I concentrated on her pleasure. She made a lot of noises, but I thought that would be good for Paul to hear considering his comments.

Although I had had two women before in one day, it wasn't with women I was so familiar with and had such loving feelings. That day would be the first for three women, all of whom I loved and found exciting. When Margo left, it was three-thirty. I felt good, and so I showered and worked a little on the painting while waiting for my third planned rendezvous of the day.

Lillian worked at the Thrifty Drug Store across the street and got off at six o'clock. The store had a lunch counter and she had worked there for several years. She was a well-educated black girl from Michigan. Her parents had moved to Los Angeles when she was in high school. She had started at the University of Southern California, but got pregnant and had to quit. Her son was 8 years old, now and she adored him, but her parents were very disappointed and now she didn't have a good relationship with them. She had had good grades in school and both she and her brother wanted to be doctors. Her brother had completed medical school and was a doctor on the staff at UCLA.

Lilly was small, beautiful, and had about the cutest little bubble butt I had ever seen. She was less than five feet and weighed no more than about ninety-five pounds but was a bundle of energy. She ran the lunch counter with precision. They had specials every day and I always went by just to see if it was one of my favorites. She would see me coming and point to a seat if she knew it was the Mexican plate or the meat loaf. We became friendly over time and one day she asked if she could see my paintings. She came that very day after work. She was surprisingly knowledgeable about Impressionist paintings. She couldn't stay very long as she left her son at a care center and had to pick him up. I asked her if she ever had an evening free and we made a date a few days later. Lilly and I had an exciting affair that night and we had repeat performances on occasion when she got off work. It was always just an hour or so with a date for dinner here and there. She worked six days a week and she wanted to spend as much time as possible with her son. It was difficult for me to understand why she would choose to work at the counter when she was much more qualified to do other things. She told me the job was easy, and she didn't feel stressed.

[Some years later, after I had opened the gallery, she stopped by and I learned she was working downtown at a fashion house, managing a large operation. She loved fashion and had done some drawings of dress designs she brought to the studio one day.]

Our six o'clock date went as planned and I enjoyed her as the finale to my birthday odyssey. She knew it was my special day and brought me a painting smock she had seen at a store near her home. It was a funny looking thing, but very practical if I was dressed in nice clothes and didn't want to change for a brief painting period. She stayed longer than usual and we said goodbye around seven-thirty.

I was spent and wanted to rest and reflect on the day's adventure. About eight o'clock I got a phone call. It was Jennifer Adams. Jennifer had a studio in the next block. She and I had met some months before when I was getting a bowl of Louie's soup across the street. Sitting at one of the three tables was a tall, blond, bombshell. Since all of the tables were taken, I asked if I could join her. She nodded that it was okay, but barely looked up. I noticed she was wearing a work shirt that had red clay on the sleeves. There was also some paint and clay on the front. It didn't match with her perfectly groomed hair and makeup. But, the hands were the giveaway; the nails had red clay under them, and there was a streak of it on her cheek.

I had asked. "Is your studio near here?"

She had looked surprised, and then laughed as she glanced down at her shirt. "And you're a painter," she said.

It was evident as I was wearing my painting clothes. I asked if she worked just in clay and she told me she had a kiln and did ceramics and sculptures. She had castings made of many of her works but had never exhibited. She was also a model and did fashion modeling and commercials. I learned later she was a Stanford University graduate in fine art and had a varied background in music and the arts. She had done some acting, singing and had writing experience, but her main thrust was television commercials. She came from a wealthy family, had tasteful clothes, jewelry, a Porsche sports car and everything a young and beautiful woman would want. She was about five-foot nine inches tall, very slim with a terrific figure. Her blond hair was shoulder length and she had a straight, perfect, nose, and full lips. Even in her jeans and work clothes, she looked like a fashion queen.

I had asked if I could see her work and she said she'd show it to me if I would show her mine. That very day she came by and I showed her what I had in the main studio. We went on to look at her work. She had a studio similar to mine in a building above the hardware store I frequented on the next block. It had the same northern light windows and slightly smaller rooms. She was impressed by my work. When she learned of my background and education, she said she had been looking for someone she could share her artistic feelings. Her work of small abstract sculptures was impressive, but she didn't have any volume of work. She had some pots and plates she had colored and fired, but I learned much of it had been done several years before. She obviously didn't have the time for a concentrated effort. She said she usually had no more than two days each week to work. As a result, she guarded her time in the studio and didn't have many guests. Over a period of months, we had several lunches, and I visited her studio several times. She liked my input on her work and took many of my suggestions. We had some interesting days of discussion and evaluation, but never got on a personal level. She told me she had someone she couldn't see very often because he traveled a great deal.

When I answered the call, I told her it was my birthday and was just going to have an early night. She said she was having dinner with a friend and they would love to have me join them.

"You can't eat dinner alone on your birthday, I won't hear of it."

We met at nine o'clock at the Musso & Frank Grill, a landmark Hollywood restaurant. Her friend was a real character, a writer with movie ambitions. She was off the wall and the three of us had an incredible time. It was almost midnight when we broke it up. Her friend Jo walked off to her car parked down the street. The attendant brought Jenn's car, and she offered to drive me to mine. I was just a couple of blocks away. When she dropped me off, she asked if I would like to follow her home and spend the night with her.

I had had many fantasies about her, but I never thought they would ever materialize. I knew if I rejected this offer it wouldn't be made again. Yet I also knew I wouldn't be a good lover after a day like the one I had had. I accepted anyway and as I followed her, I started evaluating if I could still perform. I would have planned my whole day around only this encounter had I only known. This was the ultimate birthday gift; one of the most beautiful women I had ever known wanted to make my day. But what a day it had been. Everything had gone according to plan and had met my best expectations. Now, here I was following this extraordinary woman and feeling very insecure about my abilities. Yet, woman number three had been hours before, so maybe I would be okay. I had more climaxes than that with just one woman. I decided I had to stay relaxed and perhaps mention I had a very long day. I thought again, no... no excuses; only if there was a problem.

Her apartment was in a very luxurious building and she lived in a garden penthouse. On the walls were some major modern paintings by New York school giants such as Willem de Kooning, Franz Kline, Guston and the like. I realized Jennifer was an heiress or had significant support to live in this lavish style and thought about the man she mentioned; perhaps it was he supporting her. [I learned later it was well-known comedian and actor and he was likely the source of her extravagant life style].

I declined when she offered me a drink and she asked if I wanted a hit on what she described as very special grass. I thought, maybe that would help me to relax and get my horns going. After a few hits, I was feeling it. When she told me she had envisioned me as a different kind of man, I took it as a compliment. I had never made a pass at her; the opportunity had never presented itself. I enjoyed her as a friend so I kept the relationship as a sharing of our art and emotions related to painting and sculpture. She walked me into a bedroom.

"There's a bathroom there and a robe here, if you want to freshen up a bit and then meet me in the living room."

I took a cold shower and because of the grass, it felt like jumping into an ice pool as they do in Sweden. I ran a lot of cold water over me, hoping that would revive me sufficiently. By the time, I was done and sitting on the sofa, I was high. I wanted to just lay back and dream of fanciful things. When Jenn entered the room, she was wearing the sexiest black negligee I had ever seen. I could see through it and her body was the most exciting vision one could imagine. I forgot all of my insecurities and lust took over. When she sat next to me, we didn't hesitate. We kissed and our lips merged. The grass was special as I could feel every part of me responding to her passion.

We practically ran to the bedroom, hand in hand, it was so fast. She pulled me on top of her before even pulling up the sheer black material that covered her. I tugged it clear and then could feel her maniacal thrusts taking me fully into her. I thought I could do this forever. I seemed to have complete control. There wasn't any variety; we just kept going as if it was the natural thing to do. We lasted a long time and she reached her climax so many times I felt like I was Superman.

Finally, she said, "Oh, please finish. I can't keep going or I'll have a heart attack."

I still wasn't close and started to move fast, and hard. Soon I could feel it was getting near and I felt her respond to this final burst of energy. We both met in a surreal moment, and I couldn't believe I could be at this point again. I didn't even remember going to sleep; I just disappeared after that. In the morning when I awoke, she was dressed and brought a tray with coffee to me.

"I tried to wake you before, but you were out cold!"

We had breakfast together and then she had to get to an appointment. I headed back to the studio. When I got there, I lay down on my couch and reviewed the previous day. Okay, I said to myself. Enough. I had enjoyed the planning and the excitement of this special occasion but also I had to evaluate what my lifestyle meant to my future and where I was going. I was truly over indulgent with sex, and if I didn't get hold of myself, I wouldn't be fulfilling my destiny as an artist. I felt that vigor must be channeled more in other directions. So in a way my quarter-century extravaganza was a wake-up call to settle in with one woman and redirect this energy.

I decided Jenn would be the perfect partner. She was everything a man could want and she had money and connections to boot. But it wasn't to be. During that time together, I saw her once a week or less. She was always busy. I figured out she was using me the same way I had used many women; as a lover to satisfy my needs. She had an active life with aspirations beyond anything she had shared with me. I was in love with her in a way, and not being anything more than a friend who gave her a good bump now and then wasn't enough.

[Later, Jennifer married a very well-known divorce attorney in Beverly Hills. We met quite a few times over the years at parties, restaurants, or the like. Every time we had a few words she told me, that first night with me was the most exciting of her life. She always hoped one day we might both be free and renew that experience. It was a good fantasy, but I knew it wouldn't ever materialize.]

Rae

I met a beautiful young actress by the name of Rae Odell, who was studying with Jacobina Caro, a noted acting coach, who had many successful students. She was doing bit parts, secretarial work, or whatever she could while trying to break into the industry. Rae was a talented singer, dancer, mimic, and comedian—not sophisticated or worldly—she had an instinctive feel for what would work. I had been leading a rather austere life, working very hard and concentrating on my career. When I met Rae, her very outgoing personality, her humor and warmth took me. She was seeing a well-known actor who was married and had been told at first he was separated. Then he said he would be getting a divorce and they could be together. This went on for several years. When we met, she was fed up with his promises and had decided to go her own way.

Rae was ambitious in many ways. She was an experienced script girl and valuable in many areas of production. She had stenographic skills and often worked for the Hiram Walker Liquor Company at conventions, shows, and presentations. She had been a full-time employee of the company for several years when she first came to Los Angeles.

Rae, Photo 1958

When we met, I was tired of the chase. I had found few women that didn't become boring after a few dates. I was playing tennis at the homes of many theatrical personalities and had become friends with people who Rae thought could be of assistance to her career. We hit it off, mentally and physically, and I was in lust. Quickly and foolishly, Rae and I ran off to Las Vegas and married. We got an apartment very close to my studio, a large one-bedroom place two blocks from the corner of Hollywood and Western. The next two years, we both worked hard and spent as much time together as possible.

I felt the major drawback to selling my paintings was that the tennis crowd and the clients I had developed didn't like to venture out of their comfort zone. I mentioned my friendship with Frank Feltrop previously. Frank was always terrific at introducing me to people. He would tell them of my talent and that they should see my work. And many of them would express their desire to see it, but when they learned of the location of my studio they usually never got around to it. So Rae and I moved into a large two-bedroom apartment in the center of Beverly Hills. It was a lovely building with easy access and good wall space. Soon friends and clients were coming by regularly and sales were increasing. I could see that soon I would be ready to open a legitimate gallery.

Rae was still taking acting classes and I went often to see her perform. There I met some lifelong friends in her class. Joanne Quackenbush wasn't just a great beauty, but also one of the sweetest and nicest people. I loved her from the first meeting, and we've been friends all of our lives. She almost married Frank Sinatra but turned him down. It wasn't the kind of life she wanted and she wasn't in love with him. She married Alan Kane and they have three daughters and have had a beautiful life. Ben Frank the actor and I had wonderful times together and he was a friend until he died. He was one of the great characters I reflect on often. His wife Helene was a pistol; she loved my paintings and encouraged Ben to buy several of them. I had a very wild experience with some of his friends some years later.

Ben had worked as a tout for the race track in his earlier years and had met this character named Carl. He brought Carl to my studio, and he bought a painting from me as a gift for his wife. He paid me in hundred dollar bills, all cash from a wad that would choke a hippo. I took the painting down to his car and put it in the back seat of a Rolls Royce. Ben explained to me he owned a horse racing tip sheet that was hustled at the track. The tip sheets had a phone number for exclusive information.

A week later Ben called me and said Carl wanted me to join them for a little party they were having and I accepted. They lived in a large mansion in Bel Air. Carl suggested I come alone as he had an attractive woman coming as well who was very enamored with my painting. When I arrived, he introduced me to Karen. She was very tall and quite slim, with what I immediately recognized as sizeable implants. They were pointed and stuck straight out, which was the style at the time. Her hair was blond, but it was obviously a magnificent beautician's creation. She was very striking in a skin tight outfit; beautiful teeth and a big smile, and an outgoing personality to go with it. Janet, his wife, was very attractive, and in her early thirties. It surprised me as Carl was in his mid-fifties or even older. A young man rounded out the guest list. He was obviously gay and quite flamboyant, handsome and almost beautiful as a woman. He was tiny with black hair and very blue eyes. He reminded me of the gay motorcycle toughs that hung around the county line restaurant near the surfer's beach. Carl and he seemed quite chummy, and Carl took on a bit of macho, big deal, attitude with him. Carl was very distinguished looking, but it ended there, as he was low-class and his language was crude and quite disgusting.

We had a mediocre dinner and I started to see the scene that was about to take place. I figured Carl and his wife were expecting a little ménage a trois, with the gay caballero, and the tall one might just be interested in seducing me. I would always get a little nervous when there was a gay situation forming. I had learned to avoid anything that might be embarrassing and awkward to handle. We adjourned to the living room and had drinks. Karen asked Carl what he did to make the predictions at the racetrack. What he told us in his inebriated condition was a revelation to a novice like me that had only been to the track a dozen times in my life.

He told us. "We handicap like anyone else, but we tell people we have inside information and the best experts in the business. They call us and we tell them it's five dollars for each race that we provide our picks. We do it on the honor system; they give us their name and telephone number. We call them back to verify the number and we ask them to send us the money in cash. I have five people that are good on the phone, and they make good money hustling the clients.

"At the end of the day, we make up a list of each operator's winners. We provide two types of suggestions, our pick of the winner which is often a favorite, and the best long shot we feel has a chance. The lists are followed up each day with a new suggestion for the following day. When we have a winner that has paid five dollars, we tell him we want twenty-five for the next pick, as we say we have inside information. If we get a second winner, we know we can milk the guy. We wait a few days and place a call; he answers or we leave a message. We tell him we have a special deal and we want five hundred dollars for the tip. The money must be delivered before the following day's races. We receive the money from individuals, messenger services, wives, friends or the guy himself. If he comes, we get him into a room with Jim or me. We know we need to massage the guy in case we have another winner of even if it doesn't pay off. In which case, we give him a freebie to try to recapture him.

"If we give him another winner, then I take over. I can get a guy to sell his house, his wife, mortgage everything he has to make a substantial bet. We ask for a varying amount, depending on how much he bet before, and how much we think we can get up front. We might ask for five thousand dollars, even up to twenty-five thousand if we believe he's a big hitter. Let's say we get five thousand dollars and we give him another winner. We then call him and ask how much he had bet. If it doesn't make sense with the five he has paid up front, we say we don't want to do any more business with him. That we won't give him any more information if he's not honest with us. Usually, we can get them to come clean; they think they have a money factory on their hands. After four winners, we can get them to do almost anything. We usually wait for a period, until they call us and then we say we just don't have any sure things at the moment. Then after we let him stew for a while, we tell him we have something that only happens a couple of times each season. At that point, we can get him to do anything."

I asked, "How many winners have you had for one person?"

"We had seven winners on one streak, with four people on the line. They all lost on the eighth race, they screamed and yelled and told us they had lost everything. We just say horses are animals and anything can go wrong. We're sorry, but we will make it up to them with another tip. Once they're used up, it's hard to get them back, but it does happen."

I didn't want to listen further. I thought to myself, these are low life types that prey on the addiction of gamblers. Then I started to think Karen was probably some hooker working in one of Carl's other sidelines. He went into a lot more detail as the others asked questions. He seemed quite proud of the fact he personally could milk a guy to the bone with his understanding of addiction and his prowess as a salesman. Then the gay friend, I didn't learn his name, started to describe his work as an actor and said he was friends with Rock Hudson; they had the same agent, Henry Wilson. Tab Hunter was a close friend and confidant, too, according to his stories.

As they finished their stories I was sitting on the sofa, on one side of the enormous coffee table, with Janet. She was reticent, but we talked a bit. She said she loved the painting Carl had given her and she'd like to have more. I didn't like Carl, but Janet was very soft and very sweet. I wondered how she ever got involved with such a con man, sleaze bag. The plot began to thicken as Karen, Carl, and Boy Wonder started to play around with each other. Dope was passed around and I agreed to have some grass, but I didn't use cocaine or any of the other variety of pills and mescaline they were indulging in. Karen opened Carl's fly and held his cock up. Boy Wonder started to suck him off while Karen was undoing his pants and stripping her own blouse off to expose the breast implants she was quite proud of. Janet seemed to ignore what was going on across from us. She stood and told me she wanted to get something and would be right back.

A few moments later she brought a photo album and set it on my lap. I proceeded to look at it. It was difficult as the scene taking place in front of me was quite interesting, but I ignored it. The first few pages had pictures of Janet in an evening gown. I flipped the page and the next pictures were of her sitting on the pool table, her lovely dress pulled up to the waist and her pussy positioned over one of the corner holes. Carl was in the foreground making a shot at her bush. Next was a series of nude shots, pussy close-ups, and all manner of lewd poses. As I thumbed through the pages, Janet smiled at me and asked if I liked what I saw.

"Yes," I said, "very exciting to say the least."

"Let's go to the pool," she said. "I like to fuck in the pool."

I followed her. It was just getting dark and still quite warm. Poolside, she stripped her clothes off and then helped me undress.

She was a petite woman, with a sensational figure. When we got in the water, she was all over me, rubbing and coiling like a water snake. We tried fucking on the pool steps. It wasn't working too well, so we got out and went to a chaise lounge. When we were into it hot and heavy, I felt my ass being rubbed and a hand on my balls. I was afraid it was Boy Wonder, the gay blade. I turned my head to see it was Karen.

"I like to watch you two fuck, it's very stimulating."

Janet said. "You fuck him, now and I'll watch, but you have to give him up when I want him back."

I laid on the lounge and Karen straddled me. Her long legs stretched back beside me and her body moved up and down with Janet down on her knees behind her watching at close range. Karen's bush was trimmed to a heart shape and was bleached blond like her head hair. She had a big pussy. I found myself wondering if she had been with Carl a few minutes before.

I asked her, "I thought you were screwing Carl."

"No," she said. "Valentino is fucking Carl, and he doesn't like cunts. I wanted to see what he was all about, but he didn't go for that."

Janet came behind me and lowered the lounge. I couldn't see what was going on, but I was aware she and Karen were kissing and playing with each other. I was moving inside Karen and trying to hold back but it was just too much and I reached a hard climax. Janet could feel it and brought Karen to a climax shortly after by rubbing her. I could feel it and it prolonged my own sensation.

Karen stood up after and said. "Whew, that was a good one;

nice meeting you, Chris. I have to get going. I promised to drop by some friend's house and I'm late." With that, she went into the house and I never saw her again.

Janet said, "Well, she's happy, you're happy, and I'm horny. Can you go another time after a while?"

"I can go anytime with a woman like you."

But I was disappointed when we were unable to continue right there and then. Instead, we went into the house, carrying our clothes with us into a bedroom near the pool. I suspected it was a guest room for such events as there were more intimate photos of parties and of many people, I didn't know. I was surprised at seeing Ben and his wife Helene there in all their glory at one of the nude poolside festivities. Janet went to the other room and Carl and his love mate were passed out on the big animal skin rug in front of the fireplace. It was a phony, ugly, looking thing and I could imagine the two of them on it as Janet described.

I was happy to hear they were out of the picture and Janet and I could relax a little more. We had a great session, and I learned she liked pain; the harder I would penetrate her the more she responded. I knew it must be hurting her, but she reached a climax repeatedly when I was the most brutal. It was a different evening and an adventure, but I made up my mind on my way home I wouldn't be snared into their rituals. They were just too far out there to get more involved. The drugs turned me off. I realized even Janet, who acted normal, was high at the time. She came to my studio one day, soon after, and bought another painting. She invited me to their house and said she'd like to be with me again. I deflected; not committing. She called several times after that and I always made an excuse. I never saw them again.

Ben and I continued to be friends and he would often stop by my gallery. He did very well as an actor He was a rough character and played gangster parts to perfection. But he was a heavy smoker and died in his mid-50s. Before he passed away, he made some great anti-smoking film clips often shown on TV.

***

Rae never made it big in the movies. She was active mostly in small parts. Over time I realized she had some personality disorders. She had uproarious highs, but devastating lows. When she had the lows, it was as if she was possessed by demons and didn't want to talk or be touched. She went on location often, particularly with the famous cinematographer James Wong Howe.

Since I wanted to play tennis or paint in the mornings, I set my gallery hours at noon until six o'clock on weekdays and noon until four on Saturdays. I was closed on Sunday and Monday which was a tradition with the galleries in Los Angeles. The gallery progressed very well, and I was leading the good life. One day a friend, Bud Atkins, came by the gallery and said he wanted to talk to me. We had initially met on the boat coming back from France. Bud had been a very successful motorcycle racer in Europe. He retired within the next couple of years and started a well-known shop in the San Fernando Valley.

After we had exchanged pleasantries, Bud said, "I have to tell you something I heard. I feel I wouldn't be your friend if I didn't tell you. I checked it out with several others and it seems they knew but never wanted to say anything."

It was evidently common knowledge Rae was having an affair with her agent and was also sleeping with James Wong Howe while on location. She was using her body to try to get recognition as an actress, which is common in Hollywood.

That evening when I got to the apartment, Rae was dressing and I asked her if she was going out. She said her agent was introducing her to some important people and hopefully she'd be reading for a part. I confronted her and said I knew what she had been doing, and I was very disappointed in her. Her answer was she did it for both of us so she could have a successful career. I told her if she went out that night with her agent, I wouldn't be there when she returned. She went out, and I left. I made several trips in my car to get everything back to the Hollywood Boulevard studio that night. I collapsed at two in the morning on my sofa-bed; I was at a real low point in my life.

Rae and I met and I took all of my paintings I had in the apartment, except what I felt were three of my best Fauve works. Rae said she wouldn't give them to me, as they were her favorites. I was so disgusted I just left them and walked away. I told her if she wanted anything more I wouldn't oblige. If she pursued me in court, I would name Vince Edwards, James Wong Howe and all of the celebrities she had been sleeping with.

My marriage to Rae was perhaps typical of the first attempt to live a life with a woman. I had a lot of experience with women and some short periods of sharing my feelings and space with a possible mate. There were so many excuses and reasons to bring it to an end that I doubted in the beginning I would ever marry again. I awoke the next morning and thought to myself, you have the gallery, the studio, a good income, and money in the bank. That's all you need. I shut the past out and thought of it as a new opportunity. I would have the freedom to date and move about much more freely than before, and I was sure I could parlay my freedom into new adventures.

Rae came to the gallery about eight months later and apologized for her actions. She wanted to get back together. I told her no, I had put it behind me, I was involved with several older women and I didn't want to look back.

[I didn't see Rae again for almost forty years. Until one day, I received a call in my Malibu home. I had become very successful, both financially and personally. I had a wife I loved dearly and perhaps Rae knew this. She said she wanted to see me. I agreed only because I thought I might be able to buy the paintings she had kept. They were landmark works that would fit into my plans for an art center and museum I intended to build and dedicate at some point in my future. She was living in an old run down motel in Van Nuys, that rented by the month. She was on welfare living in a room filled with useless garbage; like that of street people. When I asked her about the paintings, she said she had given them away to a young artist who admired them. She didn't even remember his name. I took her to lunch and wrote her a substantial check with the understanding she wouldn't contact me again. I couldn't understand how a talented singer and actress could sink to a position like that. She was never a very stable person; she had been raped many times growing up by her step-father. Her mother was never concerned about her, and her brother was working at menial jobs when we were together. Rae was a sad story as she had great talents, but she was used up by Hollywood, like so many others. I've never heard from her since.]

* * *

In 1958, I had a show of new work: experimental visions based on the Fauve paintings which were a remarkable transition when introduced in 1905. These raw and vibrant works got their name from that word meaning, wild beasts. I had reacted strongly to them and had for years meant to build upon the premise of pure color. I introduced a thick black outline which was partially ingrained by doing the Marchand paintings. To create them I rented a house in Guaymas in Mexico for three months. I wanted the brilliant sunshine and scenery to enhance the color and let me escape from the California atmosphere for a while.

The show was at the Perreau-Saussine Gallery on Santa Monica Boulevard in West Hollywood. Richard Perreau and his sister, actress Gigi Perreau had the gallery. It presented some of the most famous and significant works by many deceased European artists. The local artists he showed were first class. The show had moderate success, about twelve of my paintings were sold and several drawings. The reviews were excellent and Richard seemed pleased. I was paid for everything, but it took a little time, and I became aware they were not doing well financially. They represented me until Richard closed the gallery two years later. I showed only the Fauve works with him as I was showing my Impressionist work in my own Hollywood studio gallery. Richard moved to Paris and became a successful dealer there for decades to follow.

* * *

In 1960, I opened the fifteen-hundred square-foot, Galerie De Ville on Beverly Boulevard across the street from the famous Chasen's restaurant. Frequented by many in the entertainment world, it was perhaps one of the best-known high-end eateries in Hollywood. The galleries proximity to Chasen's was beneficial. Some friends helped me establish it and I had a partner, Addie Feldman. She was a trim and bright lady with many contacts in Beverly Hills. We were introduced by my friend, and longtime tennis professional, Frank Feltrop. Addie and I played tennis many times and I had told her of my plans to open a gallery. She wanted to be a part of it, so it all came together.

Galerie de Ville

Gallery Interior

Actor Barry Coe, Colleen Gray, Christian, Virginia Mayo, Michael O'Shea
(At the Marchand Opening)

Within a year, she had become bored with the long hours sitting and waiting for clientele. She was a good painter, but we agreed that neither of us would show our own work. Phillipe Marchand was our mainstay for sales and supported the gallery in the first years. Addie introduced me to many of the people of means she knew and I took her to some homes of people I played tennis with all the times we played together on the courts below his home, I was never invited up to the house. And he never once came to the gallery. No one ever seemed to know what he collected, if anything.

The gallery did well for the next couple of years and I bought Addie out. But it was a minor gallery compared to the many high-end Beverly Hills galleries. They showed the big name, deceased artists, mostly the French.

Frank Feltrop had moved from his position at the Beverly Wilshire Hotel and became the head professional at the Westside Standard Club. The Standard Club had ten courts and a large number of Beverly Hills, Westwood, and Bel Air members. Frank was a wonderful friend. I helped him when he needed a hand with lessons and classes and often played with him in his wild matches with many other pros and celebrities. I had given him a few of my paintings, including a major Marchand. Frank and Addie never knew I was Phillipe. I always used the excuse he was very reclusive and would only work through me. I had a particular company that copied the French stretcher bars, as they were quite different from the American style, and I kept the Marchand identity a guarded secret.

I had given up the portraits except for fat commissions when I would work with many sittings. During that period, I did Frank Sinatra, Sammy Davis Jr., Mel Torme, and many other well-known people. I was spending so much time producing the Marchand works

I had to hire a full-time associate in the gallery. I let everyone know I was in the gallery on Wednesday and Saturday afternoons and tried to play tennis in the mornings.

More and more I was selling works to Framecraft. They had merged with a publishing company and wanted to publish the Marchand paintings, offering a book deal with a series of twenty-four framed prints that would be sold nationally. It was excellent money and they had become the largest buyer of the paintings. This would increase it many times.

I was just getting started with Framecraft when one Saturday a nice-looking, tall dark-haired, man came through the door. He was quite handsome but a little disheveled, with dirty tennis shoes. I said hello, and he greeted me and then proceeded to view all of the work in the gallery. He said he liked many pieces and that they were very reasonably priced. He then told me earlier in the day he had visited the Stephen Silagy Gallery and had been asked to leave. Silagy was a Romanian jerk who thought just because he showed the great masters of the French Impressionist movement it made him something special. He catered to the super-rich and didn't have a use for anyone he thought wasn't a buyer. When the man told me that, I was furious. I told him what I thought of Silagy. I didn't believe this man was a buyer either, but he seemed to be intelligent and friendly. He was good company for the afternoon, very knowledgeable about art, and seemed to know Paris very well. We had an interesting talk that day, and he said he would be back. The next Saturday he came in again. This time, he was with Edward G. Robinson. I immediately recognized the famous actor and I was aware he had one of the best art collections in Los Angeles. They spent fifteen minutes or so and then were on their way.

That week I got a call from a woman representing Mr. Robinson, who asked if I did appraisal work. I replied, "I'm a member of the American Society of Appraisers." She asked if I would come to the house and do an appraisal for insurance purposes. When I came to the house, Mr. Robinson introduced me to his wife, Gladys and his secretary. He told me he and his wife had to leave and didn't have much time, but the secretary would show me the collection. I spotted a Rouault painting which I knew well, and we proceeded to talk about it. He asked what I thought about this and that type of art. When he realized I had a doctorate and had done my thesis on the French painters, Rouault, and Soutine, and spent many years in Paris, he showed a much greater interest. He sent his wife on without him and we spent several hours together discussing the paintings and their value. I had been recently inquiring about getting consignments from various galleries in Paris and I was very current on the values. There were many pieces seriously undervalued. Eddie and I became friends and he sent many people to me to purchase and to consign important pieces to my gallery for sale. He came in many times and we had some wonderful conversations about art. He was a small man and I had never realized it when he was on the screen. But he became much larger through his superb acting. A nicer man you couldn't find.

"By the Creek" godsons Christian & Jesse Powell

The unkempt gentleman who came in that first day turned out to be Marty Rackin, head of Paramount Studios. Marty came in many times and he and I became good friends. He was one of the wittiest people I have ever met. One night Marty and his wife Helen, Henry Silva the actor and his wife Ruth, and Charles Bragg the satirist and his wife Gina, all had dinner at my home. I remember that night as one of the funniest evenings I've ever spent. Charles had a crazy sense of humor, as evidenced by his work, and Henry could say the most outrageous things with complete seriousness. Marty had a special way of commenting on most everything. During the following year after we met, Marty sent many people to me.

284

"Train Station in Soller" Mallorca Spain, Oil on canvas

One day he came into the gallery and said he had talked to Stanley Kramer, who was getting a divorce and must sell his collection of masterpieces. Marty helped me arrange the collection and put it up for sale. I had a grand opening and Marty had the publicity department of Paramount Studios give me a hand in getting into the press. He had Edith Head there to host the show and every top star in Hollywood came. I arranged with Chasen's to help accommodate all the cars and we had a sign, Parking Compliments of Chasen's. That exhibit was the start of recognition and prestige for the gallery.

Years went by and the list of celebrities and profits grew.

Framecraft's efforts secured the name of Phillipe Marchand; the book was published and I received several hundred copies. Unfortunately, the partnership didn't work out and the financial obligations for Framecraft became too much and the business failed. Joe Chabot died a few years later of a heart attack and I will never forget the personality and physical change that took place.

The gallery continued to prosper and I started spending much more time as a dealer. I wined and dined some of the most wonderful older women in the area. I joined dinner parties where families fixed me up with friends and daughters, and along with the gallery, I was often in the columns associated with celebrities. During this period, Marty introduced me to David Tebet the head of television entertainment for NBC. David then introduced me to Pamela Mason, the ex-wife of actor James Mason. Pamela was an actress, writer, and movie columnist who moved in a world of exciting people. Our long history of friendship was one of the most extraordinary things in my life, as she was the most intelligent and bright in that world of exceptional people. On my trips to New York, David had me join him for many elegant affairs and gave me tickets to all the best shows. The NBC limousine was often at my service, and the dealers I visited always made a comment if they saw my transportation. Because of his introduction to men like Nelson Rockefeller, I had the opportunity to spend time with and come to know many exceptional men.

About that time, I was asked to go to Pasadena to the home of a man I understood had an exceptional collection of American paintings. I had requested a list of the works in advance and boned up on the artists I didn't know, which was most of them. I had not studied the American Impressionists, and the artists and prices were new to me. When I saw these examples of the Americans and their

Impressionist style, I was stunned, I had no idea they were anywhere in the league of the French. Many had gone there to study and to work alongside the French masters.

It turned out the man was the son of the Newcomb-Macklin picture framing company of Chicago. He had traded framing for paintings with the now known great masters of American Impressionism. I took many photos of the collection and advised him it would be a couple of weeks to do an accurate evaluation. A few days later, I went to New York to all of the known American art galleries. When I saw the auction book prices, I just assumed the bulk of the work sold had been of inferior quality and that was the reason for such low prices compared to the French. I knew those because I had been receiving the catalogs for the French Impressionists from Europe and the Parke-Bernet auction galleries in New York.

I bought all the back catalogs of this new realm of artists from the auction houses and went to the museums and the best galleries to see their work. I bought some books for further research and remained in New York for a week. It meant getting behind on everything in Los Angeles, but I was excited about the works I had seen. I went to see Norman Hirschl and bought some pieces from his gallery. I had spent over a hundred thousand dollars, a good part of my available money [it would be over a million dollars today]. The involvement in this new realm of artists stimulated my desire to perfect my own impressionism and I feel I made significant strides because of this influence.

This landmark trip secured my direction as an art dealer. I realized the Americans were superb Impressionist painters and their work was underpriced compared to the French artists of the same period. There wasn't a serious gallery in Los Angeles that represented the American Impressionist painters. Over time, several opened but they represented earlier American paintings. So I began to specialize in the American Impressionists. I had a singular interest in the group which surrounded Monet in Giverny, and I wrote articles and became an expert in their techniques and work.

My own paintings and those of the Marchand pen name were a primary source of income. The reinvestment of that income was what built an inventory to compete with the best of the New York galleries. The De Ville name became very well-known. I made trips around the country to the major cities to buy and sell to the other dealers. I convinced people the American Impressionists were a good investment, and I built many fine collections all over the country. As it turned out, my estimate of the values was conservative. The collections I developed achieved valuations beyond my wildest dreams. I became a hero, and many delightful friendships developed which made my life extraordinary.

[I've loved being a dealer. That intimate exposure to the incredible talents that preceded me led to friendships with so many wonderful people. When I was in my thirties, I came across a new book on Picasso, titled, "Picasso's Picassos" and it clearly showed he had kept much of his best works. I decided to do the same, and, as a result, I now have a great variety of my life's work. I have kept many of my favorite works of art and my personal collection grew over the years I was active in the gallery. It became a collection of the best examples of many of the American Impressionist School. My collection is a daily joy and we have the objective to eventually build an art center and museum to display it and the many works I've produced and saved for this purpose. My life in the world of art has made it something distinctive. Even after the closing of the gallery in the year 2000, I maintained storage and a showroom. To this day, my associate, Lisa Warnstedt, who has been with me for thirty years, manages the collection and many of my personal properties.]

With the considerable business of the Marchand work and the new gallery location, I began to operate in a more businesslike manner. After the first year, I added an associate to work full-time and to help with the coordination of the selling and shipping. I had purchased and made improvements to an apartment house in the valley, and the sale of that property had given me considerable cash. With the cash flow of the Marchand paintings, I was accumulating money to promote some artists I added to the roster of works available at the gallery.

Many other events added to this scenario. The exhibiting of the Stanley Kramer collection and the new interest in the American painters changed my thinking and the gallery direction. I started to spend large amounts of my savings on inventory because of my belief in the American Impressionists. I wanted the gallery to become known for their work, and I was the only dealer in the country to specialize in them. I would make several trips each year to New York to the auctions at Parke-Bernet Galleries when there was a picture in which I was interested. On each trip, I would stop a few days in a different city or two on my way. I would visit the various galleries, antique dealers, and curators to make contact and tell them of my particular interest in both buying and selling in this category.

As the years progressed, I became known as the dealer who specialized in the Americans that lived and worked in Paris and Giverny and followed the Impressionist doctrine. I always paid my obligations on time and developed a reputation for prompt payment and honesty. People wanted to sell to and buy from me. When a major painting would come on the market, I would often be the first one they called. I had continued this specialty for more than ten years before these painters started to reach a level of popularity where all of the major galleries were after the same paintings. Most of the galleries didn't want to limit themselves to a single area of the art world so they would work in a much broader segment of the market. Although my focus limited my opportunities for both buying and selling, I had no interest in the earlier Americans, nor did I wish to represent the modernists. At this point, I could see there were other areas into which I could expand.

I opened a framing operation when the opportunity presented itself. The Framecraft Corporation had folded and they had been my largest distributor of the Marchand work. And they were my sole framing source, so there was a void. To fill it I opened Museum Classic Picture Frames with several of the employees from Framecraft. I purchased a manufacturing building on Jefferson Boulevard and soon I was making frames for many clients as well as filling my own needs. I brought the quality of the frames to a new level and, although very expensive, I developed a significant business. I saw some parts that had been molded with polyurethane foam and I was impressed with this new technology. My brother came into the business and we started experimenting with a process that could produce frames cast directly from exquisitely carved frames, in flexible molds. The lack of weight and density was a problem, so we started inserting wood backing when doing the casting. We developed a method of metal-leaf with a clear polyurethane coating which after the final finish resembled an authentic gold-leaf appearance. It was a considerable cost saving without the loss of the look I wanted. I purchased a building on Melrose Avenue, a much larger space where I also had a framing department and more exhibiting space.

Other galleries and dealers across the country started to use my frames and the business grew to twenty employees. During this period original signed and numbered prints became the rage. I had developed several very talented artists, so I opened the De Ville Publishing arm of the business. The artists were very pleased as it gave them additional income without extra work. It also gave them distribution and recognition which could expand well beyond that which could be accomplished with just individual works.

The publishing business was an instant success. We grew to eight employees after the first year; mostly salespeople, as we farmed the serigraphy out to a firm which specialized in this type of hand, pulled prints. Then the key employee of this firm quit and the quality of the work suddenly wasn't what I was willing to accept. I met with the disgruntled employee, signing a contract and giving her sufficient money to set up a business of her own to do the work. This was a blessing as the quality improvement and the saving of time were significant. A young saleswoman who was a dynamo within the organization was so good at sales and running the operation.

At that time, we changed the company name to Colville Publishing, I wanted a name not associated with the De Ville Galleries. My aim was to build something that would have value as a separate entity. The result was I was making substantial money, but I wasn't doing what I loved most. And between the framing business and the publishing business, the employee problems grew. I learned the fewer employees you had to deal with, the better. I took in a partner in the framing business for a small percentage. We had met during summer sailing excursions to the Mediterranean. Their involvement helped me to maintain time to produce my personal work.

My ventures generated major cash and I began to look for more opportunities to buy significant paintings. I started to buy and sell the mainstream French Impressionists, Picasso's, and many of the French modernist painters. I found dealing in them that the income became sizeable enough that the other businesses became secondary.

About that time, I had a bad experience with the partner I took in the framing business. Evidently, when he was picking up work for framing, he was also helping himself to other inventory. Over a period of nearly a year, we had a half million dollars in missing inventory. One day we received a catalog from Sotheby's in New York. In it was one of our missing pieces, a George Bellows! We reported it immediately to the FBI and the auction house and it was pulled from the auction. Within a month, the FBI informed us the piece was sold, to the person who submitted the painting, by Don Fonger, my partner in the framing business!

I was so upset, as I had taken this sailing friend into the company, taught him the ropes and made him a partner. That fact he would steal from me was one of my big disappointments in life. None of the other missing work ever surfaced. I closed the business, washed him out, and rented the building. I sold off the inventory of the publishing company for a major sum to a cruise line supplier and gave the business to the employees.

* * *

[Several years later, I closed the De Ville Galleries and put the inventory in storage, but I continued to make private dealings, and my associate Lisa Warnstedt continued to look after the business. At that time, I was 70 years old and felt it was time to divorce myself completely from the daily pressure of being an art dealer and concentrate on my personal painting. I rented the gallery building and the factory locations. Four years later, I had a heart attack. It was mild, but I had a triple by-pass operation and decided I would simplify my life. I also made another significant change in my business life. Over time, I had purchased some storefront locations. My holding of a building on Santa Monica's Third Street promenade became an issue with a large building firm that wanted the property for development. It seemed they had purchased all of the surrounding buildings for the project and mine was the last step in the plan. Because I said I wasn't interested in selling, they offered me a list of other buildings they were holding. The Criterion Theater building and the adjoining building was in their inventory. I took the location in trade and paid them an additional sum to conclude the deal. I hired an architect and engineers to give me all the possibilities and then proceeded to design the building myself. It was a two-year project. Santa Monica made many allowances to convince me to not only build the project but to make a public walkway through the building from the parking structure behind. I completed the project and it turned out to be an award-winning design. I occupied the entire third floor of the office building with Colville Publishing. I gave up my Hollywood studio after thirty-five years and made the whole penthouse floor of seven thousand square-feet a private exhibition area and studio.

The Third Street Promenade became a very popular venue; more than a million people a month were frequenting the attractions. Seven restaurants including Wolfgang Puck, McDonald's, Subway, and a combination of very successful operators made the location the most popular spot on the Promenade. I had a full-time manager and a full-time superintendent, as well as some thirty-five other employees. The theaters were a lease situation, but the flow of traffic worked for both of us. But I had become disenchanted with the Criterion Theater Plaza, as the city of Santa Monica had double-crossed me on every promise made. Even with the assurances of many letters, the attorneys said it was a battle not worth fighting. A friend of mine who had just sold his major oil company was looking for 1031 exchanges and had an enormous amount of money he had to identify within the ninety-day period allowed by the IRS. I packaged my holdings and we made a deal. I had never had a loan in my life, all of my holdings were owned outright and without partners. I took the money and again was in the position of a ninety-day limit. If you run over this deadline, there would be a fifteen percent capital gains tax at that time.

After a lot of research and working many hours each day, I settled on Atlanta as a logical place to own property. The city was business oriented and the area I was interested in was one of the highest income areas in the country. I bought major buildings with national tenants that guaranteed triple net leases. No headaches, no obligations, just a check in the mail. I had a considerable balance and invested heavily in oil and gas leases, an avenue I had pursued for many years. I sold off all of my holdings in foreign investments and put the money in certificates of deposit with major credit rated banks internationally. All this simplified my life and my associate was able to handle all of my affairs without outside assistance, except attorneys and accountants.]

* * *

In the early 1960s, I was an art dealer, writer, artist, and ghost painter. I had given up the portrait commissions as they made my life difficult. People had no idea of what a portrait was supposed to be, they just wanted the flattery they couldn't get from a photo. If you captured the character of the person, even if it was brilliantly done, they had no interest. I really enjoyed painting people, but it became a downer. I loved life and I would never let anything depress me for a significant period.

I was involved with many group exhibits, and in 1962, I had a one-man show at the Frederic Hobbs Gallery in San Francisco. I showed with him for several years until he eventually closed the gallery. Throughout the 60s, I had shows of my Impressionist work in Dallas, Chicago, Atlanta and New York. All were successful and I continued with most of the galleries for ongoing representation. By the mid-70s, I had built a good clientele for my Impressionist work and the Marchand paintings continued to be popular. The book on Marchand and the national distribution of framed prints boosted the demand. The work I produced was all sold in advance and I was very busy as a dealer.

But the time required to develop my business interests was a detriment to my painting career. I had produced a significant body of work that was truly individual. It became a combination of my greatest Impressionist work and the Marchand experimentation. After the art dealing took on the proportions of the big ticket items, the time spent on the production of the Marchand works wasn't worthwhile. I discontinued that work and incorporated the design elements and the time and skill of my finer work into the mix.

* * *

[In 1984, I had a show at the Grand Central Galleries in New York that was successful and they represented me until they closed in about 1995. Their closing was a sad event as it was one of America's oldest and most respected galleries. Unfortunately, the dealer, although a well-intentioned person, didn't have a solid grasp of business, and the board and financiers of the gallery had become discouraged and wouldn't continue to support it.

"Mona Lisa," Oil on canvas

"Beach Picnic," Oil on canvas

In 1988, I had a show at the De Ville Galleries, the first time in my own gallery. It was a spectacular opening; the entire show was sold that night. It was the most rewarding exhibit experience of my life. Friends and clients raved about the work and I personally felt it was the best assembly of my mature Impressionist work I had ever put together. It was an evening of glory and accomplishment. It was at this point I wanted to abandon the Marchand part of my life. Although it continued to be successful monetarily, there were no psychological rewards to using a pen name. The success as a dealer and my personal work under my own name had become the mainstream of my life.]

"Mars & Venus," & "Suck Face," Oils on canvas

298

Escape to Central Park

V

THE MIDDLE YEARS

12

CLAIRE

In 1960, after my decision to separate from Rae, and a few days after moving my things into my studio, I contacted a friend, Stephanie Farnay. Her father was, at the time they came to America, the Belgian Ambassador. She was the girlfriend of movie producer Geza de Rosner and I knew she had a guesthouse behind her rented home that her father used occasionally. I wanted to see if I could rent it for a while.

I had met her when Geza and I worked on the film the *Legend of Aku Aku* with a group of adventurers. The story was about a three-month cruise aboard Lowell Thompson's sailing yacht, *Cherokee* to Easter Island where the story was filmed. I was the artist of the expedition. I sang the background music and designed the titles as well. It was an interesting project, but, unfortunately, the product didn't come together well.

Stephanie was happy to accommodate me, and I think she welcomed the company. She and Geza had broken up and she was preparing to move back to New York City. We had a long discussion about the situation between Rae and me. She had known through Geza that Rae was sleeping around. I was working so hard at the gallery, and in the studio, I was oblivious to her infidelities.

I stayed for a month in the guest house and insisted on paying her rent. I approached the landlord to see if I could remain and rent just the guesthouse after Stephanie had moved. He agreed and the little house became my home for the following year. Stephanie gave me the furnishings in exchange for one of my paintings she loved. She didn't want to ship everything to New York as she had rented just a small one-bedroom apartment. The place was furnished elegantly, and since I had left everything to Rae, it turned out to be very practical.

Stephanie gave up the house and moved into the guest house with me for the week before she left. We had an affair, but we didn't make the transition from friends to lovers comfortably. She was a lot older and was accustomed to men spoiling her. She had always had everything; she was a beautiful woman and had been with the cream of the Hollywood set. I liked her, but she was just a little too much for me to handle with the stress of my failed marriage.

***

I was playing tennis several times a week, as it had led to many of the clients I had developed. A short time after Stephanie had left I was invited to play some mixed doubles at an afternoon party at an estate north of Sunset Boulevard. Addie Feldman had introduced me to an attractive dark-haired woman named Shirley Marshall. Shirley and I had entered several Social Tournaments together and we had a lot of fun. Shirley played piano and I was still singing at times, so we performed together at various parties and developed a friendly relationship. She became my partner at many social gatherings and tennis parties and we were together the day we played at Dinah Shore's house.

There I met a beautiful woman I would be friends with for many years, Ondra May. She was married to the department store mogul, David May. I found it hard to concentrate on my tennis as I was so fascinated with her. [We had mutual friends and Swedish backgrounds, and by fate, we met many times over the years. She left David and later remarried a wonderful man named Phillip Stein.] It was a fun group that day and we played tennis all afternoon. Dinah had tennis gatherings often and I became a part of the group and had some of the most wonderful times I can remember. Dinah was, with all her fame, one of the loveliest and kind people in my life.

One Sunday Shirley and I went to the house of a friend of Dinah's to play tennis. Her name was Claire, a woman in her 40s, with dishwater blond hair and a beautiful face. Her body showed the results of the three children, as her hips were broad. She had large breasts that she played down by dressing quite conservatively. Claire's son was in college and her two daughters were both married very young. I'm sure when Claire was young she was an outstanding beauty, and the daughters were no exception.

After that day of tennis, we had lunch together served on the patio by the servants. Stuart, Claire's tennis teacher, left to give another lesson in the area, and her friend exited with him. After they had left, she asked me about my life and we talked for nearly an hour. I liked her; she was warm, sincere, and quite sexy. Although she was seventeen years my senior, we seemed to be able to talk and relate on the same level. She was well traveled and knew many of the places that were part of my life.

She asked me to have dinner with her that evening. We sat there and talked until it was getting dark. Her live-in woman served us dinner on the terrace overlooking the city. The view was spectacular. You could see all of Beverly Hills, Hollywood and the buildings in downtown Los Angeles. She asked me if I would like to take a swim and cool off. It was hot but, by the way she asked, I knew it was an invitation to something more. I found a spare bathing suit in the pool house, a little baggy, but it would do. Claire put on a two-piece suit that showed how ample her breasts were.

We were in the pool for only ten or fifteen minutes when the darkness was closing in. I could hear her housekeeper cleaning up the table and organizing the patio furniture from the afternoon's activity. Soon it was very dark and I moved closer to her in the middle of the pool. When our mouths met for the first time, I could feel how desperately horny she was. In less than a flash, she was panting and kissing me hard. She took my hand and led me to a giant chaise lounge next to the pool. She sat down and immediately stripped off her bathing suit as I did the same. The minute I was beside her, she pulled me on top and guided me inside. We made it for a long time; I wanted to show my prowess and held back. She climaxed several times and I felt totally in command. I stayed there feeling her soft, ample, body enveloping me.

"You're getting heavy," she said. I rolled off to the side. As I laid there catching my breath, she started kissing my face. It was tender and loving and I felt a real bond with her. She laughed and said, "That was quite beautiful... hold me."

She invited me to join her the next Sunday and I agreed. Yet Claire and I both knew we couldn't be a couple in the society in which she belonged. But for the next few weeks, we saw each other during the week and some Sundays for tennis. Our lovemaking took on new dimensions and she was a willing and eager participant. Several weeks later, she said she was in love with me and that she had never known such physical pleasure. She said it was dangerous; she was afraid there would be no turning back. We agreed to see each other only once a week for a while.

A mutual friend told me I had opened a door for her and she was experimenting with some younger men. But Claire kept coming back and she had me build a collection of paintings for her, which was good business for the gallery. She had excellent taste and the paintings she bought were by renowned artists. We continued our affair, and she'd call me at times and express her desire for me. Our friendship grew and we each became the standby friend in need.

13

TOBEY, DORIS, BARBARA, CHANTAL, & FLORENCE

One day I had been painting since early in the morning and I was in the gallery for the afternoon, as we were open from only twelve to four on Saturdays. A tall woman of about five-foot-eight came through the door. She didn't look at the paintings on the way in and seemed to have a particular objective. Her lean and large-boned body was somewhat sexy. Her face was angular and her eyes small, black and piercing. She was dressed exquisitely, which exaggerated her small waist and broad hips. She was exotic, not pretty, but she had something attractive about her. I guessed she would be in her late 40s with many miles of tough experience. She had a hardness that was both fascinating and disconcerting.

She immediately told me she was Tobey, a friend of Claire's. Claire had suggested she ask me to accompany her to Dean Martin's party that night. She said her boyfriend was supposed to come from New York, but couldn't get away and she wouldn't go to parties alone. It was abrupt and I had a date with a girlfriend in Manhattan Beach. I told her I had plans, but I would see if I could cancel them, and asked where I could reach her. She gave me her number and left without looking at a single painting. I could tell she wasn't into art at all, but the opportunity to go to the Martin's house was appealing so I made the call to Betty Watt, a sailing friend, who had invited me to spend the night and go sailing the next day on a Kettenberg fifty, a yacht I admired. I told her the situation, and that I thought it would be good for business and I could meet her in the morning and have the day and evening free for her. I didn't explain how this invitation had come about, and she didn't ask.

I called Claire to ask about her suggesting I accompany this Tobey to the Martin's party. I was surprised as I didn't think Claire would want to share me with any of her girlfriends. When I got her on the phone, I told her what had taken place.

"That was the work of my friend Doris. Doris is a friend of Tobey's too. I know her, but I'm not particularly friends with her; she isn't my type."

I knew the Doris she mentioned, having met her briefly when I was in Paris... and recently, again, at Claire's house. She wouldn't say anything more; just that she had shared many things with Doris and wished she hadn't done so. She told me Doris was enormously rich and spoiled, which I already knew. I figured Claire had told Doris about our physical exploits and remembered the way Doris pursued me a couple of times at Claire's house. We had talked about our meeting in Paris at The Mar's Club and had some interesting discussions about those years when she was a regular at the George V Hotel.

"Is there anything weird about Tobey?" I asked.

"No, she's just like a fish out of water in California. She lives mostly in New York."

It was all intriguing, so I called Tobey and made the date. I figured she was looking for a younger lover and the Martin's party was her vehicle. It was interesting and people of that wealth could be good patrons of the arts, and a substantial contact.

That night when I went to the house where Tobey was staying, I immediately recognized it. It was owned by Fred Clark and Benay Venuta. It had been rented before by Mario Lanza, and there was a scandal while he was there. I was a senior Fine Arts Appraiser and had been asked by an agent of Fred Clark's to make an evaluation for them. I went and inspected the house, but it wasn't for fine art. The value of the furnishings had been destroyed by the dogs peeing and pooping all over the white carpets and white furniture. I figured there would be an ensuing lawsuit and I didn't want to be involved. I recalled the condition of the house vividly, and I remembered thinking of what a complete slob Lanza must have been.

When I arrived, a male servant led me into the study and asked if I wanted a drink. I declined and he left me there. I looked at the books on the shelf and wondered if she had brought them with her or if it was part of the furnished house. After a few minutes, I realized they came with the house. There wasn't too much worth reading, and it looked as if the shelves had been assembled to be full. There was no order to it and many books were older than I was. There was a selection of magazines on the coffee table, lined up in order: Movie, Fashion, Trivia, and Trash. Maybe Tobey wasn't a deep intellectual type. I guessed by only what I knew so far that she was a playgirl in a last attempt to indulge herself to the fullest. That was okay with me. I wasn't ready for anything but adventure and fun.

Tobey didn't enter the room; she just poked her head in and told me she'd be a few minutes. She was saying goodbye to an entourage of makeup, hairdressers and the like, who had been performing the miracle of her present state, which was quite stunning when I saw her fully a few minutes later. It was an example of what can be done in Hollywood if you have the means and the time to transform the common into the extraordinary.

She asked if I could drive her limousine as her male servant had the night off. It wasn't one of those stretch limos, but it could seat five in the back on a bench seat and two jump seats behind the chauffeur's screen. She showed me where the garage door opener was, and I backed out very cautiously down the long driveway. There was a turning area in front of the garage, but it wasn't sufficient to turn the monster. Why she wanted to take this car, I couldn't figure out. My little Mercedes was a 1957 convertible custom coupe, and it wasn't anything to be ashamed of. I had just purchased it a few months before and I was quite proud of it.

The Martin house wasn't a mansion; just a very comfortable and beautiful home in the foothills north of Sunset Boulevard. When we arrived a young, very attractive, woman greeted us at the door. She was some kind of a personal manager and was hopping around arranging everything all evening. There were some fifty or sixty people already there in casual attire. Tobey and I looked a bit overdressed for the occasion. The tennis court was quite close to the house and they used it for the tent for the catered dinner.

Jean, Dean's wife, was very friendly and a very attractive lady. I had the chance to talk to her during the evening and she had a sincere interest in art. Dean was very pleasant, but he collected his cronies around him and didn't seem to care if he met everyone.

Tobey had slipped away quickly after we arrived and I spotted her with Ray Danton, a handsome dark-haired actor, I knew from the Westside Tennis Club. Ray was the kind of guy that could know you for years but never knew your name or anything about you. Unless you had some position that could be of use to him, he wasn't the least interested. Another man I knew, Ira Zimmerman, was with them. He was a real estate broker of sorts, gray-haired and very distinguished, quite handsome with his Palm Springs tan. He would break his neck to be in tight with Tobey.

I ignored her and waited until she wanted to spend time with me. I was very experienced and confident with women at this point in my life, and I knew she was either interested or not. And I didn't care which it was. I already knew she wouldn't be a long-term interest. The crowds increased and there must have been about eighty people for dinner. It was a typical Beverly Hills party with a selection of celebrities, cute starlets, and the ultra-successful.

It was around ten o'clock when Tobey came over to me. I was having a nice conversation with a lovely young actress. She would become a well-known name in the years to come, Diane Baker. I had known her briefly in Jacobina Caro's class that she shared with Rae. Tobey wanted to leave.

We were parked on the street and two other cars were now very close to the front and at the rear of Tobey's limousine. Steering that beast back and forth to get out was a royal pain. Tobey was a little blurry-eyed and acted more as if she had been smoking pot, rather than drinking booze. Within a couple of blocks, she was next to me. Without saying a word, she began rubbing my leg and then my crotch. I had to concentrate on the driving as that ungainly beast of a car took my full attention. When she felt I was hard, she took it out and started to suck on it. This didn't help my driving. In Beverly Hills I knew you had to be very careful at night so I focused on the street.

When I entered her driveway, I started to allow myself more sensation. After we had closed the garage, she suggested we get in the back seat. I opened my door and she slid out on my side. When I sat in the back seat, she got in, pulled my pants down, immediately straddled me, and put her tongue down my throat. As she rammed down on me, she murmured some strange sounds of pleasure. She was working me hard and I was asking myself if she had taken her panties off while I was driving, or if she went bare bottomed for the evening. She started grinding and grunting in an almost low-toned growl. She threw her head back and asked me to move forward, she wanted me as deep as possible. Most women found it uncomfortable in this position, so I naturally didn't thrust forward. For her it couldn't be deep enough, I arched my back and started pushing forward.

"Stay still," she said and continued her hard and methodical pounding.

I was an instrument; she didn't want personalities involved, just a prod for her pleasure. I kept my mind on other aspects of what was occurring as I wanted to control myself. She reached a frenzy, and I'm sure it must have been a final climax after a series of sensations made her so completely transfixed on the penetration. She stopped, slumped on the seat beside me and did not attempt to do anything to keep me excited. She said, "We'll go into the house in a few minutes."

We pulled ourselves together and walked to the driveway side door. She took out her keys, opened the door, turned to me, and said. "I hope you don't mind if I don't invite you in. I'm very tired."

She stepped inside and shut the door. It was the most brutal dismissal I had ever had. She was satisfied and that's all that was important. There was no kindness, or apology or even recognition I might be left uncomfortably horny. When I got to my car, there was an insult to add to the injury. It was after eleven o'clock and I had been ticketed for parking on the street.

I drove to Le Little Club in Beverly Hills where Ann Richards was appearing. Ann was a terrific singer and had sung with and been married to Stan Kenton. Ann and I had an on and off affair and had become friends. She was a woman that needed someone she could relate to and confide in. We had developed the relationship between romances. In a way I loved Ann; she was kind, loving and a good sex partner. I just couldn't spend too much time with her as she had a lot of baggage and at times, she'd depress me. At other times, she'd be on a happy high. She was available and spent the night with me.

Several days passed and I gave the evening thought. I decided Tobey was totally into herself and doubted she cared about anyone else. Thursday morning, I played tennis at the Westside Center, Frank Feltrop had arranged a game and we had a chance to talk afterward at lunch. I mentioned Tobey but didn't tell him I had been with her; only that she had been in the gallery. Frank knew her. She took tennis lessons from him at the Beverly Wilshire, and he had taken her out on several dates. A real selfish, self-centered bitch was his conclusion.

That very afternoon, Tobey came into the gallery. The limo was waiting in front and there seemed to be several people with her that remained in the car.

"I have several people coming to my house on Saturday night. Would you like to join us?"

I accepted and asked that she spend a few minutes and have her friends to come in. She declined and told me she had an appointment. Not fifteen minutes after she left, who should walk in the door but Doris. I guess she knew what had transpired with Tobey also. Elaine, my secretary, was in the back, so we sat out in the front gallery and talked for quite a while.

Doris was tall and angular, nearly my height, which was a little over six feet. She was wearing heels and this made it so I looked slightly up at her. She was quite a homely woman; aggressive but shy at the same time. She had been brazen enough to come in, yet shy enough that I had to carry the conversation. We had never talked in detail and when I told her I had done my doctorate thesis on the Expressionists, she took a new interest. I wasn't just a pretty face and stud; there was something more about me that Tobey would never understand. I knew from others she was a very intelligent woman. Everyone knew her, or of her. She was proclaimed, at the time, one of the richest women in America and there had been numerous articles and stories about her life.

"I've wanted to visit your gallery. I liked many of the works you put into Claire's home." She picked up a Picasso ink and watercolor, Minotaur, piece and asked me to send her a bill and ship it to someone in New York as a gift. She was readying to leave and said. "I enjoyed our conversation about art, especially the French Impressionists. You know so much about them." Before she left, I told her I would like to hear more of her interest in Islamic art, and hoped we could have another talk.

Saturday I dressed casually for the party at Tobey's house. She had said nothing about attire, but I remembered I was very conscious of wearing a suit and tie at the Martin's when everyone else was dressed informally. When I arrived, everyone was decked out in royal style. She introduced me to three couples from New York, friends in her society circle. I could see by their expressions they thought I was just a money grabber and was after their dear friend's bucks. I knew I had to turn this around quickly or it would affect the entire evening. I didn't want Tobey or any woman for that matter to degrade me. In conversation, I mentioned the many movie personalities I had done portraits of and the collectors I had advised in their purchases. I pointed out many friends in the museums and galleries in New York. Before long, I could see I had accomplished my objective. I concentrated on charming and making friends with the women. I knew from experience few business men and I had anything in common. I hated business, but I loved music, literature, sailing and adventure. The women had an interest in those areas. It is surprising how few men I've met that had any interest in sailing.

Everyone left about eleven o'clock; it was two in the morning for them, as they had arrived that day. Tobey sent the servants off and we went into the library. She pulled out a green folded paper from the desk drawer. When she unfolded it, there was a pink powder inside. She looked at me.

"This is wonderful; open your mouth." She wet her finger, touched the pink stuff and put it under my tongue. "Open up..." she said again and put another bit under the other side of my tongue. She did the same for herself and then neatly put the paper back in the desk drawer, locked it and put the key in a little box between books on the shelf. "Do you want something to drink?"

I was very thirsty and asked for a glass of water. I had had enough wine, and the dinner had been salty. My throat felt parched and the powder made it feel even drier. By the time, she brought the water I was feeling a little high.

"The powder was mescaline... it's working much faster than I expected."

She gave me the water and sat opposite from me instead of sitting on the leather sofa with me. She sat down, pulled her dress up, and spread her legs to show me her neatly trimmed pussy. I realized that the previous Saturday she had indeed not worn underpants that evening as well.

"Kiss me right here," she said as she spread her labia to expose her clit.

No preliminaries just get down there and make her happy. I must admit, though, it was sexy. She was a different breed of woman and I was fascinated in a way, but I didn't want to be left high and dry like the previous episode. I started to take off my jacket.

"No, I want you fully dressed."

She put her legs up and over the arms of the chair. She was amazingly flexible. When I started to perform my specialties, the powder took effect. Her pussy bloomed into giant proportions. Her clitoris became animated and joined me in returning my movements. It was so exciting I was completely immersed in her organ.

She began to quiver and then pushed me away. "No more for a minute... enough."

"Let's go and get comfortable," I told her.

We went upstairs, stripped, and the fantasies of the magic

powder began. We made every kind of conceivable love for more than an hour. She said she was exhausted, but that made me want to show her it wasn't all; it was the beginning. I took her in the usual position, held her legs up and out and proceeded to make love as hard as I could. Sometime later she became rigid, forced her legs down, her arms started to quiver spastically and her eyes became glazed over. The climax that ensued I knew was the one that would change the relationship and she'd be robbed of her Hitlerian, provocative nature. My finish with her made the union what I had planned. It was two-thirty in the morning when I got up. But I was still in no condition to drive. I had intended to get dressed and go home even though she wanted me to stay, but it wasn't prudent in that condition. It was strong stuff. I promised myself I didn't need it; it would just lead to something I might not be able to handle so I didn't indulge often. I fell asleep again and a few hours later, she was all over me. That morning, we had a slow and mutually satisfying episode. I finally left about eleven o'clock with just enough time to change and be at Claire's for tennis.

* * *

That day at Claire's was sunny, warm, and perfectly clear; not too hot and a gentle breeze came from the ocean. There was a new group that day. About twenty people showed up and I could see it was going to be more Beverly Hills social than tennis. With the group was a woman that immediately caught my attention. She was slim as a model and had a beautiful face. She wore stunning tennis clothes that looked like they were all designer creations. Her makeup and hair were perfect, as was the way she moved. She wasn't a good tennis player and I assumed it wasn't something she did very often. She had a charming French accent, but it was obvious she had lived in an English speaking country for a long time.

Chantal was an elegant woman, and she was very savvy and smart. I learned she owned a skin and makeup salon on Rodeo Drive, and that was the connection to Claire and her friends. Several others of the guests had left and the servants were serving drinks and snacks late that afternoon when Doris came by. A very handsome Italian man accompanied her. He was in his late 30s or maybe early 40s and embraced Claire in a way that seemed special. It wasn't casual and I could see he was making points. She seemed to light up when he arrived and I was happy for her. He must be one of the young men I had heard about and stayed so close I couldn't get a chance to talk to her.

Doris and I continued our conversation about Paris, its galleries, and cafes. I got very involved in our evaluations of the French Impressionists and comparison to American Impressionists. She knew little about the Americans. I proceeded to tell her about all the wonderful Americans that lived in France and assembled in Giverny, around Monet. She was particularly interested in Lila Cabot Perry, who had become great friends with the master and for many summers had lived close by. She, along with Mary Cassatt, was credited with introducing the French to many of the elite of Boston. Doris was shy, but she was in her element when she could discuss French culture and the pillars of French society. I asked her if she'd join me for dinner, and she agreed.

That evening I picked her up at her Beverly Hills mansion. The gates and the drive and then the house were something that stunned me. It was incredibly tasteful with a distinct design. Not that large but very elegant. I knew she was wealthy, but I didn't realize any single woman would live in such a grand manner.

I had made a reservation at Jean Leon's, La Scala. I knew Jean as he had been a guest with me to play tennis at Jack Warner's house on several occasions. Jean was a good player; a slight and delicate man, and one of the best restaurateurs in Los Angeles. The one thing that made the rich and famous set frequent his bistro was that Jean himself was always there and he watched the place like a hawk. If anyone ventured to interrupt a celebrity, Jean would make sure his or her privacy was protected. It became known the waiters wouldn't deliver notes, nor would they carry any message of any kind. It was Jean's rule, and it was about the only place you could go with a famous or infamous person and be confident you would have privacy. Jean knew Doris and liked her; she was always very generous and quiet. [Jean and I talked about her many years later when we continued our friendship in Malibu and for two weeks on my yacht in the Mediterranean.]

At dinner, Doris and I covered several topics. She had done some sailing and knew many of the places I had visited. It gave us a common ground. She was 50 years old and quite ungainly looking; no one would even say she was attractive, although I had seen her in certain situations where she had some flair.

I took her home that evening and she invited me in. Her manservant was still up and lurked about as we had a final drink. He seemed to be just around every corner. I remember thinking he must be her bodyguard. I wasn't comfortable, so just after eleven that evening I left. Doris asked if I would like to come for dinner on Wednesday and I accepted. I kissed her on both cheeks, and she clutched my arms briefly. On the way home, I evaluated the evening. I couldn't tell if she wanted to have an affair with me, or just enjoyed the company and conversation. I knew Claire had told her in detail about our relationship. During the evening, Doris had explained to me Claire was very taken by her new handsome Italian. I suppose

318

Doris's invitation to have dinner at her house was an offer to make my move. But, I was confused as she didn't make any advance of touching or conversation about such things as relationships or sex for the entire evening. She had shown more interest when I first met her than she did that night. I think when it came to love and sex she was shy and a little clumsy; though proud and confident in most other ways. I had heard stories about her husbands and affairs so I knew she was just having a little problem making how she felt known.

I wanted her not because she was appealing, but because I had found that women who were unattractive and self-conscious were great lovers. I liked being her friend, but I was very much aware if it became known, our relationship might be described in a derogatory way. Nevertheless, I needed reliable contacts and social friends who could be beneficial to my career. As a young artist and art dealer, I knew that it would be a long hard road without the help of others. And I found older women more interesting than the routine young ladies I had dated.

That Wednesday evening, I made my move and it was very awkward at first. But soon she displayed her passion and desires and took me downstairs to her bedroom. She seemed to enjoy it but never reached a real climax. She suggested she walk me upstairs; her subtle direction that I couldn't stay. When we said goodnight, she said she was leaving for a few weeks and would call me when she returned.

It was more than two months before she came back to LA. In the meantime, I was seeing several other, younger, women and continuing my affair with Tobey. Each rendezvous with her was more bizarre. She was trying to shock me with her antics, her dress or her considerable collection of sexual implements. She liked anal penetration and had one of the biggest pussies I had ever seen. She liked it from behind as well, along with the dildos, vibrators and the showing of various films on her 8mm projector. [Those days were very different from today where porn is so common, and the medium of exhibiting them is so sophisticated.] I never had known anyone who was as oriented to self-satisfaction as she was. She often mentioned that she depended on my discretion when we got involved. I was fascinated by her obsession with sex though I had often suspected myself of being hypersexual.

I remember on several occasions she'd be on her way to an early dinner and would stop by the gallery at five o'clock when I closed. My assistant would leave and I would lock the front door. The minute I was in the confines of the back room she was all over me. On the desk or the sofa, but the straight back chair was her favorite. She would sit me down, pull my pants to my knees and suck it until it was ready for her. Then she'd lift her dress and facing me start with her particular kind of madness. She was always ready and never wore panties. We would go at it until she'd get close. I had learned if I didn't finish with her she might just get up and consider it a done deal. Sometimes she'd be so cool she would just reach her finish and as she continued to move to bring me to a climax, would start to put herself together for a quick exit. I remember the first time we did this little exercise, she went into the bathroom and five minutes later came out and was ready to go. I grabbed her and put my hand up her dress to see what she had done about being so wet. She had put on panties and a pad which she obviously had in her purse. Tobey would make it at the gallery, in the car or her limo, in the bathroom on a sink at a party, but she'd never come to my house. It had to be on her turf or neutral ground. She wanted to see me often, but within a short period, I realized she was never going to be a client of the gallery. She never expressed any desire to own one of my paintings. I asked her on several occasions if she had an art collection in her New York apartment, or if she went to any of the galleries or auctions. I always got a very evasive answer. I was a sex partner she used when she needed her fix. As I knew her weird habits and needs, she wanted to be with me more and with others less.

* * *

In the meantime, Chantal was on my mind. I called her and left several messages that weren't returned. Maybe she didn't remember me or perhaps she knew why I was calling and wasn't interested. One day on the way home from playing tennis at the West Side Center I stopped by her Rodeo Drive salon and found she had been in Europe for several weeks. I wrote her a note that I wanted to see her and spend some time together. I knew we had a lot in common and hoped to hear from her on her return.

* * *

I had some other girlfriends, and one, in particular, was my age and always fun. Barbara was a psychoanalyst working with a senior doctor who had taken her into his practice. He was in his late 70s and was getting forgetful; not a good trait for an analyst. Only the new patients started with her since it isn't a medical profession whose patients accept change easily. She was living very modestly in the Wilshire district, just west of downtown. She was also working as staff for the city Welfare Department. That work was a scary part of her life. She needed the income, but the exposure to some strange and dangerous people was something I advised her many times to leave behind. The stories she told were real revelations for me. Although I had traveled much of the world, in some of the worst third world countries, I hadn't been involved personally with people who were as unstable as her cases. They told her intimate stories of horrible deeds, with no regrets or remorse whatsoever. The city, of course, claimed they wouldn't send her to anyone for evaluation which they deemed as dangerous. But with some of the acts performed by these people, anything could happen. It made me appreciate the quality of people I had around me in my life. They may be selfish or self-centered, but they were not borderline nutcases. Barbara and I had a sexual relationship on and off for almost a year. We always had wonderful times, but she'd want to get too involved and just couldn't accept the fact I wasn't looking for a permanent relationship.

We remained friends and she stopped by the gallery many times. She developed a significant practice of her own and moved to Westwood where she became very successful and did research that was recognized. Even after I had married again, she stayed in touch.

* * *

There was one other long-term relationship during that period. I met Florence at the Stephen Silagy Galleries in Beverly Hills. I walked in one day and started to examine several French master paintings when a voice asked me if there was anything particular, I was looking for. When I turned, there was this slender woman with sharp features and jet black hair. Her green eyes slanted upwards and gave her an exotic look. She was very formal, even rigid, but she seemed to react to me. I said to myself, she's interested. I introduced myself and left it at that.

Later that day I called and she answered. I told her who it was and asked if she would have a quick drink with me on her way home. She agreed and met me at the Brown Derby on the corner across from the Beverly Wilshire Hotel about a half block from the Silagy Gallery. We hit it off immediately and spent a pleasant hour. She was quite knowledgeable about the French artists but didn't have any formal education of them. We talked until she said she had to go as her daughter would be coming home soon.

I pursued Florence for the next few weeks and soon we had a relationship going. She was a loving and sexy woman, with some heavy baggage from a failed marriage and a child she had to support on her own. Her 8-year-old daughter, Lyn who meant the world to her, was a delight and I cooked dinner for them on many occasions. She would never tell me any of the happenings at the gallery, and although I asked some questions at times, I didn't pry. Stephen Silagy was the most prominent dealer in Los Angeles. He had an inventory worth many millions, and if you wanted a Monet, or a Pissaro, or any French master, he was the one to see. As I mentioned previously, he was also a jerk. A sour personality, and unbelievably rude to anyone who he thought might not be qualified to buy in his realm of paintings. One day he fired Florence with no advance notice. He said she wore too much makeup. He handed her a check and cold as ice after nearly a year working for him, he dismissed her.

After that, she was very helpful to me and I gained a lot of insight into the upper level of art dealing in Beverly Hills. But Florence, although exquisite, was cold and hard to get to know perhaps because she was so suspicious of everything and everyone. We remained friends for over twenty years but eventually lost touch.

* * *

It was a period of several interesting women in my life.

Claire was warm, intelligent and good company at any time.

Barbara was attractive, intelligent, and also good company. She didn't seem to have a substantial dating schedule. I think because many men felt threatened by her. She was naturally inquisitive, and only someone who was confident could make light of those first encounters with her.

Doris was very tuned in; premeditated in all that she did, she was also very challenging. I saw Doris when she came back and we had several nights together, and then she was off to New York and Paris. She called some months later, but by then I was at the end of my adventures with older women.

Tobey, well she was a piece of work. There wasn't anything good I could say about her other than she was an experience. I quit seeing Tobey because Chantal didn't like her. Not that long afterward, she moved back to New York where she belonged.

Chantal and I ended up in an exciting affair that lasted several months. I was taken with her; she looked 35 and was delicious. But when I found out she was 47 years old, I realized she was just too old for me. With that age difference, I knew there was no future.

Then I met Marie.

14

MARIE

I had purchased a home on Curson Avenue in West Hollywood at the very end of the street, the last house in the canyon. A modern three-story architectural statement across from a very steep, brush-covered hill. It had a carport on the first level with an area I used as a spare apartment for friends. The second floor was the living area, and on the third were two enormous bedrooms.

It was quite isolated, which was what attracted me. I didn't want nosy neighbors as I had in the apartments of the last few years. I was never quite comfortable with bringing people home to the little guest house I rented before buying the house on Curson; a couple had moved into the adjacent home after Stephanie left. The man worked and the woman was unemployed for most of the time I was there. She thought she was a Hollywood sex symbol and was always running out when I was alone to display her incredible figure in some skimpy outfit. She showed too much interest in my affairs, always separating the curtains a few inches and peeking out the back window. I knew she was trouble, so I never let her get too close.

The furnishing of my new house and the displaying of many of my paintings had become the props for a series of affairs. My sexual appetite, my tennis, and the business of the gallery were taking its toll on my personal painting. In a way, I had been at the easel for a very long time in my short life. I had painted an incredible number of hours, and the demands of the Phillipe Marchand works was ever increasing to the point that the work under my own name was suffering. I had long come to the realization show business and the life of an entertainer wasn't a promising future. The actresses and actors I knew were an insecure lot, even if they were successful. The artists that made real money were rare. I had opened the gallery for a particular purpose; I knew if you got into selling the high-ticket works of art, you could make enough to live on the scale I wanted. In France and then in Los Angeles I had had a lot of exposure to people with a comfortable and exciting life, who lived in magnificent homes, with the means to satisfy their wildest dreams. I wouldn't settle for anything less. I loved to travel and I had watched the people who did it in grand style in their yachts and planes.

Marie worked for Chantal. I had noticed her several times when I dropped by the shop. She was beautiful and I knew she looked familiar, but I couldn't place where we had met. Later I learned she was Miss Western Airlines. There were life-sized full-color stands of her in many of the travel shops and she was in many magazines. Her face was so exquisite just looking at her was a turn on. Every time she set foot on the street men were hitting on her constantly. I said hello to her several times, but no more than that.

I was still seeing Chantal when one day I ran into Marie at the Beverly Wilshire Drug Store and asked her to join me for coffee. She accepted and was very polite and proper. I noticed she had an accent and learned she was from Belgium. Born and raised in Antwerp her native language was Flemish; she also spoke German and French. When she learned, I had visited Antwerp and had lived in France for so many years she was immediately interested. While in Paris, there were many things I had learned about life in Western Europe during the war. She didn't know many people her age that shared that knowledge.

Marie and I had dinner and talked until the early hours of the morning. When I saw her to her door, I kissed her and she didn't hold back, I knew this was going to be something extraordinary. A few days later, we had dinner again. That night we had a hot and torrid love affair. It was incomparable. Looking into that face and those eyes transfixed me in a state of euphoria. This wasn't just sex. It was love and an understanding that moved me very deeply.

"Marie" photo portrait, 1962.

As our relationship grew, she moved into my Curson Street house. I had learned of her story and vulnerability, and I felt the need to protect her. During World War Two, the Germans had invaded

Belgium and occupied Antwerp. The people had been scared and the Jewish people lived in dread, for the tales of their mistreatment abounded. One day Marie, an only child then 6 years old, was returning from school to the apartment where she lived with her mother and father. She passed the small grocery store on the corner. The woman called her in and told her the Germans had taken every Jewish family on the street, and she must not go home. They would call and inquire to see if they could reach her parents. Later that evening, with the pretense of delivering some groceries, they found her parents were not there and the apartment had been ransacked. The people lived above their store and kept Marie hidden as the Germans threatened anyone who was harboring Jews. During the next months that became years, the underground smuggled Marie from place to place. She eventually came to live on a farm. To survive, she adopted a new background and name. She still didn't know if her parents had survived. When the war was over, through one of the many agencies that took on the task of reuniting people separated by the war, she learned her parents had escaped and survived. But her grandparents and the remainder of her family had died in concentration camps. The scars and insecurities fostered by such an experience are profound and indelible.

How haunted she was by what she and her parents went through did not show at first. Marie and I were very happy. She helped me in the gallery and quit her job with Chantal. We were married, and the success of the gallery grew. We took delivery of a cute little MGB car in England and drove all of Europe for a three-month vacation and art-buying trip. We covered northern Italy, Germany, Austria, Switzerland, Belgium and France. We just had fun and it was an enjoyable experience. Marie was alive and happy and she was a beautiful companion and exciting lover.

We had been home for several months when we realized she was pregnant. The news about having a child was perfect. I was at the age where it was good timing for me and starting to get a little late for Marie. She was just beyond the seventh month when she started having trouble and gave birth prematurely. The child, a boy, lived for five days in the incubator; his lungs were not developed enough. We both took it very hard. We had fixed the extra bedroom up into a nursery and I was in the process of getting it decorated for the baby. The doctor said it was just a mishap and there was no real physical reason, but he suggested we move to a home on one level where Marie wouldn't be constantly going up and down the steps. We decided we would buy a new single-level home that was under construction. In the interim we went looking for a puppy; I thought a dog would take her mind off the tragedy. We found an ad in the paper and it said the puppies' father was a combination of a German Shepherd and Sheltie, and the mother was a Poodle. It seemed an interesting mix, and the puppies were just as cute as could be. We took a light colored one home and named him Becket; not only for the distinguished Thomas Becket but also for the shaggy tail of a seaman's knot.

The gallery continued to grow and the Marchand paintings gained in stature. It was 1961. I was 29 years old and while my father worked as a pharmacist and made forty thousand a year, I made over two hundred thousand. Summer was coming up, and I planned a trip to Greece and Turkey and Egypt. I had been to these places before and I wanted to share them with Marie. We spent two and a half months on the trip and Marie seemed to forget the disappointment of our loss.

During our journey, the builder was finishing the house. We had made a deal and he took the Curson house in trade for the new and much larger home in Bel Air. I had concluded the arrangement before I left on the trip, and the builder agreed to leave the furnishings until our return. My mother, who was a great animal lover, kept Becket. The trip was fun and we purchased some paintings in Paris on the way home.

Our new home was perched in the mountains and had a beautiful view of the city. We put in a distinctive pool I designed with fountains and a wall made of stained glass tile created by an artist friend of mine. I bought Marie a new Jaguar XKE roadster which was the latest hot car around town. I sold my Mercedes coupe and got much more than I had paid for it. Convinced that foreign cars would hold their resale better than the American cars I bought a Mercedes sedan. We were starting fresh with a wonderful new home and new cars. It had taken some time and real effort to get Marie back on track, but everything was now okay and she was functioning at a healthy level. Our sex life had suffered for a while, and that was difficult for me. Marie again got pregnant and that seemed to make her happy. She took it very easy and didn't try to do too much. She took walks with Becket and occupied herself while I was continually busy, both in my studio in Hollywood and in the gallery.

Because of the evening traffic from Chasen's restaurant, I stayed open on Wednesday and Friday nights. The parking attendants at the restaurant were friends and they often suggested that the people take a stroll along the boulevard, and not miss the De Ville Galleries. Many of these regulars always came by to see what I was exhibiting and to say hello. I made many friends and loyal clients with the Chasen's crowd during those years. The Marchand paintings that kept me so busy were a mainstay. They were decorative and since I did them myself, I could use them as a draw by pricing them well below the other galleries. I had many galleries at this point showing the work in San Francisco, Carmel and Palm Springs. When people saw them at much lower prices than they had seen in other galleries, they assumed everything was priced well. This was accurate, as mostly I wanted to develop a following that trusted the prices and me. Paintings are always a mystery to the buyer. Equating quality with price is something the average person cannot do.

The evenings I was gone disturbed Marie and she objected to the two nights each week. Understanding the economics of business, painting, and paying for a house and cars and vacations was something she couldn't fathom. During this pregnancy, she was quite evasive sexually, even though, in the early months, the doctor said that it wasn't a problem. I dealt with the frustration and felt once the baby was born things would get back to normal.

When Marie reached seven and a half months, the same thing happened. A little girl lived nine days; her lungs were not sufficiently developed. We went every day to the hospital, and Marie spent a great deal of time there. One night I came home and she told me. "The baby died today." She was stone-faced and didn't cry as she had the first time. During the next months, she wouldn't speak of the loss, nor would she discuss hardly anything at all. I tried to get her to help me plan for another trip to Europe, to no avail. I had to keep working hard as the hospital expenses were horrendous and had taken a significant amount of my savings.

I tried to get Marie to see my friend, Barbara, and see if she could help her. But Marie wouldn't go to her or anyone for that matter. She moped around the house, stone-faced, cleaning, making food but never speaking. Our obstetrician called to see if she was okay, as she had not returned for any of the follow-on examinations which were required. He called me after his conversation with her and was concerned she might be suicidal. I talked to my friend, Barbara. She gave me some insights, but that would not help unless Marie was willing to help herself.

Our relationship went downhill, and for months, she became like a zombie. I told her I couldn't continue this way and she must make a decision to seek help, or put this behind her and start our relationship again. She responded but only to say that if I wanted her sexually, it was okay. She wouldn't object, but she'd be back on the pill and would also use a diaphragm to be sure she wouldn't get pregnant again. We tried this and it was like making love to a corpse. Barbara said since she couldn't help Marie she'd be happy to help me. We had always been good lovers and enjoyed each other in that respect. Barbara was then living in Westwood, which was on my way home. I stopped by there a couple of times a week.

Marie didn't care if I made love to her or not. She escaped into her own world to hide from society and me. This lasted for about eight months and then I made an ultimatum: She would snap out of it and become a person again or she'd be on her own. She didn't care. I went to an attorney and told him the circumstances. I wanted a divorce, but I wanted to be fair. He said she was entitled to half the value of the house if I chose to sell it. Even though most of the money to buy it was mine from before we were married it was considered a gift to the marriage. He told me considering that we were married for three years it would be a good settlement.

I told Marie and we found an apartment for her. She didn't argue. I used much of the furniture from the house and many European paintings I had purchased and made the apartment very attractive. It was considerably nicer than the place she had lived in when we started to date. I paid the rent for a year in advance for her.

The house sold very quickly. Her half amounted to more than ten years' salary at what she was earning when we met. I gave her the Jaguar. She didn't contest the divorce in any way. I thought she knew how generous I was, but she never expressed it. I heard through friends that eventually she got a job as a sales person in a store.

I recovered emotionally and financially. The gallery began to grow rapidly and I met someone with whom I would spend the rest of my life.

[I saw Marie once thirty years later. She came to meet me for lunch one day at the Criterion Theater Plaza. She was very complimentary about my success and my happy marriage to Joyce. She was still single, still very attractive and had regained some of her sparkle. About ten years after that my fortunes had grown considerably and I wondered if there was anything, I might do for her. I guess I carried a certain amount of guilt because of leaving her. I learned from a mutual friend she had married and was living in Vancouver. I wrote to her and expressed I was most happy she had found happiness and a new partner. I received a letter back that shocked me. She told me that I hated her for losing the babies, and she should have taken me for all I was worth for abandoning her. She had absolutely no appreciation for the kindness and care I took in leaving her without worries. Never had I ever expressed any blame for our loss. She never mentioned all the great times and wonderful traveling we had done, or the tremendous expenses I had with our losses and our travels. It was a vicious and hurtful letter. I had only contacted her because I was concerned for her welfare.

This is one of the lessons of life. No one perceives one's actions as others see it, and few are ever honest enough to let you know where you stand. Marie had deep scars from her abandonment as a young girl. When she lost the second child, she assumed I would abandon her and that I hated her, and she acted accordingly. She never had the capacity to evaluate most of what had taken place, and over the years, had distorted it in her mind.

Her close girlfriend and I had dinner one night before I received the letter, and she told me more about Marie's childhood. Her interpretation of what had happened in Antwerp was decidedly different from what Marie had explained to me. We discussed it and I understood the horror of what had happened to Marie had grown to monstrous proportions. I realized that unless you can put a tragedy behind you, it will grow with time. The more it grows, the greater the weight one carries. But when I now evaluate my actions and the resulting life, I've had. I know my decision was the best for me. For I met Joyce and at this point in our lives we've been together well over forty-eight years, unequivocally happy and enjoying every day together.]

15

JOYCE

After settling with Marie and rebuilding my capital, I bought a townhouse condominium in Marina Del Rey and purchased a forty-foot yawl, which I named *Clochard*, the French word for a vagabond. I began sailing again; partying, dating and I started a sailing club called the "Sundowners." I rented a room at a local yacht club facility that looked out over the water and the boats. I set up a studio in the condo and I began painting all the Marchand works there. The gallery was very successful and I started working three days each week. De Ville Galleries had become known as one of the premier galleries specializing in American art, and the only gallery specifically targeting the American Impressionists. I avidly studied this period and began to write articles and brochures praising the merits of the American concepts and accomplishments in the field of Impressionist paintings.

As my success grew, I started to buy estates of the most talented of the Americans and bought the best works I could find. There was a particular prejudice of the art historians and major dealers in New York against artists of the Giverny School, and the group that clustered around Monet. The unfavorable bias came about because the Americans wouldn't abandon their structural integrity, and many historians and dealers considered them overly decorative. I disagreed and still do. I've always felt that the decorative aspects in the works of artists I favored were the highest form of the pursuit of impressionism. Time has shown I was right. The Giverny

Impressionists have become in such demand they bring incredible prices in the market today.

My time was filled with many endeavors, all of which I enjoyed. The sailing club grew to over three hundred members, about sixty-five percent of which were women, mostly under 30 years old. We had parties and many sailing events. I recruited many local guys with sailboats that wanted to make extra money. On some weekends, we had thirty and forty people going out with us. Many girls met guys and it was a melting pot of individuals and relationships. My friend John Powell, who was a fellow artist and a longtime friend, made up the sailing schedules, loading my boat up with the most attractive girls. We met and pursued a gaggle of lovely ladies, and life was exciting and fun.

It was just about that time we got a notice from the Coast Guard. They informed us we couldn't take people out for hire; the club wasn't legal to take people out on the water if they were paying for it. We discovered there were many technicalities we didn't know about. I had consulted with an attorney, but he didn't give me proper information. When I made further inquiries, I realized with the kind of approvals necessary, insurance, and liability factors; it wasn't a viable business to continue. I hadn't started it as a money-making venture but only to introduce many people to sailing that otherwise wouldn't have the opportunity. It was also a fun way to meet and mix with many people. All the members wrote letters and complained but to no avail. We shut the club down and its closing was a great disappointment for everyone.

I continued to paint the Marchand paintings in my condo and the personal Impressionist paintings in my Hollywood studio. One day while shopping at a new market that had opened across the street, I encountered a very attractive blonde girl, with a knockout body. I asked her out sailing for the following weekend, and a relationship started. Pat was very outgoing and an excellent hostess on the boat. She and I got along very well; she was well-adjusted and very open. She had been married before, but it had lasted a very short time. Although I never stopped dating others completely, I did see Pat much of the time. We made a two-month trip on *Clochard* down to Mexico and had great fun. When we returned, we were together as much as I had time, three or four nights each week. With my work, I went to the homes of clients and mixed with an elite group of people that often fixed me up with a daughter or friend for events that were both social and business for me. Rarely did I attend as a single.

A month or two after we returned from our trip, out of the blue Pat said she wanted to discuss some things with me. She didn't want to share me with anyone and it was all or nothing. Pat was slowly gaining poise and grace, dressing well and she had great potential. I truly loved her and we spent many pleasant times together. But I wasn't ready. I had been through two marriages, and I needed a lot more time. I told her if she wasn't interested in giving me that time, it would have to be over. I felt inside we could become real partners, but I didn't have any idea how long it would be before I would be comfortable enough to make a permanent commitment. And so it ended with Pat. I guess it was fate because that very week I went to dinner and met Joyce. She was someone that seemed to fit instantly into the same mold of life I wanted for myself. And with such ease and comfort, that in only a handful of meetings with her I knew we would spend the rest of our lives together.

* * *

My friend, Ron Ely was starring in the leading role as Tarzan, for Sy

Weintraub Productions. He had rented a home in Mexico City, as the television series was filmed at a studio outside the city. I went down and joined Ron for ten days, making the rounds, and becoming familiar with the galleries and museums. I often went with him to the studio and watched the filming of the series. Ron was a big, very handsome, man and an incredible swimmer. I enjoyed the filming and met many of the guest stars. One of the actors I met, Henry Silva, was one of the stars in a landmark movie, *The Manchurian Candidate,* with Frank Sinatra. [Usually cast as a heavy, Henry spent an entire career playing bad guys. He became one of Sinatra's famous *Rat Pack.* He's a fun and good man and we've remained friends since that meeting.]

One evening when I was in the condominium having a rare quiet night. I received a call from Henry.

"Let's go to dinner at Chuck's." Chuck's was a local Marina Del Rey restaurant and hangout. The owner, Dave Alderman, was a friend and we had spent some time together talking about our mutual interest in sailing. Dave had not had the opportunity to do any extensive cruising, but he had many dreams of doing what I had already done. He was always promoting me with his friends and the array of ladies who frequented the restaurant. I was tired and only agreed to have a quick dinner and then off to bed early. Henry was of the same mind since he had an early call, on set, in the morning.

We sat in the bar area at a table by the window. Soon after Dave seated us, he came back with three lovely ladies. He introduced us to them, knowing our names but not the women's. They immediately recognized Henry. A conversation started and Henry, being a charming and entertaining type of fellow, began to enthrall them. He turned his seat toward them and they all were quickly engaged with him. I sat on the other side looking on at the laughter and listening to Henry's storytelling.

40th Woodbury University reunion

At the helm of Clochard, 1968

One of the women, from across the table and further down, looked over at me. She glanced at the other girls, walked around to me and asked if I would join them. When I accepted and brought my drink with me to their side of the table, she moved a chair up for me to sit beside her. I thought to myself, this is a bright and thoughtful girl; she sized up the situation and immediately rearranged it to her liking. Joyce had jet black hair, white skin, a bombshell body, and a beautiful face. Her eyes twinkled with energy and spirit. When we started to talk it was a natural conversation that flowed smoothly and I knew she was special.

I immediately loved her face; it was so bright and expressive.

I asked if she'd like to go sailing with me the following Sunday. She said she would but that I should call her on Saturday and confirm. I thought about her for the next four days until I made the call. I couldn't get her out of my mind; it was just that certain something about her and our communication that sparked a chord. In our conversation, she had told me she was a nurse at Cedars-Sinai Hospital and the head nurse of its important Dialysis Unit; a position of great responsibility. I immediately thought of Carolyn. We had shared a love and respect I had never repeated since that boyhood experience. Joyce was about an inch taller, but a replica of her body and the same hair color and eyes. So many things in her demeanor were also similar. At 25 years old, she was a very sharp lady. She dressed like a model and drove a little sports car right out of Butterfield 8 [the movie with Elizabeth Taylor].

Head Nurse Joyce, 1967

On our first date out sailing, just the two of us, she smiled and was enjoying herself as I handled the boat with ease. My dog Becket was very attentive to her. He immediately liked her and I could tell it was a good match. I thought, wow, here's a woman that loved my boat and my dog! I could see she was confident in all respects. No excuses for anything, just at ease with herself and the people around her. She dressed with class and taste and carried herself with elegance.

Completely taken with her, I abandoned several other ladies I was seeing regularly and arranged every moment so I could be with her. It was amazing that we had such similar tastes and desires. She loved to travel and had been many places most of the women I knew had no knowledge of. Her enthusiasm for art and adventure were very much as mine. In my adult years, I had never met anyone that shared so many similarities. An interesting note was that hanging in her bedroom at the time we met were two framed prints by Phillipe Marchand.

We saw each other continuously for three weeks. I didn't press the issue of my physical desire. I figured it would come naturally, for both of us when the time was right. I knew that when you cared and your feelings developed with love and understanding, the better it would be. When it did, it was nothing less than magnificent. I knew at that moment that she'd be my life's partner. Joyce was very unusual in many respects compared to the many women I had known. She came from a happy family that lived in New York. Her sister was married and lived there with her husband and three children. Her father was a teacher in the New York City school system and on the weekends was a Presbyterian minister, giving one Sunday sermon in the Welsh language and one in English. Born in Wales, he came to the United States when he was a young man. He had finished his education in the U.S. and had a master's degree in education and a Doctorate in Theology. Her mother was a head nurse at a nearby hospital.

Her balanced and happy childhood had been the factor in her constant reflection of joy. She awoke every morning with a smile on her face and a bounce in her toes. It seemed we enjoyed the same foods, music, theater, travel, and other things in our childhoods seemed to coincide. I had never met anyone that was so comfortable and compatible from the start.

She was strong-minded and definitely a head nurse-in-charge type. But she wanted our relationship to work; she always remained flexible and never became overly confrontational. I think she had the best sense of humor of any woman I had ever known. She entertained me with comical routines, always spontaneous and hilarious. I had at that point in my life loved and enjoyed many women. But they all had some baggage from bad experiences or unfulfilled dreams. Joyce was different. She knew where she was going and didn't need a partner to get there. If one came along, that would be a plus in her life, but it wasn't a need. She was popular and had dated many very successful men.

[After forty-eight years I can say that she is the most well-adjusted person I've ever known. She can be explosive when she thinks something that's been done isn't fair. But she never carries it away with her, it's put behind immediately. It is my recommendation to all young people when considering a permanent relationship look for someone who is intrinsically happy.]

I realized as my love for Joyce grew daily, that I had previously based relationships on the wrong criteria. I looked forward to seeing her happy face and experiencing her personal joy on a daily basis. Soon I didn't date nor see anyone else. I found I was happy, in fact, happiest, with just her. Joyce helped and worked with me on charity and social projects and was a charming and popular partner. My friends and associates all loved her and made it known they liked my choice. She became a part of my life and my dreams. We shared everything and spent an incredible amount of time together without ever a doubt. She quit her job after a couple of years so we could travel and experience the world together.

Christian and Joyce 1970

The San Juan Islands

Early in our relationship, Joyce and I chartered a thirty-four-foot sailboat in the San Juan Islands, off the coast of Washington state, from an individual for one month. We drove my new Mercedes sedan up and Becket was with us. He was a good sailor and always with me on *Clochard*. We met the man and he seemed a nice person. I asked him if we could leave the car somewhere and he told me we could park it next to his garage and he would start and run it occasionally while we were gone.

We spent the month cruising all of the San Juan's and

Vancouver and points north. We had never caught crab before, but we were great fans of the Dungeness crabs in the area. After a few days of getting used to the boat, we put a crab pot over the side. I asked Joyce what we should use for bait; we had bread, bacon, cheese and a large assortment of groceries.

Joyce said, "Let's just put the pork chop bones left over from dinner."

"They're not dogs," I scoffed. "They don't eat bones!"

"Just try it," she said. So we did.

The next morning the crab pot was full and they were hanging all over the outside of the trap trying to get the bones. From that day on, we had cracked crab meat, crab sandwiches, crab omelets, and everything we could possibly make with crab meat. Even Becket shared in many of the dishes.

We loved the islands. Joyce and I had many romantic and unique experiences on this trip. One night in Friday Harbor, we frequented a local country music nightclub. When we arrived, there was a table in the corner with a group of card players. One fat guy with his back to us was wearing a green visor; the others were other notable characters as well. It looked like an Edward Hopper painting.

We had drinks and a wild looking, long-haired, young man started to bang away on a homemade string instrument. It was just a handle attached to a wash tub. Within a few minutes, several of the guys sitting at the table set their drinks on tables or on the floor and got out guitars and other, beat up, instruments. The girls in the place collected at the tables around them. They started to play and I couldn't believe what I was hearing. This group of grubby hippies was talented. They played a little while and then sat down again. I continued to drink, thinking about what I'd just heard. I said to Joyce, "I'm going to call Bill Robinson, a top agent in Hollywood and get him up here to hear these guys."

I went to the bartender to get some information. I asked him. "How often do these guys play?"

He replied. "They're just up here for a break from touring; they're a group called *Alabama*." I had heard of them and was embarrassed for not knowing who they were and thinking they were just some local guys jamming.

After we returned and cleaned the boat up, the owner picked us up in his station wagon. We said our goodbyes and were on our way. My Mercedes had been washed and cleaned inside, but there was something wrong. I don't know exactly why I sensed it, but there were a few nicks and scratches I thought weren't there before. As we drove along, I asked Joyce to get the service record out of the glove compartment. I had had the car serviced just before we made this trip and the invoice had the miles noted. We figured our distance from Los Angeles and a little extra for the sightseeing we had done. But, no matter how you calculated it there were at least two thousand extra miles on the car. I wrote the man we'd chartered the boat from, about my disappointment in his dishonesty, and sent him a bill for racking up miles on my car. But I never heard anything in reply. I just chalked it up to another lesson learned.

* * *

Joyce and I lived in my townhouse in Marina Del Rey until 1979. Then we moved into a house we had planned and constructed over a period of three years. Our new home was in a canyon just a thousand feet from the beach in Malibu, on a parcel of three acres. I designed the house and we put everything we loved about Mexico into the project.

Our Michoacán ranch house was much like many I had seen in Mexico. We imported seventy-thousand pavers for the front courtyard, forty-five thousand large handmade bricks, and seventeen thousand hand-painted tiles. I purchased the roof tiles from a friend who owned the Cleveland Wrecking Company; they were from a 1908 school that was condemned. We imported hundreds of Saltillo tiles used in the house and the outdoor passageways and porticos, and for the pathways around the property and in the rear patio areas. Even the stairs to the upper bench, which circled that part of the hill, was finished with Saltillo tiles with hand-painted tiles on the face of the steps.

We hired a very talented stone carver from Guadalajara. Using the native lava rock, he carved a massive fountain in the center of the ten thousand square-foot courtyard. The fountain was twelve feet across in a basin of hand-painted tiles. A small wall fountain was in the entry of the front door. In the central courtyard, we put another wall fountain which was quite large. The rear fountain, surrounded by hedges and lawns and tropical palms, was done in a much denser type of material called Guadalajara stone. The carving was exquisite and the basin alone took him seven months to sculpt. The centerpiece of the rear gardens was an oak tree that was three hundred years old; a massive and beautiful specimen. Running through the property was a four hundred-foot stream. We constructed an elaborate bridge with a giant planter at the front of the front courtyard and put in a twelve-trunk specimen palm. On the creekside courtyard there was another oak; it spanned ninety feet growing from the side of the creek. The front doors were purchased from a dealer in La Jolla and came from the San Capistrano Mission. The doors to the master suite were from Lake Chapala and were exquisitely inlaid with bone. We bought the all the roof beams from a church in Tlaquepaque and had them kiln dried for ten days to be sure no termites or critters were left. All the other doors and woodwork was made from this two-hundred-year-old hardwood.

The interior had wall outlets for every painting in our American Impressionist collection; they were all on rheostats, so the lighting could be adjusted for dramatic effect. Our collection of paintings is a very special selection of art collected by an art dealer and artist, with explicit knowledge of this group of painters. It's not only by great American artists but the finest examples of their work. The interior reflected our personal taste in antiques, fabrics, and sculptures: bronzes by Remington, Chaderoff, Miller, Zajak, and others, with pre-Columbian statues and artifacts from many states in Mexico. The list goes on, but it was a showplace with the distinctive touches and personalities of Joyce and me. It was a great compliment when Johnny Carson told other friends it was his favorite house.

We loved our new home but planned for many adventures away from it.

China

On our first trip together to China, Joyce and I stayed at the Peninsula Hotel in Hong Kong. Our third evening there was our anniversary, and we wanted to find a special restaurant for the occasion. The concierge at the hotel recommended a place which he said was the hot spot of the city. We took a cab there and found it crowded but unappealing; the front had the look of a modern corner drugstore. The furniture inside was Formica and polished aluminum; the place looked like a cheap hamburger joint. But in China at that time, this was really high-tech and different. The food might have been good, but we didn't stay.

We checked several other places and couldn't get in so we returned to eat at the hotel. The dining room was enormous with a central dance floor. Each table was decorated with a candelabra and a half dozen burning candles. It was elegant and we admonished ourselves for not just going there in the first place. It was nine-thirty and the crowd was beginning to thin out. By the time, we got our food it was ten o'clock and we were still eating a half hour later. The waiters started to collect the candelabras and put them on a central table in the middle of the dance floor. I became a little pissed that they were cleaning up while we were still eating. I called the maître de Maison to the table and told him I thought it coarse to be cleaning up all around us while we were finishing our meal. He was embarrassed and quickly motioned to all of the waiters to cease their work. They lined up on the opposite side of the floor space and stood side by side waiting for us to finish.

Joyce looked at me and said. "Let's have some fun."

"What do you have in mind?" I asked

We put our heads together made a quick plan and proceeded to execute the Fire Dance. We each took one of the lighted candles from our table and started to sing *A Bushel and a Peck*. We flitted around lighting all of the candles they had put out and left in the center of the floor. The staff looked on in horror and likely thought we were insane. When all were lighted, we did an Indian dance around them. Many of the staff started to laugh then. I think they

348

began to understand we were just having fun. After the Indian dance we sang, *Oh How We Danced on the Night We Were Wed* and waltzed around the candle display. After one chorus, we sat down at our table and toasted with a glass of wine for our celebration. They recognized the song and now were all smiling and wishing us good cheer. It had turned from a stiff and impatient scene to a festive and fun time. I could always count on Joyce to remedy a gloomy situation.

We had decided to venture into mainland China, even though it was long before people were traveling there and we would not be allowed to go very far in their tightly held communist environment. But we wished to visit an art professor at the University at Canton. We took the train, which was crowded beyond anything I had ever experienced. It traveled so slow you could get off and run beside it without a problem. All the seats were taken and Joyce and I were jammed in tight. There wasn't an inch more of standing space. People were carrying all sorts of boxes and paraphernalia, which made standing even more uncomfortable. Once onboard the train and settled as best we could for the ride I was questioning the wisdom of spending over an hour like this. But it was interesting, and the throngs of people around us were fascinating.

Then I felt a funny sensation on the back of my leg. It was as if someone was scratching me from behind. I ignored it for a while but suddenly it was jabbing me painfully. I was much bigger than other people were and stood nearly a foot taller than most of them. I reacted by pushing people away and glared at the man standing directly behind me. When I looked down, I had the answer. He was carrying a chicken in a plastic bag. The chicken's feet were hanging out the bottom, and the head was protruding from a hole. The live chicken was pecking at my leg. I put my hands together clasped in front of me and bowed slightly, an expression of apology. Everyone had been watching these strange foreigners and at this occurrence, they all laughed. These experiences were the beginnings of our understanding of these good people.

Many years later, when China had become more open and travel there more acceptable, we made our first driving trip from Shanghai to Beijing. We had been on the road for quite a few hours after an early start. We looked for a restaurant in what appeared to be an area appropriate for stopping. It was a village in China, but there its population could be a half a million people! There were few private vehicles then and we parked directly in front of the restaurant. We entered a large room about three-quarters occupied. No one spoke a word of English, so I used my sketchpad and a few hand gyrations to get my message across. The owner made gestures making us understand we could leave it to him. People looked at us, smiled and made it a friendly atmosphere. Though I'm sure, it was rare for foreigners that didn't speak their language to come in.

Customers continued to enter and we didn't pay much attention. Then a man came through the door carrying a large rectangular basket. He slipped on the floor and went sprawling. The basket was full of live eels and they went slithering in all directions. The women jumped up on their chairs or ran out the door while the men started running around picking up the eels to help the delivery man refill his basket. Joyce and I got up and started helping; she was the only woman lending a hand. By the time all the eels were collected everyone was having a great time. Men went to the door to inform the women that all was clear to rejoin their friends for lunch.

Everything slowly returned to normal, but there was still an air of fun and excitement. While everything calmed and we waited for our food, I did a sketch of the scene which had taken place. The food was served. It looked excellent and we started to eat. As we were well into our meal, the owner came to see if everything was to our liking. We motioned yes, and I gave him the drawing. He was so excited he showed it to everyone in the place. They all smiled and gestured to us their appreciation.

When the time came for us to continue on our journey, we asked for the check. The owner, through pantomime, said 'no, please, my guest!' He wouldn't accept any money. We thanked him and went to the car and he accompanied us out the door. We got in and when we looked around the entire restaurant, customers and employees had come out on the street to wave goodbye. A heartfelt and touching scene that fostered an ever-loving feeling for the people of China. We have returned several times and always have felt the warmth of these friendly people.

VI

BACK TO SEA AGAIN

Tarquin in the Mediterranean

16

TARQUIN OF MALIBU AND OTHER SEA ADVENTURES

Over the many years of living and traveling in Europe, I had become addicted to the social atmosphere and international ambiance. But since living in France during my art school years, I had spent only a few months at a time traveling and enjoying the various countries of Europe. I wasn't only missing the life in Europe. I had sold my Sparkman and Stevens sloop, *Clochard* in California and hadn't owned a boat for a considerable period. I had the itch to feel the thrill of a well-found boat under my feet. The business was going well. The Japanese gallery was selling an astonishing number of paintings and the Grand Central Galleries in New York was making regular sales of my personal work. The De Ville Gallerie was going into the slow summer season and I made it a regular practice to leave during the summer months.

When Joyce and I had met, I told her of a promise I had made to myself. At 35 years old, I was going to take at least one month off each year to travel, and I was going to increase that by one month each five years. The time would be spent just enjoying life. I had seen so many people consumed by their professions, never having time for pleasures. I didn't want my life to lead to that kind of existence. It didn't because I had stuck to my promise. By 1983, I was taking four months each year to travel, paint and live the good life. Joyce and I had long before opted to be selfish and not have children so we could

353

have the time to travel, study and play.

I had loved cruising with *Patience,* my topsail ketch and I wanted Joyce to experience the Mediterranean with me that same way. I decided we would shop for my next boat in Europe. We traveled along the coast of France and saw many boats, most of which were not in good condition. Finally, in Port Grimaud we saw a one-year-old Peterson 46, cutter-rigged, center cockpit cruiser. The design was well-known and I was pleased to find it had all the right credentials. The owner was a professional boat surveyor who had gone to Taiwan and supervised the building himself. He had installed the refrigeration and many of the systems with knowledge and precision. It was perfect for us, with a large comfortable cabin aft, and a roomy forward cabin with its own head and shower. There was little required to give it the personal touch, some fabrics, cushions, and items we liked to cook with to equip the galley.

We named it *Tarquin of Malibu* and during the next eleven years, we spent four months of every summer in the Mediterranean. That first time with her, we stocked the boat and within a few weeks had trial sailed enough to feel confident with the rig and the gear. We felt ready to explore. We set off traveling east along the coast of France until we got to San Remo. We spent a few days there and met a couple on an older, larger, boat moored next to us. He had been a successful attorney in the Midwest. She was his secretary and they had fallen in love. He sold everything, left his wife and nearly grown children and bought a camper van. The two of them drove down to the tip of South America. This took them two years and then they sold the camper and went to Europe. There they bought the boat, which he had named *Good Jump* after her. They were a special notation in our log of people met along the way, as they were conventional people, which suddenly broke the mold and took a flying leap at life.

We saw them again seven years later. She had contracted a viral infection which had almost killed her. She was well on her way to recovery, though still so thin we hardly recognized her.

The Mediterranean

On our cruises, there were many encounters with interesting people and many exciting and fascinating places. Just about the most remarkable harbor, visually, we visited was Bonifacio in Corsica. Pirates used Bonifacio in its early days because its entrance couldn't be seen unless you were very close. You entered through a passage in the cliffs that turned and twisted for about three-quarters of a mile. When you cleared them, you found a harbor and the lower part of the city. Above the harbor the old drawbridge, isolating the upper city from the harbor, can still be seen. Around this peninsula, it's all cliffs so the dwellers couldn't be attacked from the sides or behind. The city itself existed on the upper part of the mountain. From the sea, if you were in close, it looked as if the city hung out over the water. The cliffs curved inward to the sea below. The city and the way it was built was very fascinating and unlike anything I had ever seen before.

The Corsicans were a friendly lot and seemed to have an old-fashioned, easygoing manner. Corsica had many areas that looked as if they were frozen in time. In contrast, nearby Porto Cervo in Sardinia was the elegant resort yacht haven that Prince Ali Khan had developed that we visited many times.

From there we went to Capri. All of my life I had heard stories of this elegant little island and the rich and famous that frequented it. It was indeed an extraordinary place with the finest shops and the most delightful restaurants and hotels. The harbor was new and we moored next to a restored schooner from the early 1930s. The brightwork was spectacular and I loved just sitting next to her and spending my time admiring a yacht with so many stories to tell. My imagination ran wild thinking about its possible history. Abeking and Rasmussen in Germany had built her when Hitler was coming to power. I couldn't imagine there were many people during that period that could afford an eighty-foot masterpiece such as she was. We met the captain and some of the crew, but they knew little of her history.

We spent some very special times in Capri and on the Island of Ischia. We anchored there under the castle which was built at lands' end. Alone in a beautiful bay it was one of those times we hoped would last forever. The nights were pleasant and we took many swims in the bay, as the water was quite warm. Joyce and I were in love and everything in our lives was beautiful. The people and the marketplace were picturesque and I spent considerable time sketching the market and the harbor. It's one of those places you can only reach on a boat and not any other means. It was a wonderfully private setting.

We made the trip up the west coast of the Peloponnesus to the Greek islands of the Adriatic Sea then through the Corinth Canal to Athens. The Greek islands were spectacular with their white houses and the deep blue sea. But the restaurants left something to be desired, although there were a few good ones in Athens. Mostly the food was poor quality, and the wines were not much better. They had wine, called *Retsina,* the Greeks thought was unique. It was the worst wine I have ever tasted. After so much time in France, Corsica, Sardinia, and Italy, we were spoiled. There we had found excellent restaurants everywhere. In Greece, even going to the markets to buy our own food to cook was limited and very meager compared to the previous countries.

Summer after summer we sailed all the islands of Greece, and then would leave the boat in Turkey at Kusadasi, where they had built a wonderful marina. At the dock, we met liveaboards from many countries and lifestyles. We are still in touch with some of them nearly twenty-eight years later. We loved the coast of Turkey. The weather was always warm and perfect and the people were kind and very helpful. The charter trade was just beginning there, but we saw few charter boats.

The southern coast of Turkey in the summer was usually close to a hundred degrees much of the time. But when sailing with good winds in the afternoon, typical of the Mediterranean, it was comfortable. But once we endured a heatwave which killed hundreds of people. I remember one day when it was a hundred and twenty-five degrees. We found an anchorage and spent the day in and out of the water every few minutes to maintain a comfortable body temperature. The water was probably ninety degrees, but it felt cool compared to the air. That night it was over a hundred degrees and we kept the fan blowing on us all night. The next day was down to about one hundred fifteen, and we stayed put so we could spend most of our time in the water. It was an experience to think about when people complain that it's hot. Ashore, thousands of people packed the beaches and the water was crowded as I had never seen before.

When we got to Turkey, we were very surprised that the food was good. It wasn't international, or on the level of France and Italy, but considerably better than Greece. I always think back on how much Arugula we ate there; they call it *rocket*. It was about five cents for a large bunch. It was strong and about the best I've ever had. The fruit and peaches there were also excellent. I think the heat makes them so sweet.

Christian and Joyce, coast of Turkey 1988

I remember our first entry into Kusadasi, and I'll relate the procedure so you can understand the dilemma. First, we went to the Port Captain. He gave us some papers which took about fifteen minutes to prepare and then we were off to customs. There we went to several offices before someone reluctantly had us sit down at a desk. The man asked for our passports and the paperwork from the Port Captain. He had about ten different rubber stamps, each with a wooden shaped head. They were not labeled so he would take each one, put it down on the ink pad and stamp a blank paper to see if it was the right one or to see if it worked. He proceeded to fill out about five sheets of paper, which he stamped about six or eight times. Finally, when he completed the task it had been about an hour. He then gave us back the passports and several sheets of paper including the ones from the Port Captain and instructed us to go to immigration.

Each of these offices was four or five city blocks apart. At the immigration office, we waited for about an hour. Finally, a man showed up that spoke some English and told us it was too close to lunch time. We'd have to come back at two o'clock. We returned then and were there for another hour. A man took our passports, filled out some papers and asked us to wait. He was gone for about forty minutes. Tired of waiting I went to see if I could find out what was happening. I found him in an office down the hallway having coffee with some of his cronies. When he saw me, he said, "I'll be with you shortly." After ten minutes, he came and apologized for the delay, but something urgent had required his attention. When we finished there, we were instructed to return to the customs office.

At the customs office, the routine was like a bad joke told the second time. The same man proceeded to take all the papers and go through his stamps again. We were then instructed to take all of the papers he gave us to the Port Captain. The Port Captain was gone for the day and the associate said we must return in the morning. When we finally finished the next day we had spent a full day plus several hours. This episode was the worst we had ever experienced, but there were other times in Greece and Turkey nearly as bad. If you wonder, why these countries have financial problems, the answer is their inefficiency. To put things in perspective when we cleared back into France, it took twenty minutes!

We bounced back and forth between the Greek islands and Turkey for a couple of years. The several years spent in Greece and Turkey were memorable; their cultures stick in the mind. [But, when we crossed the Pacific on our future boat, we marveled at the fact even the smallest of islands there had better procedures for ships landing on their shores.]

***

[Since my Paris days I've considered myself knowledgeable about food. While, in France I had attended many classes at the Cordon Bleu and met Gaston Gate, who was labeled the Premiere Chef de France. It was the only class he conducted at the school because it was such prestige that he lent his name to that institution.

The class was asked one evening to make a dish that was typical of their country and several of the students from various lands made a specialty representative of their heritage. Everyone tasted the results. Monsieur Gate would then pass on his comments about the dish and would discuss its ingredients, tastes, and how he felt it could be improved. When my turn came, I prepared southern fried chicken. My step-father who was a professional chef came from Texas and often made this meal. I loved it and had watched him many times until I knew how to make it. When I completed the dish with mashed potatoes and country gravy, everyone liked it. Monsieur Gate was particularly impressed.

It was different from anything in France. In those days you bought the whole chicken, they didn't sell parts. The French chopped their chicken and when I brought it to class and cut it American style. Gate loved the dish and asked if I would come on a Sunday and help him prepare it for some friends. When I went to his home, it was one of the most beautiful chateaus in the country. The kitchen must have been fifteen-hundred square-feet, with a staff of about four people. That was when I realized he wasn't just a teacher. This had been a lifelong hobby. His father had founded an aeronautical parts company which he had run most of his life. His father also was very interested in cooking and had built this extraordinary kitchen. It had a rotating oven that could roast twenty large pieces of meat at one time. I had no idea he lived as he did and that there would be such a sophisticated group of people. The guests that night were the famous French singer Charles Trenet and his young sister Lucky (who I've mentioned previously), several political figures of the day and Mrs. Gate. They all raved about the chicken. It was so commonplace in America I was embarrassed with all the attention. Hardly what I would call gourmet compared to the elegant and superb dishes in France. But it was different and American folk type fare. Of course, Americans were very popular this short time after the war, as everyone still remembered the liberation and the kindness of the soldiers.]

***

The Dalmatian coast and the islands were so exciting and unique that we spent two seasons there. The first year we stayed at the Mon Falcone Marina about twenty miles west of Trieste. We found many great restaurants in Trieste and the food of the area was exceptional northern Italian cooking. The surprise was the little café in the marina that was open for breakfast and lunch. A Mama and her

361

daughter ran the place and I had the best pesto sauce and melanzanie of my life there.

The following year, after cruising northern Italy and the Yugoslavian coast again, we went into the inner harbor up the river from Dubrovnik. We spent less than a week there and went into the city every day. The city was spectacular with beautiful sights and restaurants. There were many people just wandering and enjoying this picturesque and ancient place. We had been there a few days when people started talking about a truce in the conflict in the region. And that a new proclamation was supposed to be agreed to before the deadline of midnight the next day. If they didn't reach a peace agreement, I was told that war might break out as a result. But we were assured everyone in the marina would be safe. The next day at six o'clock in the evening the agreement had still not been signed. I told Joyce I didn't want to be there in that situation so at eight that evening while it was still light out we headed across the Adriatic in high winds and heavy seas. I thought it would be better to handle a little weather than to take a chance on the unknown and be trapped on land between two sides in an armed clash.

It was a scary night. A large ship only a couple of miles away started heading directly at us. We changed course to avoid them, but they changed course as well and continued directly at us. It was very heavy seas and getting dark. We maneuvered several times and each time we changed course they changed as well. I got on the VHF radio on the prescribed channel sixteen and queried them; asking them to state their intentions, but they didn't answer. As they approached very close, we saw a group on deck waving at us. They passed by and went on their way. They had just been curious but were too stupid to realize they were alarming us with their actions.

At first light on a very dark morning with thick black clouds, I was sleeping below when Joyce yelled. I rushed on deck. She had just cleared a large platform abandoned on the sea. Because of the poor light and the large seas, it was difficult to detect. We were thankful Joyce had seen it in time. It was a large steel-bound raft made from fifty or more strapped together oil drums just floating along without lights or anyone aboard. The Albanians made these rafts and when the wind was favorable they launched them with many political refugees aboard. The Italian Navy would rescue the people but could do nothing with the dangerous rafts so they were left at sea where they became hazards to navigation. We both stayed up at that point. We could see the coast of Italy and as we approached, the sky got even darker and bolts of lightning started to form a web of lightning strikes into the water all around us. I quickly disconnected all of the electronics and we were careful not to touch anything that could be a conductor to the water. Using the remote control of the autopilot, we wouldn't have to hold the stainless steel wheel. We arrived safely in Siberi, inside the heel of the boot of Italy. That afternoon we learned rebel forces had come into the Dubrovnik marina and had machine-gunned and sunk over two hundred boats.

We left the boat in Siberi for the season and spent a week in Paris on the way home. The following year we cruised around Italy and stayed in Gaeta near Rome. We met many friends every time we visited and this was no exception. Alex and Gina were there on *Menbihan*, his thirty-six-foot motor-sailer. We had some great times, just as we had in Turkey. We continued through many of the favorite places of our previous journey ten years before.

* * *

Joyce and I visited every island and country in the ancient regions of the Mediterranean, trekking the land and sailing the coasts. On our annual visits, we often took international flights to visit a host of other countries and cultures on the way. It was my philosophy that the rewards of travel were more important than business and had become a stimulating factor in my writing and painting.

We ended our cruising on *Tarquin* in the Mediterranean in September of 1993. After eleven years and eighteen thousand miles, we felt we had covered the history and locations that were of interest. We sold the boat in Palma, Mallorca and returned to California. Our new boat was being built to fulfill our dream of a Pacific Ocean crossing. The sixty-eight-foot high-tech vessel, designed for major cruising, would be finished by April of 1994.

* * *

Touché m'Dear was built as a sophisticated fast cruiser, with every amenity available and many custom features of my own design. It was rigged so two people of our age could manage the boat in any weather. It was built specifically for our crossing the Pacific and visiting all of the South Pacific Islands. We took delivery in March of 1994. We spent two months adding the extras and learning the new navigation systems. The systems aboard were high-tech and well beyond any we had used in the past. The learning curve was mind boggling for a couple of old-timers.

The boat actually became much easier to handle than *Tarquin*. The accuracy of our computerized navigation and the maintenance was a marvel. The equipment gave us the complete weather picture and the fax capabilities gave us the latest in communication. We could now keep in constant touch with home, and if there were any emergencies, we could respond and plan.

Touché anchored in Bora Bora 1999

First, we needed to spend a lot of time at sea learning the sail handling and the systems. We took the following three months to travel the east coast and some of the Inter-Coastal Waterway. We stopped in New York, anchored near the Statue of Liberty; saw Baltimore, Annapolis, Charleston, Savannah, Jacksonville and St. Augustine, ending the season in Fort Lauderdale.

An exciting event occurred after leaving Annapolis. We stopped in Norfolk, Virginia, where many boats were waiting for a weather window to round Cape Hatteras, a notoriously dangerous area. With us were two other Sundeer yachts, both our size but with various layouts and equipment. Ten were built and customed out for people from all parts of the globe. The captain of a large schooner became the guru of the fleet on our morning net radio. He predicted that a low sweeping in from the Gulf of Mexico would be slowed down by the land and wouldn't present a problem by the time it reached the east coast. The weather predictions agreed and the entire fleet left together. We remained; I could see no reason for gambling when a two-day wait would give us a guaranteed window.

As it turned out, the low slowed across the south but began picking up force as it hit the east coast. By the time, the fleet got around Cape Hatteras they were hit with sixty and seventy-knot winds. One Sundeer called the Coast Guard and a South American man and his pregnant wife were rescued at sea by helicopter. Their boat had to be abandoned and the man had set it on autopilot, motoring at about three knots for the rescue. He and his wife then jumped into the rough seas. He thought it would be better to be plucked out of the water by the Coast Guard helicopter and its man on a cable. Instead, it was far more dangerous than remaining on the boat. Fortunately, they were okay, but it was a foolish decision, which could have cost their lives and maybe that of the rescue crew. Their boat was recovered in the North Atlantic about five days later cruising along at three knots and unscathed. The other Sundeer lost a fifteen-thousand-dollar tender from its davits, and when he finally cut it loose, there had already been considerable damage done. His decision of not putting the tender on deck wasn't good seamanship. This owner gave up cruising and put the boat up for sale in Fort Lauderdale. No lives were lost, but many boats had severe damage. All because they couldn't wait two days and took the judgment of one man who seemed to know what he was talking about.

Since my very beginnings and my experiences on my other boats I had learned the most important lesson of the sea, always err on the side of safety. If you want to get there in a hurry, take an airplane.

The Caribbean

Incident at Sea

In April, we continued through all of the islands of the Caribbean. We had made some of this trip before with a boat we had chartered for a month and with friends on their yachts on several occasions. On one such occasion, Joyce surprised me with a feat of physical prowess while in Tortola, anchored in Cane Garden Bay. We were with a friend and several couples and had ventured ashore. A steel band was playing in front of a large beach bar. Nearby a group of young crew from the various yachts were displaying their talent for rope climbing. A man with a stopwatch was timing each of the young studs as they made their climb. Watching them was a large crowd of yachties and the people in the café. After each climb, if a new better time was set, they all clapped with recognition.

We watched for about five minutes and Joyce, who was a rope climber in school, couldn't resist the challenge. When she approached the man, he said dismissively. "Women can't climb ropes as they don't have the upper body strength."

Joyce didn't budge and told him. "Just time me and we'll see!"

He gave a barely tolerant look but pulled his watch out ready to push the button. The crowd of young sailors yelled and gave her support. I think they just wanted to see how she would struggle up the rope. She started from a sitting position and scampered up the rope like a monkey. The man read the time and she was the fastest of all of them. Several of the young men objected and said the timing couldn't be correct; he must have made a mistake. There was a fuss, but many also said they thought she had done it in record time.

Joyce told them. "Time me again." She went up the rope like a bullet in even better time! All the women were so proud and congratulated her. It was a moment of great pride.

After a week in Fort Lauderdale, we were prepared and ready to go. Stocked with food, we were joined by a couple who had moved to Savannah from Los Angeles and they made the trip to the Bahamas with us. They were our first guests aboard *Touché* and we had a marvelous time. We found the boat with its much larger quarters perfect for entertaining.

For three months we sailed the Caribbean; diving, dining out and entertaining guests from home. We loved the warm climate and revisiting many familiar places. It had changed considerably since our first time. Back then there were few charter companies and most of the bays were sparsely populated with cruisers. Now it was chock-a-block with inexperienced people who were a constant concern. To avoid them we found ourselves picking anchorages which were not on the main directory list of the charter companies or recommended in the cruising books. The adventures and experiences through these islands were enough for another book so I'll just say we had many friends join us and we had memories we cherish.

We spent some time visiting a friend in the Dominican Republic and left there about six o'clock one evening. With winds from the southeast, we would be on a close reach to Puerto Rico. Estimating a wind speed of about twelve knots would put us in the harbor at first light, which was our objective. It was always better to clear customs first thing in the morning. About two hours after our departure the winds started to increase. I had based my timing on a sailing speed of eight knots. We were now approaching twelve and the winds were up to twenty knots. I didn't adjust sails to reduce speed but decided to make a long port tack south and increase the time, to arrive as planned. We had a rule of never entering an unknown harbor in the dark.

It was about one in the morning when I picked up a boat on the radar about five miles behind us on the same course. I thought this strange as we were killing time and a destination point on this tack was open ocean. Joyce was below sleeping and I kept an eye on the radar. The boat was gaining on us and I became concerned. I put the tracking device on (Marsat) and got a direction and speed of the other boat. We were now making about fourteen knots and the other boat was making twenty knots. I knew it must be a power boat.

When he was within three miles, I called for Joyce and told her the situation. I didn't want to tack and startle her while she was below, nor do it without her on deck. We tacked and set a new course for our destination in Puerto Rico. Within five minutes, the other boat changed direction and our tracking told us he was on an intercept course based on our speed. It was at this point we really started to worry. Just to be sure we tacked again and within five minutes he was on our track. We tacked again to get as close to Puerto Rico as possible and started the engine to give us greater speed. We adjusted sail and with full throttle were making eighteen knots. When he changed again, his intercept direction was directly into the seas and I realized he had to give it much more power to maintain twenty knots. Even with his speed he wouldn't intercept for about an hour and a half.

I got on the radio, international channel sixteen, and asked him to identify himself. I said I was aware he was tracking me and asked what his intention was. I never received an answer, but another yacht heading for Mono Island and the Dominican Republic picked up the call. He was a German with his wife and son on board and they were heading for an anchorage. He said he would remain out to stay in radio contact until we knew the circumstances. He also was a seasoned cruiser with a citizen band commercial radio license and would try to raise the Puerto Rico Coast Guard. I began also to use my single sideband long-range radio and attempted to reach them or customs. Although I didn't reach Puerto Rico, the Coast Guard in Miami picked up my distress call. They also would monitor the situation, and would try to raise the Puerto Rico Coast Guard to alert them.

Joyce was at the helm as I was more adept at operating the radio. The other boat continued to gain on us and soon we could see them bashing toward us through heavy seas. White foam with every wave was visible in the partial moonlight. Joyce and I planned that when they were quite close we would alter course directly into the seas at full throttle. When they closed on us, we let the sails flap violently and the boom swing wildly from side to side. We were crashing into every one of the ten-foot and larger seas sending a monster wave to each side. The boat pursuing us was about a fifty-footer; what we call a cigarette design. With red lights flashing, they pulled alongside. We saw a man facing us who looked to be in some sort of uniform. He shined a flashlight on the badge he held up. They had a bullhorn and instructed us to heave to. They were getting thoroughly drenched with the waves from our bow as two men on their foredeck looked to be positioned to jump aboard. The swinging of the boom and the bouncing and violent motion prevented that.

Joyce zigzagged and every time they closed she turned us away. They raced ahead and tried to block our path. I told her, "Ram them." They pulled away just in time as we had a gigantic anchor on a substantial sprit of solid stainless steel which would have gone right through their hull. They turned again yelling that they were with customs. We knew customs didn't go out and board people at sea when they were heading for port. They were probably pirates. Our tempers were up and we screamed that we wouldn't heave to and to follow us into port if they needed to board us.

We were at that point where we were scared but going to fight to keep them from boarding. They made a second run at us to come alongside. Just as they were catching up with us again, they suddenly made a hard right to starboard and headed for the Dominican Republic. We didn't understand why until I checked the radar and saw a large vessel was approaching us rapidly from the port of our direction. We were relieved as we figured the U.S. Coast Guard had arrived. The boat approached us downwind doing sixteen knots off about two hundred meters. It was a commercial fishing boat going out for the catch. Regardless, we were sure this was what scared them off.

I got on the radio and the German cruiser was happy we were safe. I told him the story and he said he would report it to the Dominican Republic authorities. He had tracked the boat and was sure it came from there. Joyce and I were exhausted; the strain and stress of the episode wiped us out emotionally. When we got to port, we went alongside where the books instructed us to go. But we didn't go to the check-in. Instead, we both collapsed and slept for several hours. When we got up, we checked in we confirmed they didn't have any customs or patrols out in that area. They asked if they had weapons, but we never saw any guns. To this day, Joyce and I wonder why they didn't have guns. And if they had pointed one at us, would we have heaved to and let them board us.

We sailed as far as Trinidad and put the boat up on the hard until the next season. Trinidad was a bad experience. We liked the people but the boatyard was poorly run and when we returned, the dehumidifier had been unplugged for a considerable time and the boat was ripe with mold. It was a two-week job of cleaning and remedying the situation. The boat yard would not take responsibility.

The Night Intruder

The next year we returned and made another jaunt through all of the islands for several months. We attended, Race Week in Antigua, and it was a party time unlike any we had ever experienced. The Bacardi Rum Company held an exceptional party aboard a reproduction of an old galleon. The dance band was loud and raucous and the drinks flowed like water. Cute little hostesses with trays of drinks actually took your drink away if it was low, and stuck a full one in your hand. It was the only time in our years of marriage that Joyce and I were really drunk together.

When we left, we staggered down the dock wobbly and without much balance. We got in our tender and I attempted to start the outboard. It wouldn't start, and then Joyce said, "I think you have to turn the switch on!" We laughed hard realizing we were so inebriated. Once started we headed to where we had anchored. Many boats had come in since we went ashore and there was no clear view of ours. There were perhaps fifty boats in the bay and we checked half of them before we found *Touché*. We were laughing most of the time and people on many boats were signaling for us to come and join them for a drink. We just waved and finally were aboard and safely in our bunk. We had a sizeable headache the next day, but it was worth it and fair exchange for so much fun and laughter.

On the way back south to avoid the coming hurricane season,

we anchored in Dominica, a small and beautiful island. We had another couple aboard, friends from Malibu. We had a pleasant dinner, drinks in the cockpit and retired about eleven. Joyce screaming awakened me suddenly. As I opened my eyes, I saw a naked man running out of the cabin. Joyce was after him in a flash with me just behind. In seconds, he was out the hatch and dove into the sea. I got a flashlight and scanned the waters around the boat. I didn't see anything so we turned all the lights off and I used my night vision binoculars. There were no dinghies or boats in the area so we concluded it was a person on a boat in the anchorage.

When we had arrived in port, I had noticed a rather derelict sloop with a French flag. In our many years in the Mediterranean, the yachties routinely warned about any shabby looking French boats, as often things disappeared when they were present. We had on many occasions re-anchored because of one of these vessels. When I studied this boat with my night vision glasses, I could clearly see a nude man drying himself in the cockpit. He was tall and lanky like the intruder. I shined a powerful searchlight on him, just to let him know I saw him drying himself at two o'clock in the morning. But I didn't hold it long as I didn't want a confrontation. We investigated below. My wallet which had been in my pants on the settee had been taken out and the money removed, then put back in the pocket. My friend's pants which he had on the bunk in the other aft cabin had been disturbed, but he had nothing in it to steal.

The next morning, I contacted a friend by radio on the morning net. I had heard that he had been robbed and learned it was in the same bay. I asked him if a French boat with a peppermint rolled jib was in the bay when he was robbed. He said, "Yes it was, and I was suspicious of the guy aboard." It added up. The afternoon we entered the bay we had come from the south. We had passed it and he had seen the direction of our entry. Early the next morning at first light he headed north. I guess trying to make us think he was heading the same direction as we were as I watched him from my foredeck. That evening we arrived in Guadalupe, the capital of the French Islands. As we cruised into the anchorage, there was our friend on the French boat. He had gone north and doubled back to the south. This confirmed my suspicion and I went to the police and reported the incident. Because I spoke French, they were very polite and took me seriously. They said they couldn't arrest him on that evidence, but they would add it to their records and keep an eye on him.

The Caribbean was becoming more dangerous all of the time. Night robberies when people were not aboard and the stealing of dinghies and outboards were becoming common. We had heard of some burglaries and some scary stories of natives robbing people. The charter boats and cruisers were often careless and left their boats unattended and unlocked. Some of the poor people of the islands, invaded by people of wealth on their yachts, resented them and saw it as an opportunity. The situation was particularly bad on the coast of Venezuela. We locked our tender to the boat and lifted it on the davits every night. We installed a motion detector after the intruder affair and made up a dummy that we put a light behind in the cockpit so it looked like someone was sleeping in the pilothouse at night.

We backtracked through all of the Caribbean islands having friends join us and investigating areas we hadn't visited previously. When the season ended, we took the boat to Puerto La Cruz in Venezuela. The yard there was more equipped for long-term storage and we had no problems when we returned the following spring.

In 1997, we covered the southern Caribbean and again had

many friends join us. We anchored near our friends aboard *Royal Eagle*, a magnificent 150-foot Feadship. We had another couple with us and they were a party of three couples. We were all ski friends from Vail, Colorado and spent three days diving, eating and partying. The Los Roques Islands were the perfect setting for fun and games. We spent time in all of these islands which we found to be the most comfortable of our adventures. The sea was pristine, plenty of fish, lobster, and crab, and few cruisers to crowd the bays. At the end of the nearly five-month season, we returned to Puerto La Cruz and put the boat back up on the hard.

The following year we decided we wouldn't have guests but would spend our time meeting other cruisers until we got to the San Blas Islands. Guests were fine when you were remaining in a given area without a schedule, but trying to cover long distances with people aboard was difficult. We found they became scared when there was any sea running, and the long sailing periods that we enjoyed were not appreciated by most.

We spent a week in Bonaire in the ABC islands, well-known for the fantastic scuba diving there. There are excellent restaurants and the Dutch population was efficient and helpful. We sailed on to Curacao and Aruba and moored right in front of a sidewalk café and restaurant where we could also view the interior of the casino. There were wonderful markets, restaurants and supply stores for our every need. We knew the islands off the Panama coast would have meager supplies.

We had a fast three and a half-day passage to the San Blas Islands. September was still the hurricane season and high winds built up high seas, all in a westward direction. We were below the hurricane belt, but still in an area where you have to be very cautious.

This became evident some weeks later when Hurricane Mitch started developing in the exact track we were on. We watched the weather pictures and reports carefully. Although we loved Aruba and wanted to spend a little more time there, we also wanted to take advantage of the weather window. A low had passed through followed by a large high-pressure zone pushing up from the southeast off the Venezuelan and Columbian coasts. The first day and night on the tail end of the low-pressure moving west gave us winds of twenty-five knots and twenty feet seas. Our course with the seas on the aft quarter was a little bumpy, but the strong winds held us firmly. We had set our course more north than a direct route called for as the waters close to the Columbian Coast have a reputation for piracy.

The first twenty-four hours were very fast and we covered two hundred and sixty miles. The second day the wind dropped to fifteen knots and the seas calmed to ten feet. Mostly we only needed to keep a lookout as we made the entire trip on autopilot. It was our second visit to the archipelago. We had helped the restaurateur, Jean Leon of La Scala fame, to take his fifty-five-foot sloop to these islands in 1992. It's one of our favorite places in the world and after over a hundred countries that's a very special recognition. These islands and their inhabitants, the Kuna Yala nation, are truly extraordinary. They are the second smallest people in the world. The men average about four feet seven inches and the women about four feet four inches. But, they have generous hearts and a friendly and happy spirit. They are very creative and their molas, indigenous art, are known around the world. Each day they'd come with lobster and crab from the reefs bringing along the trinkets and molas they crafted.

We didn't dive on the reefs that protected the islands as they were sensitive about the cruisers invading their territory. We always purchased the sea life from the men in their palm log Cayucos (dugout canoes). The water was eighty plus degrees and one could spend the entire day swimming and enjoying the beauty of the islands. The San Blas consist of three hundred and sixty-five islands, most of them within twenty miles of the east coast of Panama. The area covers about a hundred miles of coastline and is about one hundred miles south of the Panama Canal. The further you move south the more primitive the culture.

The coast is steep and the mountains rise to five thousand feet. This causes incredible cloud formations and flash rain storms which last only a half hour or so. The skies are the most dramatic I have ever seen. The islands are low, often only a few feet above the sea, and covered with dense palms with crystal white sand framed by the aquamarine and light blue waters. There is very little tide or current and the water was perfect. It is interesting to note many of the photographs used to advertise the South Pacific are actually the San Blas Islands. We made this observation in comparing our personal photographs with posters. The area was a favorite place for cruisers and we met people we had known in previous years in various parts of the world. One couple we met were good companions of ours in Corsica and Sardinia. We had spent many fun times together and to suddenly meet them again was very special.

We lingered in these islands for a month before continuing on to Isla Grande in the Portobello National Park, a resort community about a hundred miles south of the Panama Canal. There was a small beach enclave of expatriate Americans who wished to escape the buzz of the cities and the hassle of daily life in the United States. It was an inexpensive area to live, and one could drive to Costco in Panama City in two and a half hours. We spent several days there before the canal transit.

We waited for our transit reservation in Cristobal. We hired two extra line handlers and the required pilot for the passage through the canal. Two days later we made our second transit. It was different from the first one before the canal had been handed over to the Panamanians. Now, the deterioration was evident. Transit was much more expensive and poorly organized. It was a revelation to see what the United States had given away. We owned it, built it and cared for it, and it made a profit of a half billion dollars per year. It was also strategic to world economics. Thank you, Mr. Carter, for your generosity. The strange part of the equation was the average local citizen resented the fact we gave it to their country. The American presence there had brought many jobs and wealth to the country.

When we arrived at the Pedro Miguel Boat Club, we put the boat in a protected berth. This quaint little historical spot was old and charming, unlike any marina we had visited before. It is located between the Miraflores and Pedro Miguel locks, one step down to the Pacific. We left the boat in the care of another cruiser who was married to a Panamanian woman.

17

PACIFIC CROSSING

Why the sailor goes to sea has always been a mystery to many. I can only, in part, describe the enormous revelations that invade one's mind. It's hard to explain the ebullience of momentary thrills which invariably occur while at sea. In what one person finds dull to the point of unbearable boredom, another finds nuances that bring pleasure to the core of their being.

Imagine yourself at sea, with dark overcast skies, your body reacting automatically to the methodical rolling motion because of your years of riding the wind. Your mind is free and wanders through a labyrinth of sensations. The heel of the boat, with the steady force of the breeze holding you firm, centers you and supports a feeling of contentment. Then from out of nowhere in the bleak gray environment a small swallow flutters around the boat. He looks for a place to land and finds his perch on the bridge deck near you.

This scene played out in real life for Joyce and me. We watched him carefully and knew he was exhausted. We were forty or fifty miles from the nearest land. Joyce went below and got a plate of bread crumbs and a small bowl of fresh water. She set it close to him. He sensed she wasn't a threat and let her get very close. He drank and ate looking up and watching us with small, jerky, motions. He quivered at first, but as he settled in his fear passed. After a while, he flitted about inside the pilothouse then sat on the instrument console. Slowly he lowered his body and shrugged down into his feathers. He knew we accepted him as our guest. He trusted us and slept for a couple of hours. When he was ready to continue his journey, we went on deck to say goodbye. He seemed to have his bearings and circled the boat quite close before heading south toward Colombia. There is a beauty in that experience that is hard to describe. It happens at sea because your world has shrunk to the setting and that moment.

After a month of living on the boat, all sense of time was lost as we knew it in the context of our life at home. We watched clouds; they kept changing more rapidly than any other landscape, forming new shapes and forms, shadows and colors. Their essence could not be captured on canvas, or even on film. It's life at the moment; an experience, a phenomenon yet just one of nature's many incredible dramas played out in our world. If you're willing to watch it until the final act of departure, if you look closely, you'll find every color in the prism reflecting and reaching out for a new dimension. The memories of our sailing adventures are treasures of the mind. We stored them away for the time when perhaps the body rejects such a life for the comforts of a softer time.

It was March 20, 1999, when we returned to Panama and started provisioning for our Pacific crossing. We knew there wouldn't be a good supply point until we reached Papeete, Tahiti. We had fifteen cubic feet of freezer and ten cubic feet of refrigeration, so it was enough to sustain two people for a year. Our range under power was twenty-four hundred miles or more if we didn't use the generator consistently. On the 26th, we made final preparations and transited the last locks. We made a shakedown cruise around a few of the islands to the Balboa Yacht Club. On the Fools day of April, we set sail for the Galapagos Islands.

380

Christian & Joyce, South Africa 1993

April 29, Thursday

The hull groaned and creaked from the constant pressure of the sea. The waves were running ten to twelve feet in a confused pattern from the changing direction of the trade winds. The bouncing and plunging motion kept us hanging on with every move. I had slept for seven hours and felt refreshed. Usually, we would take three or four-hour watches, but Joyce knew I was fatigued and let me sleep until I woke. She made penne with ham and vegetables, garlic, ginger, peppers and spices, which was a creative concoction that was truly delicious. At three a.m. Joyce went to bed and she slept until eight or nine that morning.

The first three days the winds were light or none at all, so we motored much of the time. It was a relief to make nine and ten knots instead of seven. We didn't power over that speed because the fuel consumption was much higher as the rate increases. At that point, still early in the trip, with more fuel thousands of miles away, it became a careful study of miles to go and fuel on hand. We had to consider the future needs of the generator, water maker, and main engine. At night, with the multitude of instruments giving us all the pertinent data, our electrical usage was considerable. Everything was determined by the conditions. We didn't keep more than three hundred gallons of water in the tanks, as this water ballast shifted to the windward side, to keep the boat more upright and comfortable. If we had light winds, we could pick up a little extra speed by running the main engine. And at the same time the large alternators were generating electricity for the batteries, making water, and freezing the holding plates for refrigeration and the freezer. If we had good winds and were making significant speed, we would use the generator as it consumed much less fuel.

We hadn't seen another boat for several days and were happy watching the marvels of this beautiful planet. Two days ago we had gone through a school of fifty to a hundred porpoise. They greeted us and played around the boat for twenty minutes before they got bored and went on their way. Some big ones bumped the bow. They liked to stay right in front of it, dashing in and out of the wake and then scooting off and jumping high in the air. The faster we went the longer it held their interest. They could swim at forty knots or more so even if we were making thirteen or fourteen knots it wasn't a challenge. The skies were spectacular and, like watching a fire, it fascinated us for long periods.

We watched the sea and reflected on the beautiful eight days we spent in the Galapagos Islands with cruising friends; some new and some we'd been meeting for many years. Much of that time was with a new group we had met at the Pedro Miguel Boat Club. Among that group were a couple with their nine-year-old daughter and a single-hander named Larry. We took several day cruises to other islands to see the beasties. We especially marveled at the giant tortoises. There were some good restaurants and we ate out most of the time. Joyce would cook daily in the weeks to come, so it was a break for her.

May 3, Monday

The last few days had been a period of adjustment for both of us as we settled into the solitude of a long passage. We were cleaning out our intellectual tubes and leaving the *basura* of civilization behind in our wake. Each day we tuned in more to the wind, sky, and sea. The vastness of this undulating mass of liquid wilderness wasn't our natural habitat. We were aliens out there. When in steady winds and peaceful seas we began to feel it was a friendly new world beckoning us to its honesty and purity. When she commands respect the friend departs and her demanding ways thwart even the strong willed. We made our alliance with time and started to understand the beauty of solitude. It was our environment for another week or more until we made landfall in Atuona, in Hiva Oa.

Three days before I had heard the screeching sound of the fishing line. "Wow," I said, "it must be a big one!" We quickly rolled up the jib and feathered the sails. I took the pole from its holder, keeping a wire hooked on the rail pulpit. It took me an hour of testing my arm strength to reel him in. Joyce took over the pole to bring him alongside while I gaffed him. We brought aboard a three and a half-foot Dorado. The sun would soon slide beneath the horizon, so I quickly started to prepare him for the freezer. It took over an hour and I had to finish it under the mizzen flood lights. We filled thirty bags which we then vacuumed for freezing; each bag contained a full meal for two. Joyce put aside the food we'd earlier planned to cook that evening and we had large fish steaks for dinner. The following day's lunch and dinner were sushi.

To that point, the winds had been kind. We had experienced a few rain storms during the transit from Panama. They were always fun; we would get out the shampoo, soap and washcloths and take the ultimate shower. We looked like a couple of clowns frolicking in a downpour in the middle of the ocean. Most of the time was spent reading, listening to CDs and viewing an occasional movie. Sunday afternoons we would have a matinee with popcorn, candy bars, and all the junk food we generally didn't eat. I had received regular weather reports via satellite, but the information from other boats on the single sideband radio told us what they were experiencing both in front of us and behind. That information was the most valuable. As we exchanged weather reports we made friends, we would meet shortly on the islands ahead.

May 7, Friday

Our 12th day out the same, old, trade winds, light and variable pushed the seas to our destination. The big mounds of water seemed relentlessly determined to get somewhere with their white caps breaking and rolling toward some unknown rendezvous. We were only four days away from our next destination but in no hurry. There were many more books to read and thinking to do. It was all becoming clearer. The world was looking bigger, and our lives and the people in them smaller.

Marquesas Islands

The Marquesas Islands are volcanic with steep walls of green rising to the sky; every anchorage was lush and beautiful. We visited Hiva Oa, Fatu Hiva, Tahuata, Oa Po and Nuka Hiva.

We arrived in Hiva Oa after a passage of seventeen days. Several of the cruisers in smaller boats had been at sea for as many as forty or fifty days. Many didn't stop in the Galapagos, as the currents demanded a good engine and adequate fuel. Some misjudged fuel consumption and had to go on directly. Without additional fuel, they were forced to wait out the doldrums which, in the intertropical convergence zone bordering the equator, could be windless for a week or more. Others had come directly from points in California and Mexico, a considerably shorter distance to the Marquesas.

We had now cruised throughout each of these spectacular islands. On the island of Nuku Hiva in Toilhae Bay, the most awe-inspiring sights had surrounded us in anchorage after anchorage. The islands were young and the raw beauty of the volcanic formations towered above us with their covering of tropical lushness. The cloud formations lingered on the peaks, adding a natural beauty beyond which we had ever experienced before.

In Fatu Hiva, we dropped two hundred feet of chain in a natural mountain crevice, the steep-walled bay leading to a small village. The bay was filled to capacity with seven boats. Because of the three-thousand-foot ridge line and a steep rise on both sides the wind funneled down into the anchorage with a fury, often causing boats to drag their anchors. But that added to the excitement of our stay. We had hefty ground tackle and didn't have a problem, but we did help others to reset. At one point, a Frenchman left his boat to go to the village and while he was away his boat started dragging toward the rocks. With two men from other boats, we were able to push him from disaster with our tenders, but he continued to float out to sea. Another yachtie went ashore to find him in the village. We couldn't start his engine so it was a matter keeping him from drifting too far before he returned. Finally, after hours of running our outboards and towing against the wind he returned.

The bay in Hana Vave had many high spires rising out of the water and from plateaus which served as pedestals. The vision was so incredible as to seem unreal, like someone from Disney studios had just made it up for a magical movie. We stayed for four days admiring and enjoying what we agreed must be the most beautiful anchorage in the world.

Our final anchorage was Daniels Bay before the four-day transit to the Tuamotus islands. A cruising book recommended the hike to the waterfall for those who were fit enough to make the trip.

We met fellow cruisers that had walked the trail several days before and wanted to go again. This was a great advantage as firsthand knowledge was essential. But the group, all much younger than us, were concerned the old geezers might not be able to make it. They assured us we could rest or turn back at any time.

As it turned out, Joyce and I didn't consider it very difficult. The hike up the valley mostly followed an ancient Polynesian rock trail about six feet wide. It had deteriorated considerably over the centuries since it was built. There were many old altars where the king would hold court and the remnants of carved stone Tikis had fallen by the wayside. It was evident very few people had walked this trail, as it appeared untouched. For three hours, we walked through pristine forests of ferns and exotic plants and trees. We forged the creek seven times in each direction, often up to our waists. The current was swift and the crossing was exciting. Joyce, without very much body weight, would ride the rapids at an angle to cross in several places. We came upon a grove of Banyan trees in a swampy area. The floor was rocks and mud covered by a blanket of flowers. The trees twisted, turned, and formed an animated scene like something out of Fantasia with the sun peeking through to make them dance in the shadows of the moving leaves.

As we made our way up into the canyon, the cliffs above us closed in on the trail. The walls, sheer cliffs, and spires rose well over two thousand feet. When we approached the final quarter-mile, the walls seemed to overhang the trail. The path ended at a two-hundred-foot wide pool that spanned to each side of the sheer stone walls. It was eighty to a hundred feet long and led to a large rock in the center of a closed canyon. On both sides were smaller stones many feet in diameter, but small enough to be scaled. The water poured into the pool equally from both sides. We swam fully clothed with tennis shoes on across the pool to the rocks. We remained fully dressed because although the temperature of the air was eighty-five degrees, the water was seventy degrees. The mosquitos were the other reason, as well as for protection from the rocks if you were swept away by the current. We covered our skin with Deet and re-applied it many times on the journey.

We climbed the lower part on the left side of the rocky opening. After another twenty feet, we came to another pool. The second pool was so close to the waterfall that the mist was thick and hovered over it. We had been forewarned and brought our diving goggles with us. The wind created by the volume of cascading water dropping two thousand feet was enough to produce white caps in the small pool. We plunged through the waterfall into the cave behind. The weight of the water was like a shower of small stones. Most of the cruisers didn't attempt this, but Joyce and I needed that charge of adrenaline to complete the experience. It was truly one of our most beautiful and exciting adventures.

The four-day passage to the Tuamotus brought quiet seas and light winds. We left the autopilot on a single course with the engine pushing us at seven knots. We entered the pass at nine o'clock in the morning with the sun high enough to spot the reefs on both sides. Kauehi is a small atoll off the beaten path. Several other cruising friends were making this their landfall and we decided to join them. It was our first calm anchorage since we had left the confines of the Pedro Miguel Yacht Club.

The volcanic Tuamotus are sunken craters, forming saltwater lakes in the middle of a series of small motus and reefs. Seventy-six islands stretched for a thousand miles, forming a barrier between Tahiti and the Marquesas. The reefs on the eastern and southern sides of each motus are difficult to see. The northern sides are low with palm trees a recognizable feature from the sea. Because the current enters from the south and east over the reefs and exits out of the only passes for entering you could encounter currents of more than eight knots. Many boats waited for a slack tide before attempting to enter. We always waited for enough light to enter any of these motus. The many reefs and coral heads required that Joyce sit up in the spreaders in a bosun's chair and guide me in with our headset walkie-talkies.

The Tuamotus were known as very special scuba diving areas and we made many dives. It had now been two months since we left Malibu. We had met many wonderful people that had all shared a dream of this paradise. All the natives through the Marquesas, Tuamotus, and the Society Islands spoke their Polynesian language, and many spoke French as well. Since French is my second language, it was easier for me than most of the other cruisers. The village in Kauehi was picturesque and the color of the water something to dream about. Strewn about the bay were little houses set up on stilts with porches that served as work areas for harvesting the black pearls for which the area is famous. When the first ships arrived, the islands were plundered for the rich oyster beds and abundant natural pearls.

We loved the people. They were friendly, smiled and said hello on every occasion. They were not money oriented as there are only a few small stores, within houses, that sell essentials. They were very interested in trading for anything that caught their interest, but mostly for liquor. The government levied such a high tax on alcohol that a bottle of rum was fifty dollars. We learned about the black pearl industry in the islands and how the expert pearl divers cut and plant the symmetrical bead particle into the living oyster. When they harvest the pearls, they again plant the particle. This continues until the third implant after which the oyster will not produce a good quality pearl. At that point, they eat the shellfish and use the shells for jewelry. The oysters have a small hole drilled in the hinge of the shell and are attached to a long wire with fabric tails. They are then submerged up to ninety feet for a year or more. Some of the divers can hold their breath for up to four minutes. They dive straight to the bottom, with weight for the deeper dives. They then work the line and rise to the surface. Pearls are judged by how symmetrical they are as well as the color and smooth surface. We made some trades for black pearls which were good quality, but we didn't really know their value.

The 13th of June was my birthday and I had never known anyone with this same birth date. As it turned out, another cruiser with us did. Several of the other boats got together and threw us a party with a big Happy Birthday sign strung across the cockpit. It was an evening to remember, incredible sunset and all.

After four days in Kauehi, we made a mid-morning departure for the atoll of Fakarava. The entry was calm and we anchored close to a small village on the east side of a motu. It was a superbly picturesque little haven of about two hundred fun and loving people. We quickly made friends of the locals and were pleased to see the young German couple we had met many times, starting from the islands of the Dutch Antilles. After a week of diving and playing with the locals, we headed through a series of islands and then on to Papeete. When we arrived in Tahiti, we anchored at Maeva Beach, close to the Tahina Marina. We spent a week eating at good restaurants and stocking up on goodies, fuel, and water. We checked in the jewelry shops and realized what a wonderful selection of black pearls we had acquired in the Tuamotus.

Our godson Jesse Powell had graduated university and as our

gift to him we flew him and his girlfriend to join us for ten days. We sailed with them around the island of Tahiti for five days, experiencing some deserted and excellent anchorages. We spent their remaining days in Moorea anchored on the reef at the entrance with a view of the entire bay.

After returning our guests to Papeete, we headed for Luahine. We did an overnighter and arrived in the small village of Fare. It was a relief from the more touristed areas. I would recommend to anyone coming to the area to make a special effort to spend a few days in Fare; it's an insight into the Society Island Polynesian heritage. We found lovely anchorages through Raiatea, Tahaa and a selection of sophisticated quality restaurants in most of these French governed islands.

We arrived in Bora Bora on July 9th and anchored right in front of the village in ninety feet of water. It was a deep, but good holding and we had a short dinghy ride to the small basin that made landing very comfortable. The village had prepared for an upcoming holiday celebration, on the 14th, and the arena for the dancing contests was only a few feet from the basin. The area was a temporary village made up of elaborate huts constructed of palm leaves and all were either restaurants or bars. The entire community was on silky white sand and the bars had temporary wood dance floors. Usually nothing started until 3:00 pm, except on Bastille Day, a major holiday in the Islands and France. We were fortunate to celebrate it there. The audience for the festivities was primarily Polynesian, but there were many yachties and tourists. The dance contestants represented many islands throughout Polynesia and they danced in large groups with their own drum bands. On the last night of dancing, each village or island that had sent a troupe was represented by the best of their individual dancers. The atmosphere was pure joy and the dancing was something to behold; a glimpse of the Bounty days in all their glory.

The Unknown Paradise, the Cook Islands

After Bora Bora, we visited Rarotonga, the capital of the Cook Islands. All of the Cook Islands are protected by New Zealand and have been given the citizenship of that country. As a result, there's been a tremendous migration to New Zealand from the Cooks and other islanders who hold citizenship.

The winds had been gusting to more than thirty knots and the mainsail was still full on a close reach into Avatiu Harbor. Joyce headed the boat up into the wind with sufficient speed to hold her on course with the autopilot. We went forward, dropped the main and cleaned up all the lines so they wouldn't wash overboard and into the prop. The twelve to fourteen foot seas were breaking over the bow and washing down the decks as we plowed directly into the waves. As soon as we returned to the cockpit we set a new course off the wind by forty degrees making for an easier ride to a point a half-mile off the entrance to the port. Within a few minutes, while safely sheltered in the pilot house, the winds started gusting to well over forty knots. The rain was so heavy we couldn't see the bow. For two and a half hours we motored, guided by radar and waited for a break in the weather.

When we entered the harbor, we were directed by radio to tie up to a steel survey ship bouncing against the concrete wall, just behind a giant freighter. Once inside the port we realized there was little maneuvering room. While I jogged the boat around from side to side, Joyce got out all the ropes and fenders, put them all on the port side and readied the lines from the various positions. I was fully occupied with the positioning the boat around the bow of the freighter and alongside the survey ship. We lined things up nicely and a group of about four or five robust young men jumped aboard and helped us secure everything.

When it stopped raining, we were able to evaluate our location. With large swells rolling directly into the harbor, we had excellent protection from the freighter which was blocking most of the seas. Others in the harbor were bouncing violently and all hands were aboard every yacht watching in case something broke loose. A precarious several hours later the winds backed to the west and things calmed. We stayed on the boat until the harbor director, the immigration officer, and a customs official came aboard. These were rolled into one laughable and lovable Kiwi character by the name of Don Silk.

I must admit it was the most entertaining clearance we had ever received. He started the process, pulling out dozens of sheets of paper with volumes of questions, instructed me that this sheet and that sheet must have eight copies each, and each must be hand written. He said the authorities didn't trust copies! Just as he had me going and really frustrated, he started to laugh. "If you give me a cold beer, I think I can simplify the requirements." After a few simple forms, we were finished. We spent a couple of hours talking boats, ships, and the Cook Islands. When I said we would be there for three days, he said, "I came here on my boat for three days also, but people have a tendency to stay longer than they planned. For me, it was forty years ago." Don Silk was well-known in those islands. He had run inter-island shipping for most of his life and his adventures were a legend. His book, From Kauri Trees to Sunlit Seas, is a delight to read.

Rarotonga is one of our favorite destinations in the world. The people are beautiful, the beaches are superb and it is probably just as Bora Bora was thirty or forty years ago. Lushly green and dramatic vistas are the norm. It is the perfect mixture of primitive culture and the accessibility of a civilized lifestyle.

After Rarotonga

We spent a week on Rarotonga and could easily have been there a month. Unfortunately, it's a tentative harbor and very vulnerable whenever the winds back around to the north, as the swells rolled directly into the basin. We left reluctantly for the two and a half day voyage to Palmerston Island.

Palmerston Island is an atoll populated by the descendants of an Englishman and his three Polynesian wives. William Marsters settled here with his Penrhyn Island women in 1862. He fathered twenty-six children and divided the island into separate reefs and sections for each of his three families. He established strict rules regarding intermarriage. There are seven sets of islands scattered along the coral reef that surround a large lagoon. The main island that's home to the families is a jewel of white sand beaches and dense coconut palms. Their homes are quite comfortable and the people possess a warmth and love that are hard to explain. When we arrived in stormy weather, they came out in a skiff to help us put our anchor in the best location. There was no entrance to the lagoon deep enough so we anchored outside in the lee of the island. A passage of even a small boat requires local knowledge and great skill. Every morning they came out in the boat and picked us up, and in the evening returned us aboard. At night, it was miraculous how they could weave their way in and out around the coral through an intricate path.

The people adopted us and we became like family within a few days. Their supply ship comes only once every six to eight weeks and we had been told what supplies were hard for them to attain so we brought an ample amount of food and goodies. They had VCRs and monitors and told us they watched the movies they had as many as twenty or thirty times so we gave them many of our cassettes. They had only one guitar on the island, which they shared. About half a dozen of the men had learned to play it very well. I hated to give up my guitar I kept aboard, but I knew it would bring them great joy and happiness. So I gave it to them as a gift with the promise the men would teach the children to play. We spent a week diving, fishing, playing volleyball, laughing, dancing and feasting with these unique people. When we left, about twenty people came out in their boats to see us off with much hugging, kissing, and crying as we bid farewell to our new family.

Beveridge Reefs

We were in high winds and it was a fast ride to Beveridge Reefs. This area hadn't been written about and wasn't in any of the sailing books except for warnings to avoid the area. The charts also gave specific warnings to stay clear. Don Silk had sailed these waters for forty years and told us the entire area was a diverse paradise. Over drinks one evening he told us of the reefs everyone avoids. He explained there was a channel which could take us into the lagoon. The entire lagoon for miles was a sand bottom with coral heads that were easily avoided in good light. The perimeter of the reef had a circumference of about fifteen miles. We anchored near the breaking waves on the east side of the reef. A large fiberglass trawler lay on her side in a few feet of water just over the ledge of the reef. Over the years, the pounding waves had partially dismantled her and she gave the scary impression of a ghost ship in the moonlight. The ship was the only landmark we could check to determine that our position remained the same.

The combination of a challenging entrance and its isolation from any inhabited place gave us a glimpse of what it was like in these islands before it was fished out. The Japanese had purchased the rights to fish many of these island territories and the ignorant local authorities put no restrictions on fishing activities. They came in with their factory ships, small boat fleets, using fine nets, and raped the seas. In many islands, the people lived easily on the abundance of the sea, but for many years, and even now, they spoke with great resentment about what was done to the area. The deep water fishes were still difficult to hook and the islanders now eat many varieties of reef fish, such as the parrotfish, that they did not eat before.

Waters of the area were the clearest we had ever seen. With the anchor out 120 feet, I could clearly see if it dug in properly for good holding. When we started diving, we were awestruck by the beauty and colors. It was like swimming in an aquarium; there were so many fish, turtles, and sea life species of such varied colors. All juxtaposed against the backdrop of hard and soft coral. There were numerous large sharks, but we knew they had such an abundance of food that they wouldn't be interested in our strange life form. We didn't fit in their food chain, but we were most careful when taking lobster or fish. After five days of isolation, two of our friends on *Moonshadow* and *Total Devotion* came to join us. These couples were full of energy and fun. We dived all day and partied with a lobster feast until late each night. The wine reserves dwindled rapidly and after another three days we needed the rest of going to sea. It was a difficult place to leave.

Two days and 400 miles later we sailed into Niue, one of the smallest independent nations on the globe. The people there have developed a society, more so than many of the other more primitive islands, significantly influenced by different religions, which made them a docile and friendly people. The religions, with their social pressures, have also driven many of them to New Zealand, which also protects the island and offers citizenship. When we were there, there were little more than 2000 people living on the island, but it was said there were 12,000 Niue Islanders living in New Zealand. There were empty homes and derelict structures across the land. Niue had a few adequate restaurants and some small hotels and motels. One very plush hotel, with a magnificent view, became a hangout while we were there. After *Moonshadow* had arrived, we had many evenings of drinks and dinners at the pool which overlooked an incredible coastline.

Niue is the highest coral atoll in the world. Its limestone caves and pools surround the island and make for fascinating swimming and diving. The one drawback is that it is rampant with sea snakes. On every dive, we would see dozens of the little devils all around us. On one occasion, a large one went after Joyce. She flew out of the water like a missile. The locals told us they could be very curious but rarely bit. When they bit a human their fangs, which are situated deep in their small mouth, rarely inject enough venom to cause death. Sea snake bites claim only a few lives each year.

We picked up a mooring on arrival. These moorings are in over 100 feet of water and were placed there to bring in the boating world, where anchoring is difficult and dangerous. There were twelve boats including *Total Devotion*. When we arrived going ashore was a complicated procedure. The tender had to be bridled for lifting, and the dock approached through heavy swells. Joyce would jump ashore and hold the boat with the tether while I placed the giant hook from the crane lifting device. Then I would jump ashore and use the crane to haul the boat on the dock. Fortunately, we had folding wheels on the stern and that made it much easier to then move to the storage area.

Tonga

After a week in Niue, we had our usual reluctance to leave a beautiful place and new friends behind. It is one of the most challenging aspects of a Pacific crossing. Most of the places you visit hold pure and loving people. We tried to get to know a single family and their friends at each place rather than getting involved with too many and knowing none.

Following two days of easy sailing, we entered the Neiafu Bay in the Vava'u group of the Tongan islands. Neiafu is the last gathering place after the crossing. From here some will go on to New Zealand, some to Australia and others will continue into the Indian Ocean for a nonstop circumnavigation.

Every friend we'd met from the Panama Canal through these islands would get together again to say goodbyes or to make plans to meet in the future. Most of the cruisers have shared many experiences, hikes, dives and meals aboard their boats. We met so many wonderful people it was sad to say goodbye to the ones going a different route. As all cruisers say we will meet again, but although we exchanged information we know many are gone forever. They're from every country in the world and without exception all speak English.

The mix of paths and backgrounds is truly impressive. One

evening while there, with friends aboard, we counted the professions we could think about offhand. We met several medical doctors, two psychiatrists, three dentists, several builders, and developers. There were also numerous CEOs of large companies and some educators, including some famous professors from the great universities. I was the only professional artist, but writers were among the most numerous. Americans comprise the largest number of travelers we encountered, about 40%, of which more than half were from California. Many others were from Washington state and 20% came from Canada. The English were next with boats from Norway, Sweden, Denmark, Germany, Italy, Switzerland and many from both Holland and France. There were one or two from odd places around the globe, but these mentioned made up the vast majority.

The Final Leg to New Zealand

It was a fast and uneventful sail from Tonga to Fiji in just less than four days. That included some hours of killing time waiting for enough light to traverse the reef strewn area. Suva was another gathering place for cruisers. Some took the more northern route to Australia, but many went by way of Suva to both Kiwiland and Oz.

We waited and carefully picked a weather window to New Zealand. That transit was one where most people got into trouble as it was an area of quickly developed storms, often with the wind against the current causing steep, challenging seas. We had some nasty winds and seas only hours out of Suva. Because we were pinned down to a southerly route between islands and reefs we had to plow headlong into the maelstrom. It was a wet and miserable six hours before we could fall off to the west and ride comfortably. The winds subsided overnight and we made a slow circuit back to the south as the winds backed.

For the next five days, we had good winds and made a six-day passage covering the 1200 miles to our destination in the Bay of Islands. The little old whaling port of Russell became a favorite and we rested there for five days joining several boats that had become our closest friends on the journey across the pond. We covered the coast of the North Island from Russell to Gulf Harbor and stopped at the magnificent and picturesque towns, bays and islands. At our final mooring, until March of the following year, we cleaned, repaired and made improvements to the boat. Some of the work would be done while we were away so we were organizing everything in advance. The boat would remain in New Zealand for at least the next two years while we saw more of the western Pacific.

We'd been gone for over eight months. We had covered many thousands of miles; it had been a demanding adventure, both physically and mentally. Out of the nearly 100 boats we estimated we met we were the largest boat being sailed by a couple. We were also the oldest couple. The average age was 50 to 55 for men and 45 to 50 for women. It was interesting that many very young couples that had worked a few years were now making two or three cruises before they settled down and took on the responsibilities of raising a family. There are also many others that had been out there for years and had their babies on the way. It wasn't unusual to find a young couple with two or three children who started out as just a pair.

The Mind's Eye...

In the months we had been cruising, some forty days of it had been spent at sea. Most of that was spent reading more than twenty books, contemplating my life and surroundings, evaluating every aspect of my existence and planning all forms of future endeavors. The time spent actually navigating and handling the sailing chores had been less than 10%. It's, for this reason that the crossing of more than 10,000 miles of ocean was difficult. The physical aspect, although demanding, isn't the primary hurdle. The use of the mind to understand the situations and cultures, to make evaluations of them as it relates to our own personal world, is necessary. It enabled one to combat boredom from the endless expanses between cultural experiences.

But not all of this had been enough to ward off the lack of inspirational experience we were accustomed to in our sophisticated lifestyle at home. In this respect, I spent endless hours sketching my elaborate fantasies about the human condition, the male sexual drive, and the female response. The intricacies in these drives and their answers have provided me with material that's developed beyond anything I had previously been able to develop in the strictly mental sphere. Although I continually visualized aspects of the finished painting when drawing or planning it, I hadn't, however, been able to complete a work of art in my mind.

With the long hours on watch at night, my eyes tired from reading during the day, I started to paint in my mind's eye. The more I developed the picture in full color, trying to place the paint stroke by stroke, the better I was able to execute its full character. In the beginning, after an absence from the minds easel for hours or even days when we were occupied ashore, I would return to the image in a remembered and more complete state. The capacity to sustain full pictures and return to them with little loss of the previous minds work has been very rewarding. I had a collection of works now in storage which I was sure would manifest quickly when I physically faced that blank canvas. That facility, which is my passion in life, has grown. The adventure of our Pacific crossing was exciting and I didn't experience the loss of time well spent that I had feared. Time without disruption had added a dimension to my life.

Every year we planned a cruise to islands that we had not seen.

Opua, New Zealand

We had waited a week in Opua for a weather window to make the voyage to New Caledonia and it looked like the moment. We would move out on the tail end of a low knowing the winds would be strong, but would give us a fast start for the crossing before us. It was a very unpredictable stretch of sea. We knew if we got out far enough in the next twenty-four hours, we would be able to ride an oncoming high before anything else had time to develop. I watched a seagull as he teetered on the rail, trying to resolve the dilemma of web feet on a small rounded surface. His body moved back and forth in cadence with the roll of the boat. He seemed determined in his discomfort. Soon I would be performing the same acts. Here I was, escaping from an abstract digital world, a refugee from the suffocating toxins of my other life. Soon I would be nestled in the tropics, where daily rains withdrew to allow fiery sunsets, squeezed between clouds and sea. I felt myself starting that slow slide into the mellow zone. I had put my watch in the drawer, it needed rest.

The wind was fresh and approaching twenty knots. The sails seemed to embrace the force. The speed log advanced to eleven knots; the wall of wind made us steady and powerful. The hours raced and the wind built, twenty-five knots and gaining. The boat heeled to twenty degrees and a constant spray was sweeping across the decks and off to leeward. We got the message and moved quickly to the cockpit. We furled ten feet of the mainsail into the boom. Now, the mizzen; eight feet of the taut Vectran material disappeared into the boom. I thought to myself how much easier the new automated system was. A year previously, that routine would have taken fifteen minutes of physical effort instead of five minutes of managed judgment.

Another hour and it was time to reef again; we reduced sail to half of our two thousand square-feet. It put us back in the comfort zone, but we still were pushed above the twelve-knot mark. The wind had backed another fifteen degrees and was creating a multi-directional sea. The beam seas were fifteen feet and the wind over thirty-five knots. It was time to make some decisions; the weather reports said it was going to be more of the same. I changed course to windward of my rhumb line. Though we would be beating more, it would be more comfortable to take the seas on the bow. It stopped the heavy beam roll. We reefed again as the winds went over forty knots. The jib was rolled in completely, in a tight tube, and the staysail was out and sheeted hard. We rolled the main another eight feet and the mizzen five feet. The motion was better now, but the winds continued to build. We would make as many miles on the tack as we could; leaving us the option to take the downwind course with the stronger winds and larger seas if they developed. Joyce heated up the pre-made filling for some delicious burritos, and we ate our fill. A full stomach was the best way to fight fatigue and nausea.

It was getting bouncy now. The seas looked angry and the blue skies were turning gray with the sun dipping into the horizon. When the darkness closed in the seas seemed like mountains. The sun with its never-ending journey around the Earth made one continual day, leaving in its wake the past lurking in its darkness. We made our phantasmagorical alliance with the night. The seas seemed fluorescent with white breaking crests that loomed above as if to swallow us into its darkness. I had set up the lee cloths to keep us from being spilled out of our berths. Joyce sat up watching the radar for other ships while I tried to get a few hours' sleep. I half dozed for a couple of hours, my mind aware but my body sleeping. Joyce woke me; the winds were over forty knots now, and we were getting into major storm conditions. We altered course downwind until the seas, now over twenty feet were on the stern quarter. We furled in the mizzen until it disappeared. We left the main, which was down to less than a few hundred square feet. With the staysail rolled in a couple of feet, the motion was much better. The autopilot seemed to take it in stride. We were surfing down the face of waves at up to eighteen knots. We had done this in daylight and had a mental picture of what it looked like.

It was a long night and we resolved ourselves to a destination of Vanuatu on our new course. A spectacular sunrise found us in twenty-five knot winds from the southwest. We had slowly moved back to our original course as the winds moved around. It was New Caledonia again on the agenda. It wasn't a comfortable time, but we had covered two hundred and sixty-five miles. The next days had good stern winds and we had a record four-day crossing of eleven hundred miles.

4 Days to Noumea

Noumea was a fascinating city, less island-like and more French than the other Pacific islands cities except Tahiti. In port we tied up, settled and made a trip by taxi to the customs and immigration offices across the Bay. They were quick and efficient like the French usually are. We took a long walk through the city; found a local bakery and bought some Pain du Raisen for the freezer. This was always a special treat while out in the islands or at sea. We washed the boat down, got things settled and took a long siesta.

In the late afternoon, we made the rounds of the boats at the dock and saw a few cruisers we had seen before on the journey across the Pacific. We hadn't developed any friendships but nodded to them. Kyle Wallis was an American from Seattle. He was a little man and quite out of shape looking. His wife was even more unlikely as a cruiser. She was quite plump and looked as if she didn't have a muscle in her body. We went aboard for a beer and sat in the cockpit under an awning. Looks were deceiving as Kyle and Barbara had been cruising for eleven years and they had circumnavigated once and were on their second time around. We exchanged stories and they confirmed our earlier decision to skip Australia as a cruising destination. It had too much shallow water and not enough interesting anchorages to make the journey worthwhile. As we suspected the time in Sydney was the best of their trip. They were on a stringent budget and it didn't allow for meals out in an expensive place like Noumea. We went out to a place they had heard about and it was excellent. Auckland and New Zealand had some good restaurants, but none quite at the level of this first class bistro.

We left the restaurant fat and happy. When we got to the dock, a large ninety-foot sloop was there with her towering mast standing above the fleet. We couldn't wait to get to the boat and rub in the fact we had beat them by some ten hours. When we left Opua, the sloop owner had gloated on the VHF radio on the morning net. When the group of some thirteen boats had decided to leave he announced, he would be waiting for us when we got there. He had a crew of five for the trip and the owners were joining the boat there. When he saw us, he didn't believe it. When we said we had been in for ten hours he laughed and said, "No way." We told him to check with the Harbor Office, they'd confirm our arrival time. By that time all the crew was on deck and it was obvious we were dressed for dinner and had been there for some time. It was one of those moments when it felt so right to rub it in, as he was a cocky know-it-all captain.

The other four boats heading for Noumea arrived over the next two days except for the thirty-seven foot *Jaga Two*. They had been caught in a severe low that had them weathering the front by lying ahull for two days and being blown well off course. They came in on the thirteenth day, nine days after us! It just again confirmed that speed is a big factor in the comfort equation.

A Reflection

A year after the completion of our second voyage in the South Pacific I had this to reflect upon. *Touché M'dear,* our 68-foot Sundeer Ketch, was nearly 8 years old. We had sailed her some 23,000 miles. In real time, that represented 18 weeks or 3285 hours at sea. Back in the reality of terra firma I reflected on the endless hours beyond the limits of an earthbound dimension, in a realm of enchanted revelation where the mystery of existence was solved in the beauty of the cosmos. I recalled a particular night, during that last time at sea, when the impact really struck me:

That evening was warm and deliciously comfortable. I was wearing a light T-shirt and light cotton, knee-length, shorts. Joyce had only a long cotton shirt on and she flashed the reddish glow of her bare bottom as she turned away from the fiery sunset to the west. She fetched the dinner that had been cooking below. We ate as the sea and sun performed their magical display. It seemed to last for hours. We toasted the cast of this drama with a glass of Chilean Tinto Rosso. I could perceive the curvature of the Earth as the sun brought light to the other side. The exit was slow and graceful, colors ever changing to the darker tones. I watched and concentrated on the last vestiges of light in its deepest form. We were heeled slightly to starboard as the trade winds seemed ever warmer. I watched the slow appearance of the stars, a few at first, and then a massive invasion lighted the heavens. The Milky Way became the autobahn of space travel.

The evening deepened into night. Alone, I had as few or as many hours as I wished before I had to wake Joyce. Should I contemplate Einstein's theory of general relativity? Was his passion for dinghy sailing a contributor to his mathematical sphere? What would he say if he were here with me now in this complete luxury of solitude? What should I have chosen to contemplate that night? I thought about friends that had occupied so many pages of these adventures. The moon would be rising soon. It was certainly worth that night's contemplation. That night I actually looked at it. I mean I really looked at it!

I imagined everything possible in my wildest dreams, and it changed my perceptions.

VII

THE LAST WORDS…

18

TWILIGHT YEARS

Every year we sailed to all of the Pacific islands or to magnificent bays and islands around the very unique country of New Zealand.

In 2003, Joyce and I were strolling in Gulf Harbour on Voyager Way, an avenue with spectacular views eighty feet above the marina. There was a property for sale, a quarter acre overlooking the marina and the Hauraki Gulf. From there you could see the north shore, the islands, and coastline to Auckland. We loved the spot and decided to build a house there and join the golf club. I did some drawings, but the confines of the land parcel were too limiting to create something that would make us happy. I found the owner of the lot next to us and made him an offer he couldn't refuse. I made over a hundred drawings with every detail down to the design of the ceiling moldings and baseboards. I had a well-recommended draftsman who was familiar with the regulations bring the plans to code. Then I took his recommendation of a builder to construct the house. It was finished in one year, and he did a quality job. It was seventy-three hundred square-feet with a studio of over a thousand square-feet; I had designed the exhaust system and the skylights to become the best studio of my life.

The light in New Zealand is unusual, the air is clear and the sunsets from my studio and the entire house are spectacular. We have spent every year there, since, during January, February, March, and April, often even well into May. For the following four years, we maintained the apartment in the Viaduct Harbour, but as the years rolled on we spent less time there. Some years only spending eight or ten day's total, so, alas we sold the apartment and decided we would just get a hotel if we planned to spend the night in the city.

Each year after our time in New Zealand we made extensive journeys around the world, often renting a car and driving the country to feel we had experienced the culture. On some occasions we rented an apartment in Paris for several weeks each time in a different quarter. My love of Paris has always been part of my being, and now that passion was shared with Joyce. We always had romantic and memorable times there. My language skills have diminished over the years with the lack of use, so I especially enjoyed my time there to regain some of my lost vocabulary. Paris is the city that has changed the least over these many years.

In 2005, we purchased a twenty-acre ranch in Somis, California. It was formerly part of the Burt Lancaster Ranch and had been gated and sub-divided into thirty-six parcels of twenty acres or more. The home we bought was a sprawling estate with a sixty-foot pool, tennis court and a private three-hole golf course and driving range. Nine months later in 2006, we sold the Malibu house and moved to Somis. We had in the meantime taken up golf as a sport and joined an elegant club there. Over the years, we had played considerable tennis and having our own court allowed us to get out and play nearly every morning. We also played golf as it had proper greens and sand traps and a putting course next to the house. It had a six-car garage and I converted three of them into an office and studio during the period of changing homes. The studio wasn't as large and didn't have the skylights I had designed in Malibu, but it was a separate building, convenient yet apart from the house. It had good north light, and I had seen the potential when we purchased the property. I had retired from the gallery in 2000 and because of energy and age was painting fewer hours. Golf had become a passion, at seventy-four years old the knees and body were reluctant to endure the stresses of both tennis and skiing.

In 2007, I had a retrospective exhibit at the George Stern galleries in Beverly Hills. About two hundred and fifty people attended. It was a glorious night, and although a significant portion of the show wasn't for sale, a large number of pieces sold. I had framed the show with the best frames on this planet and published a catalog that was like a small book with everything in color. I spared no expense in promoting the show. The owner and I had made some agreements, but when my brother picked up the paintings in George Stern's personal office as agreed, he also returned a large portion of them that were the mainstay of the exhibit. He kept mostly those that were for sale and the retrospective aspect of the show was lost. George's focus was on promoting his gallery with a dealer he knew was very successful and had many contacts. I knew some people that were on his mailing list and so I eliminated them from mine. I was told the mailing went to his client list, but I found out he was only interested in getting my clientele, and not promoting my work to his own.

I canceled the many favors I had called in from all the major magazines and friends; canceled the lunches and all promotion that would benefit his gallery. What happened to the over 1,000 brochures was a question in my mind, as it seemed no one I knew ever got them unless they were on my list. Five years later he had a delivery man drop them at the storage facility that my associate Lisa managed for me. He never made a compliment about the show and his brother, also a dealer I knew well, breezed by with a cursory look at the work and said nothing. It was a mentally crippling event as the man wasn't honest with me. I thought then and still do now that he doesn't really care about art, but just money. I could tell he had contempt for my more abstract work. I never saw or spoke to George Stern again.

This event was essentially the last major exhibit I will have in my lifetime. I'm a successful man and comfortable with my life and my talent, the glory and disappointments are lost in the wealth of my loves and passions.

In 2012, we sold our precious *Touché*. We were getting a little long of tooth to handle a boat of that size without problems. We were returning from a trip to the Barrier Islands when we encountered some nasty weather and managed all right, but it made us realize the time had come to make a change. We sold our beloved yacht and closed a fabulous chapter in our lives. When we returned home, we made the decision we would then add another dimension to our lives. We searched the Coachella Valley for the right country club home, from Palm Springs to La Quinta. After a massive search and looking at an incredible number of homes we honed in on a modern residence designed by a well-known architect. The Quarry Country Club was the highest-rated golf course in the desert and considered by many as the number one desert golf course in the world. On the eighteenth fairway we had a view that was nothing less than incredible; it overlooked the course with several ranges of mountains in the background. We joined the club to find there were some internationally known people who were friendly and interesting. The golf course was the best we had ever played and it has brought us great satisfaction and joy. The house is as unique as our other homes and we now plan to limit our international travel and spend about four months in each. We are very fortunate we have excellent people to look after them and they maintain our homes without worry.

The excitement, love and romance have continued through the years and I now know that love can be sustained for a lifetime. Joyce and I have shared so many adventures, experienced the ultimate passions and held each other as a part of a singular being. We are just one... together. I can't think of a better word to say how I feel about Joyce. We are... together.

19

CLIMBED THE HILL

It is five o'clock in the morning; my mind is awhirl with what I should write as a conclusion to my story. I'm in my home in Gulf Harbour, New Zealand, a beautiful home on the bluffs overlooking the harbor and the Hauraki Gulf. I designed it with everything that brings me pleasure. I feel this place has become my second home both physically and mentally. For many years, I felt this way about Paris, and my many trips back to stay there were among the most pleasurable of my life. But Paris has become difficult because of the crowds, and going there when we leave New Zealand in May isn't the ideal time. In the future, we'll go and just rent an apartment in a quiet arrondissement in the late fall, which to me is now the best time to visit Paris.

When I look back, it's hard to believe almost eighty-three years has passed. It seems to go by more quickly each day. But I will, as in the past, plan a new adventure to look forward to. It has been my philosophy to always have the next adventure planned, even before the current one is complete. Often the expectation is as exciting as the realization. I've been in over a hundred countries. I have lived and traveled in foreign lands for many years of my life and I will continue, albeit in a slower more selective way. I just want to put on my rose-colored glasses and enjoy the magic of the world and the elegant and sophisticated places in my memories.

Christian Title

I've climbed the hill and I find at the pinnacle that there is no place to go. Death is just above me, but I will stay here for a while. The view is uncluttered by the future. I can see clearly the wealth of beauty and youth, bound up in impulse. Since there is no future, I must give my full attention to the solving of problems in retrospect.

Silence now walks in the deserted valleys of my mind; on mute feet, the settlers have abandoned me. There is an emptiness in knowing I have left nothing behind for them. I must investigate this elevation, find all the views and cherish them. The key is to recognize nothingness and somethingness. I'll give up the secrets of my heart here, perhaps I'll put them under a rock, and I will not let death take them. I've lost the fear of losing and I think within I have accumulated some time I can use to reach out and steal back lost creativity. I must conquer the resentment and lust made devious by a desperate need. Why does it not come out in the open? I've been conditioned, trained, educated, why do I not understand it? Do I want love? The little boy inside wants love and admiration without this exhausting communication. I don't want to be responsible for others' lives or even my own. I'm tired of self-denial; I want to enjoy to the limit of my creative manifestations.

There is a sign up here on the very peak, it says: "For sale cheap! For a few dollars a week you can be a child of God." Maybe that's the answer!" But in the end... I can only say, "Thank you World for my time aboard, it has been as good as it gets."

ABOUT THE AUTHOR

Christian Title was born in Los Angeles, California in 1932. He has lived most of his life there. In his early years, he lived in Paris for five years, and over the many years he has spent an additional four or five years there, and throughout Europe.

He has traveled in over one hundred countries and lived a total of nearly twenty years in foreign lands. His extensive travel and sailing experiences have been paramount in a life dedicated to art and philosophy, and the gift we've been given to understand the diversity of this planet. It is impossible to record completely a life such as the author's; this book is but the highlights of his desire to live the fullest life possible.

Highly educated, he has authored many articles, essays and contributed much to the field of American Impressionism. His personal paintings and creative work have had considerable recognition, and he continues to contribute to the understanding of the art world.

He has committed to his desert community and is currently planning his legacy to the art world. An art center and museum housing his personal collection of American Impressionist paintings, his personal works, and space for international exhibits. The Center will have studios to fulfill the desires of aspiring artists, with an extensive art library for reference.

www.ingramcontent.com/pod-product-compliance
Lightning Source LLC
Chambersburg PA
CBHW021038090426
42738CB00006B/134